Gendered Universities in Globalized Economies

Gendered Universities in Globalized Economies

Power, Careers, and Sacrifices

Jan Currie
Bev Thiele
Patricia Harris

LEXINGTON BOOKS
Lanham • Boulder • New York • Oxford

LEXINGTON BOOKS

Published in the United States of America
by Lexington Books
A Member of the Rowman & Littlefield Publishing Group
4720 Boston Way, Lanham, Maryland 20706

PO Box 317
Oxford
OX2 9RU, UK

British Library Cataloguing in Publication Information Available

Library of Congress Cataloging-in-Publication Data

Currie, Jan.
    Gendered universities in globalized economies: power, careers, and sacrifices / Jan
Currie, Bev Thiele, Patricia Harris
        p. cm.
    Includes bibliographical references and index.
    ISBN 0-7391-0364-4 (cloth: alk. paper)
    1. Women college teachers—Australia—Social conditions—21st century.
2. Universities and colleges—Australia—Faculty—Social conditions—21st century.
3. Women in higher education—Australia. 4. Sex discrimination against women—
Australia. 5. Globalization—Social aspects—Australia. I. Thiele, Bev, 1955–
II. Harris, Patricia, 1943– III. Title.
LB2332.34.A8 G46 2002
378.1'9822—dc21   2002029673

Printed in the United States of America

♾™ The paper used in this publication meets the minimum requirements of American National
Standard for Information Sciences—Permanence of Paper for Printed Library Materials,
ANSI/NISO Z39.48–1992.

We dedicate this book to our

Mothers, Daughters, and Female Friends,

and those men who struggle with us to change the world.

Contents

List of Tables

Acknowledgments

The impetus for this research started with our working lives in a particular *corporatized* university. There was a dramatic change in the culture of this university during the 1990s that affected all our lives. This book tries to capture what we were feeling and what many of our colleagues told us about the changes that were affecting them. We are grateful to the respondents who were interviewed on different occasions at Curtin University of Technology, Edith Cowan University, Murdoch University, and the University of Sydney in Australia; and Florida State University, the University of Arizona, and the University of Louisville in the United States.

This research caught the imagination of many of our colleagues. Over the past decade we owe our inspiration to many friends, too numerous to mention by name. However, we would like to acknowledge their contribution to this book as well as those who directly worked with us on several projects on the nature of gendered universities. We are grateful for the funding we received from the Australian Research Council and the two main participating universities. We also received a publication grant and administrative assistance from the Centre for Research for Women. Our colleagues, Susan Hall and Lesley Parker, were beneficiaries of one of those grants and helped us administer, interview, and write papers on aspects of this study.

We have had several research assistants/directors during the course of this project—Harriett Pears and Anne Butorac—and appreciated their energy, insight, and patience in helping us analyze the data. Paul Snider took over from Harriett Pears and continued to analyze the NUD.IST data for us and did a considerable amount of editing of our chapters. In addition, we thank the interviewers, James Bell, Annie Goldflam, Helen Olivieri, Jane Pearce, and Joy Puls, as well as the transcriber, Stephen Robson. We want to thank Loraine Abernethie who had the most difficult job of bringing our work together into a camera-ready version for the publishers. She also checked all of our referencing and grammar. Thanks must also go to Jasmina Brankovich for preparing the index. Our editors, Serena Krombach and Hedi Hong, encouraged us to publish this book and were most helpful during all the publishing stages.

Family, friends, and our lovable dogs have supported us throughout this work. We appreciated their emotional and physical labor and their patience while we toiled on the book: Paul, Serena, John, Anna, Ewan, Casley, and Tarka.

Perth, Western Australia

August, 2002

Introduction

Why are we writing this book? We would like to see universities become more sensitive to the lives of the women and men who inhabit them. We would like to see universities become more aware of the way in which their increasingly managerialist culture marginalizes women. We are worried about the current direction universities are taking in many countries. Adopting global practices changes the very nature of universities. These practices devalue critical bodies of knowledge and threaten values that we would like to see as central to universities.

As feminists and senior academics in our university, we have been upset with the dominant managerial ethos that pervades our institution. We are not retreating and passively witnessing this. We are struggling within the institution to resist the worst excesses of a hegemonic, patriarchal management. This book, therefore, in part tells our story as well as the stories of other women and men caught up in what we are describing as corporatized universities. The corporatization of our universities is a result of politicians and bureaucrats accepting the challenge of a globalized economy and thrusting nation-states and their public agencies into adopting neoliberal economic practices.

We seek to describe what is happening to our universities from the inside and with a gendered lens. We are telling these *insider* stories with an aim to understand and seek change in the current organizational culture, our working environment. We conclude with visions of alternative scenarios for universities.

Gendered Universities

Based on our study and review of the literature, we conclude that universities are dominated by masculine principles and structures that lead to advantages for male staff and disadvantages for female staff (whether academic or general). The most valued activities in universities are those that reflect male patterns of socialization: individualist rather than collective, competitive rather than cooperative, based on power differentials rather than egalitarian, and linked to expert authority rather than collegial support. The masculinist culture is a particular type of culture and, set in the context of globalized universities, it has devel-oped into a more competitive, aggressive, and entrepreneurial culture.

In addition to the masculinist culture that has characterized universities for centuries, a managerialist ethos has begun to pervade universities in this global-ized era. This means that universities are rapidly losing their collegial commu-nities and scholars are becoming more individualized. This culture tends to benefit men more than women; yet not all men benefit from this type of univer-sity culture. Some men resist these global trends and decide that they will not compromise their values. Others are not aware of making sacrifices or compro-mising values because their socialization has suited them to this culture. In the end, it appears that more men identify with this culture and are able to engage with it more easily because of their determination to succeed, no matter what the costs.

Our study has some similarities to one that the Massachusetts Institute of Technology (MIT) completed in 1999. That study grew out of conversations in the summer of 1994 by three senior women in the School of Science about the quality of their professional lives. The report on the status of women noted:

> While each of them had come to realize, individually, that gender had probably caused their careers to differ from those of their male colleagues, they had never discussed the issues with one another, and were uncertain about whether their perceptions were in fact accurate or their experiences unique. Once they began the discussion, they realized that their experiences in fact formed a pat-tern, and the idea of a full-scale study was born. (MIT 1999: 5)

The committee found, in the words of Professor Lotte Bailyn, chair of the MIT faculty, "that gender discrimination in the 1990s is subtle but pervasive, and stems largely from unconscious ways of thinking that have been socialized into all of us, men and women alike" (MIT 1999: 3). Our study came to similar conclusions. However, we were not focusing on women alone and their differ-ences from men. We were trying to understand the organizational culture in which both men and women worked. We discovered that there was *a peak, male* culture that dominated the universities we studied. That meant that most women and some men were denied entry into that culture. The peak male culture was not the only one operating in the university, but it had the hegemonic power within the institution.

Australian sociologist Don Edgar draws a connection between globalization and emotional labor. He theorizes that one of the underlying problems affecting many workers, especially female workers, is the masculine structure of work. "Successful careers require long hours, building a reputation while you are young, minimizing family work by finding someone else to do it (a wife or a paid carer), and children are a beloved impediment rather than a shared respon-sibility" (Edgar 2001: 11).

Edgar's observations and those of the MIT Status of Women Report were not the first to draw such conclusions. The literature on gendered careers and gendered institutions goes back at least three decades. Feminists have come to similar conclusions in their studies of universities worldwide. What is new is that universities have entered into a new era. They are adopting, almost without reflection, without hesitation, global practices that emanate from neoliberal economic policies that will make the lives of women within them even more difficult than they have been in the past. As affirmative action officers eliminate the more obvious gendered practices, the constraints on women's careers become more subtle, as the MIT women faculty reported.

These writers point to the underlying theme that drew us to studying the gendered nature of American and Australian universities. There was a normalization of the masculine structure of work in universities and a denial that anything was wrong with that situation.

Many *liberated* women since the 1960s went into marriage with the belief that they would share the domestic work, and they thought that their marriages would be partnerships of equals. So, too, women went to work in universities believing in an equality of treatment, an assessment of their work on its merit, and a belief that they would rise to the top in the same way that men rise to the top in their disciplines. However, women leave universities more frequently than men do. The burden of being both wife and worker is becoming unendurable as globalized economies develop even more aggressively masculine working cultures. Professional, married women in many fields are expected to be totally committed to their work, work long hours, and still be loving wives and mothers and give quality time to their families. Some women are able to achieve a balance between work and family commitments; however, many are finding the burdens of work and family life unsustainable. It also appears that those who rise to the top in universities are those who can put in the long hours (single women, divorced women, or those whose children have left home). This is not the same for men who can rise to the top, whether married or single, with or without young children.

This kind of analysis is made by men as well as by women (for example, Ann Brooks 1997; Jeff Hearn 1999; Louise Morley 1999; Bob Connell 1987, 1995, 2000; Ann Brooks and Alison Mackinnon 2001). Richard Collier (2001) describes the shift in British universities from a *paternalistic* masculinity to an *entrepreneurial* masculinity. He describes this new managerial style as one which is "aggressive, top-down, resistant to dialogue and exchange, and singularly lacking in empathy as to the human costs of the changes which have been and are being instituted in many institutions" (Collier 2001: 23). He is equally concerned about the direction universities are taking which, he argues, raises questions about power, politics, quality of life, and social justice for both women *and* men. These are issues about

work/life imbalance, long hours, unsympathetic corporate culture and weight of
workload, about physical and psychological health, about the quality of and,
indeed, ability to sustain interpersonal relationships; and about the sacrifice of
family in order to pursue a career—issues each of which, it is all too clear,
continue to be gendered in some far-reaching ways. (Collier 2001: 31)

Universities are often thought of as neutral organizations where men and
women can succeed on their merits. We argue in this book that despite the ideal
of universities, where equality should exist between males and females, this
ideal has not yet been attained by most universities. What is surprising is how
many people working in universities are in a state of denial about how women
are treated in most universities in the world. Bittman and Pixley coined the term
pseudomutuality in their 1997 book, *The Double Life of the Family*. They argue
that we take refuge in pseudomutuality—where we say we are equal, but act as
if we are not. Denial is a way we keep up the illusion of control in the face of
overwhelming evidence to the contrary.

Morley uses the conceptual framework of micropolitics to unmask the organizational culture of universities and "disclose the myriad ways in which
women are undermined and excluded from access to resources, influence, career
opportunities and academic authority" (Morley 1999: 4). We agree with this
analysis and the conception of universities as patriarchal institutions, imbued
over time with structures of hierarchy and male dominance. Overlaid on these
structures are global practices, creating the entrepreneurial universities of the
1990s and 2000s. What is it about the globalization era that has ushered in a
managerial climate and led to a lower quality of life for most academics in today's universities? Some describe this new globalization era as an era of heightened capitalism or fast capitalism. Others describe it as corporate capitalism or
corporate globalization (Barlow 2000). Sennett (1998: 9) refers to it as flexible
capitalism where "workers are asked to behave nimbly, to be open to change on
short notice, to take risks continually."

Sennett (1998) writes about the personal consequences of work in the new
capitalism. One of his questions is similar to the underlying theme of our study:
How can mutual loyalties and commitments be sustained in institutions that are
constantly breaking apart or continually being redesigned?

Many Anglo-American universities are in a process of restructuring. Individuals in these universities work with the fear of their jobs being terminated, as
do most workers in corporations today. What does this do to the character of
universities? Just as Sennett argues about the impact of the new capitalism on
the corrosion of character in the United States, we make the same argument for
universities. We have witnessed the erosion of our university's character. Also,
when we have talked with academics at conferences and interviewed them in
American and Australian universities, we heard their despair when they spoke
about the threat to their universities' core values.

Our concern is that university administrators adopt these changes with an
earnestness that makes these practices almost above criticism (Rees 1995). Ex-

emplifying this trend, Hecht quoted a University of California at Los Angeles (UCLA) administrator as stating, "Can a university be run more like a business? You bet it can. . . . Most universities can do a significant job of cutting costs through the same re-engineering of processes and work that have characterized the best for-profit corporations" (Hecht 1994: 6).

Another idea coming from business is that change has to be the order of the day. This is in line with the idea that managers should make the most important decisions and make them quickly. When applied to universities, this means that collegial decision making is bypassed. Managers also have a penchant for restructuring institutions and molding them into streamlined operations that allow only a few people access to the information base on which decisions can be made. More decisions are made in secret. University administrators are now reading management books written for the corporate world, which explain how managers can bring about reforms quickly. A New Zealand academic whom we interviewed in 1997 talked about one such book. He said that it could have been describing the changes that were occurring in a number of American and Australian universities:

> If you read Roger Douglas' [former Treasurer in New Zealand] book, *Unfinished Business*, he talks about the politics of successful reform, and he articulates a number of principles for successful reform. I can quote them to you off the top of my head. One of them is institute the reforms in quantum leaps, big packages neutralize opposition, once you start the ball rolling never let it stop, speed is essential, just keep on going, and consult with the community only to improve the detailed implementation of decisions that have already been reached. (Male, Education, New Zealand University)

In the voice of another academic, across the world from the University of Auckland, the rapidity of change was noted in response to a question about the current style of decision making in an American university:

> It seems that bureaucratic tendencies are increasing. The faculty has a lot less control over the institution. There were a number of changes imposed on the faculty: not electing deans, changing the definition of what we do, making teaching-only and research-only streams; a post-tenure review, evaluating what you do which could lead to termination; increasing the proportion of faculty without tenure. The faculty met for the first time in donkey's years and voted against these proposals, like 495 to 15, and these were faculty from all the colleges: the medical school, the law school—they all said, "This sucks." The Board of Trustees said, "We don't care, this is what is happening." There is contempt for the faculty. But also a sense that they are running a business. You know when you are running an auto plant, you don't ask the workers how to run the plant, at least in America, and if you are running a university, you don't ask the faculty how to run the institution. (Male, Social Sciences, American University)

We experienced the same kind of rapid change when our university appointed a new vice-chancellor in 1996. Within the first three months, he eliminated thirty-two committees. Within the next six months, he wrote a new vision statement, preparing the university for the twenty-first century. He wanted twenty-three actions voted on within three weeks, actions that, among other things, would restructure the university into larger divisions, create a hierarchical management structure with appointed (rather than elected) executive deans, and eliminate small programs and courses. Before the end of the year, he had achieved most of his objectives. To continue the momentum for change, he initiated a merger with another university, which ultimately failed. Nevertheless, the pace of change has not halted as major new initiatives are debated at each council meeting. It is clear that managers talk to each other, read each other's books, and discuss ways of baffling staff so that their initiatives can succeed. What will universities look like in the twenty-first century? Will they be changed so much we will not even be able to recognize them?

Our Study

By interviewing women and men in different positions (secretaries and managers, technicians and academics) in two universities, we were able to describe in some detail how they perceived the university. We found that the views of the managers, whether males or females, differed from those of academics. There were different ways of viewing a career, depending upon one's position within the institution. Many secretaries felt they were in dead-end jobs, rather than on a career ladder. Junior academics viewed their career prospects differently from senior academics.

We began our interviews asking our focus groups and individual respondents about their careers and what it takes to be successful within the university setting (see appendix for the interview protocols). We asked about the attributes of success and examined whether it was more difficult for women to achieve success in these universities. We then moved on to look at issues of power, who has it, and how do people attain it. We wanted to examine the way power is seen in universities and the way it is used or abused. Another topic we asked about was if individuals had to make sacrifices to get ahead. In addition, we wanted to know whether they had to compromise any of their values within their work setting. These two case studies allowed us to analyze at a deeper level the organizational culture of the institutions.

The study took place in two Western Australian universities from 1995 to 1998. It revealed the differences between males and females in their working styles and the sacrifices both males and females have to make to either further their careers or just maintain their current positions. The interviews included managers, academics, and general staff, 89 males and 113 females.

The book sets these issues about the nature of gendered work in universities within the context of globalization and the globalization practices most common in American and Australian universities. It identifies the differential impact these are having on men and women, mainly because of their location within these institutions. Female academics are more often in junior positions and teaching in areas more distant from the market, so it is more difficult for them to be winners in the university cultures of this globalized era. It also details the anatomy of power within these institutions and how it is seen from different viewpoints: managers, academics, and general staff. It details the subtlety of how male working styles are normalized within universities. Finally, it offers policy options for universities in which it describes organizational cultures that can most benefit women.

According to Bacchi (1999), the construction of policy problems can be better understood as competing interpretations of political issues. We bring this *What is the problem?* approach to our study of gendered universities and the impact of globalization on public sector institutions. By examining how different countries adopt, alter, or resist globalization practices, we can elucidate alternative constructions of the problem. Why are Anglo-American universities so readily adopting corporate, entrepreneurial practices and European countries, largely, resisting or adapting them to suit their organizations? Why have universities maintained their patriarchal structures and cultures? Our prediction is that globalization practices are likely to favor male cultural practices and leave gendered universities unchanged, despite the efforts of equal opportunity legislation and feminist activism within universities.

Overview of the Book

Part 1 of the book gives the Anglo-American setting for the book in two chapters: one on globalization and the other on gendered universities. Chapter 1, "Globalization and Higher Education," examines the term globalization and how global practices have penetrated universities. It reviews the literature on globalization and suggests that there are winners and losers in the global economy, both in terms of countries and in terms of workers within each country. Certain countries are deregulating their economies and opening their doors to free trade without qualms. One of these countries is Australia, and we examine the way in which it adopted global practices and how these affected higher education policies. Global practices turned the universities into corporate bodies competing against each other for research dollars and marginal funding grants. This chapter sets the context in which Anglo-American universities are restructuring their universities to become more competitive in the national and international race for prestige and dollars. They are competing for international students, for research grants, for patents and other types of intellectual property rights, and for online students. This is a race that is in its initial stages and will only become more competitive as borderless education and the mobility of scholars increase, with the global economy extending across most national borders.

Chapter 2, "Gendered Universities," begins by relating the gendered nature of universities to the global practices that are becoming more dominant in American and Australian universities. We describe the type of gender discrimination that exists in western universities. We then relate findings from a study of three American and three Australian universities, investigating whether men and women were treated differently in their universities. In this chapter we also elucidate our theoretical approach to understanding the subtle ways universities construct their organizational cultures to marginalize women. We use the concept of the normalization of a male culture to understand what happens to women within the academy. We describe how male practices are taken as the norm and, in this way, they become invisible and difficult to alter.

Part 2 focuses on our Australian study of the gendered nature of two universities. Chapter 3, "Context of the Australian Study," gives the setting for the in-depth study of the organizational culture of two universities. It describes the sample and the methodology. We used qualitative research methods, interviewing administrators, academics, and general staff in small focus groups and individually. We then analyzed the themes that emerged from these interviews, investigating the microprocesses of organizational culture.

Chapter 4, "Normalization of Male Working Styles," uses Eveline's (1994) conception of the "normalization of male culture" and analyses whether that was the situation in the particular universities studied. We conclude that the normalization of male culture was not only present in the peak management culture where it was strongest, but it pervaded the organization. It was detected in responses from those who were satisfied with the gendered status quo and in those who were seeking to challenge it. We also look at the reasons people believed there were so few women in senior positions in their institutions. The findings analyzed four kinds of responses: those that provide structural explanations; those which deny the problem; and those which either blame the past and tradition/nature or blame women themselves for their absence from senior ranks. Women were more likely to see structural reasons that impeded women's advancement within their universities; whereas men were more likely to proffer the other explanations. Included here were the pipeline effect, sociobiological reasons and women's mothering responsibilities.

In chapter 5, "Anatomy of Power in Universities," we continue the line of argument about male norms through analyzing the gendered nature of power within two universities. We look particularly at the discourse of men and women when they discuss the attributes of those who have power. Power, of course, is seen differently depending upon one's position in an organization. We look at the different ways in which academics and general staff, men and women, view power. The current climate of entrepreneurialism is one of the metaphors shaping behavior in universities impacted by globalization. In such a climate, the more aggressive staff members will be rewarded and those who are *the good campus citizens* (many women) will be overlooked. We conclude that it is more than likely that the entrepreneurial academics will be males and that promotion into higher ranks and into the ranks of management will become even more difficult for females. It is also likely, then, that women who do move into those positions will be those who take on masculine values to survive in that climate. Therefore, power is likely to become more, rather than less, gendered as Australian universities become more integrated into the global economy.

In chapter 6, "View from the Top: Captain of the Ship," we turn to a picture of managers steering their ships through troubled waters and enjoying the challenge with some degree of excitement and self-satisfaction. Here we describe how the senior managers in the two institutions in this study thought about the changes affecting higher education, patterns of success and exclusion within their universities, and the position of senior academic women. We also recount their reflections on their own career paths: the planning and sacrifices involved and their regrets and aspirations. We found that while there were distinct differences among the senior managers (who were all male), there were also common patterns. These centered on a general acceptance of political changes, a marked tendency to explain the relative absence of women in senior positions in either historical or sociobiological terms, and an optimistic assessment of their own careers, past and present.

In chapter 7, "View from Below: Sacrifices and Success in Greedy Universities," we hear the responses of academic and general staff about the same issues we canvassed with the senior managers. However, the *view from below* is distinctly different from the *view from the top*. We use Coser's (1974) concept of the *greedy institution* to describe the hold which universities have over their staff and to detail the range of personal and professional sacrifices which academics and general staff make in order to be part of their university's culture. We compare females and males and general and academic staff. The impact of the current neoliberal discourses minimizes the differences across the two universities, between males and females and by rank. We conclude that this apparent uniformity is the product of a peak masculinist discourse used mainly by those in the more powerful positions in these institutions, which acts to disenfranchise all those who do not operate within its restricted and restrictive boundaries. In terms of how the promotion and advancement system is viewed, we look at who gets ahead within the institution and which attributes they have. We also ask about who does not get ahead and why. In interviewing academics and senior managers about their perceptions of success within one of the universities studied, distinct differences emerged. However, the divide was not only that between managers and academics, but there were also academics who viewed the system as reasonable. Those who felt the system was reasonable saw the successful academic as someone who was productive, hardworking, strategic, and able to adopt a university-wide perspective. Those who saw the system as flawed, identified success in negative terms, speaking of *careerism* and selfishness. This group also spoke of institutional discrimination. These responses were differently articulated among the participants. We conclude that the pattern of academic and managerial success within universities is profoundly gendered with production privileged over reproduction and output over process.

Finally, our conclusion, "A Critical and Conserving Agenda for Universities," provides a vision for the kind of university that we think would be more hospitable to women. In other words, we propose a university that would be a more attractive workplace for both women *and* men. We envision a university that will conserve the best of traditional values that universities have embraced in the past and will also be critical of those values, searching out of curiosity for a better, more just society. We see the role of the university as critical for maintaining a democratic society and for educating a questioning and informed citizenry.

PART 1

THE ANGLO-AMERICAN CONTEXT

Chapter 1

Globalization and Higher Education

Introduction

The new millennium is marked by protests against globalization in countries around the world. Between 2000 and 2001 there were major demonstrations in Seattle against the World Trade Organization, in Washington, D.C., against the World Bank, in Melbourne against the World Economic Forum, in Quebec City against the expansion of NAFTA to the Americas, and in Genoa against the G8. The protesters—who included students, academics, unionists, political activists, members of nongovernment agencies, and church groups—rallied against neo-liberal economic reforms, centered on privatization, deregulation, and free trade practices. These developments, they said, bow to the interests of transnational capital and damage poorer nations and working people around the world. Accordingly, when protesters marched against the September 2001 meeting of the World Economic Forum in Melbourne, they assembled under the banner *S11 Carnival for Global Justice.*

While there is no agreed definition of globalization, certain key features predominate in most accounts. These are the compression and deregulation of a world economy through liberalizing trading and banking policies, the increasing power of transnational corporations able to locate wherever the advantage of the global market dictates, a hollowing out of the nation-state, and a dissolution of national cultures as well as national economies. The loss of sovereign power is a predominant theme. Kohler (2000: 3), for example, suggests that globalization has reduced the sovereign power of nations through the flight of manufacturing capital, financial deregulation, and the development of electronic technologies that create international markets in a matter of moments. From a different tack,

Sklair (2001: 8) suggests that a transnational capitalist class, composed of executives, bureaucrats, politicians, professionals, merchants, and media owners, displaces national goals by supporting economic competition at the expense of social and community development. There is, though, considerable disagreement about how far globalization has proceeded. Hirst and Thompson (1995, 1996), in particular, warn against exaggeration. However, even they concede that the past three decades have seen significant erosion of national, political, and economic autonomy.

Political responses to globalization vary. Conservative leaders in Australia suggest that there is no turning back, that the country is fully enmeshed within the globalized economy, and that politicians have to accept this path. The Prime Minister, John Howard, argued, "In a globalized economy you can't turn your back on change and reform. It's going to happen anyway. It's a question of whether you manage change in an intelligent fashion, a sympathetic and compassionate fashion" (cited in Kelly 2001: 23). Similarly, Rob Borbidge (cited in Kelly 2001: 23), when leader of the Queensland National Party, maintained, "The simple fact is we can't stop globalization. What we have to do is manage it. There is no way we can go back to the 1950s or the 1940s. The simple fact is that Australia is part of the world." Another pro-globalization spin on matters was voiced by former President Clinton (2000) during a London Television interview: "We need to keep opening up our markets; let's not close off opportunities to increase the flow of wealth around the world."

Pro-globalization sentiments are more marked in Anglo-American nations than in countries with a longer tradition of opposition to international capital. The French stand out in their opposition to both cultural and economic encroachment—witness, for example, their opposition to McDonald's and American movies. They have also moved to reduce the working week from thirty-nine to thirty-five hours. Turnbull (1999) describes this as a defiant move designed to safeguard the quality of life against the demands of Anglo-Saxon efficiency and the drive to work crazy hours. Contrary to the predictions of the American Chamber of Commerce in Paris, the first year of *les 35 heures* has coincided with 3 percent growth in the French economy, increased consumer confidence, and reduced unemployment (Anderson 2001). More importantly, a survey of French workers found that their personal and family life had improved (86 percent); they had more time for personal growth and development (74 percent); and there was better morale at work (50 percent).

Finally, we should note that the costs and benefits of globalization are unevenly spread. Poorer nations, with economies wide open to exploitation, are the great losers. Such benefits as there are accrue to the nations of the North, particularly Anglo-American countries. However, even in their case, there are workers who are losing badly. The growing army of low-paid workers in the United States is a case in point.

Australia stands somewhere in the middle of this winner and loser spectrum. In the main part of this chapter, we describe how it has responded to globalization pressures. We start by outlining the broad thrust of government responses to globalization, particularly in the economic arena. We then turn to policies specifically directed at higher education. After outlining the main initiatives of the federal government, we describe how universities have responded to these developments. Here we consider the patterns of control operating within universities and the sites of resistance to them. We conclude by looking ahead to the rest of the book and by commenting on the gendered implications of globalization.

Australia's Response to Globalization

Australia's response to globalization has been influenced by a number of interlocking factors. These include its reliance on agricultural and mining products as exports, the comparative weakness of its manufacturing sector, its pattern of tariffs and other protective measures, and its historic reliance on the minimum wage. Because of these circumstances, the impact of globalization—or at least the way in which governments have responded to it—has been more pronounced in Australia than in countries with more resilient trading patterns, particularly those with firmly entrenched social democratic traditions, such as Sweden, Norway, and the Netherlands.

In the early 1980s, a Labor government moved to deregulate the Australian economy and open it up to competition. It floated the dollar in 1983, admitted foreign banks and lifted various financial controls in 1984, and substantially cut tariffs in 1988. Workforce reform and labor market deregulation came to center stage during the 1990s, particularly under the Federal Coalition Government (Liberal and National political parties). Over the same period, governments embarked on far-reaching programs of public sector reform. They attempted, above all, to achieve a significant extension of market values and practices. To this end, they transferred services or whole corporations from the public to the private domain, aiming to produce a leaner public service that achieves competitive neutrality with private enterprise (Hilmer 1993). Many techniques were employed including privatization, corporatization, contracting out, managed competition, and purchaser-provider agreements. Where privatization was not politically feasible or could not be pursued any further, governments concentrated on intrasectoral relations in the public domain (thus, for example, on the relations between schools, universities, or welfare agencies). In this case, they worked to establish markets or quasi markets leading to heightened competition, improved performance, reduced costs, and a consumer ethos. This has led to a reduction in the welfare state and a shift of power from the state to the private sector, especially through privatization of public sector agencies. One of the ironies of these deregulatory and privatization measures is that they confirmed and encouraged the very features of a globalized economy to which they were originally responses (Quiggin 1998).

At an individual level, governments encouraged personal initiative, private medical insurance, the user-pays principle, and the prevailing philosophy of "mutual obligation." The prime example of this is the "work for the dole" scheme, introduced in Australia under the Howard government. These "workfare" programs have parallels in New Zealand, Britain, and the United States. Edelman, a former Assistant Secretary at the United States Department of Health and Human Services, resigned in protest over the welfare bill because he felt it paid no attention to the job market and warned that it would end in increased homelessness, malnutrition, drug abuse, and violence. He said that for "60 years Aid to Families with Dependent Children has been premised on the idea of entitlement. But now 'entitlement' has become a dirty word" (Jobs Letter Editors 1997: 1).

With this as background, we may summarize the steps taken by Australian political parties to adjust to the global economy as follows.

Events in Australia Illustrating Globalization

1983:   The Australian dollar was floated. The Hawke Labor Government opened the way for a wider program of deregulation.

1984:   Deregulation of the financial sector began when foreign banks were admitted to Australia and controls were lifted on the operation of banks.

1986:   Labor Treasurer, Paul Keating, stated that Australia was in danger of becoming a banana republic. Commodity prices fell and triggered a currency crisis, and the government response was to cut federal programs.

1987:   The Industrial Relations Commission ratified a two-tier wage system, beginning steps toward deregulation of the labor market. Part of the increase was to be negotiated between individual unions and employers (enterprise agreements).

1988:   The Hawke Labor Government cut tariff rates to 15 percent and, for those already below 15 percent, to 10 percent. It made an exception for cars and textiles, but these were already under huge pressure from imports. Loss of manufacturing jobs began. The federal government committed itself to the privatization of enterprises such as the Commonwealth Bank.

1989:   Formation of Asia-Pacific Economic Cooperation (APEC), a group of twenty-one member countries formed to assist economic liberalization. Concerned about the formation of international trading blocs, Australia pushed hard for a regional organization with a free trade agenda in which it could participate. The result was increasing Australian exposure to Asian markets.

1990: Short-term interest rates rose to 18 percent in an effort to deflate the assets price boom following the relaxation of bank lending policies in the wake of deregulation. The "recession that Australia had to have," as Paul Keating described it, was much deeper than anticipated with unemployment rising above 11 percent. The two-airline agreement came to an end, and the basis was laid for competition in telecommunications.

1991: Privatization commenced on a large scale with the sale of a block of shares in the Commonwealth Bank, the sale of Aussat to form the basis of Optus, and the sale of Commonwealth Serum Laboratories.

1992: The Keating government sold Qantas and Australian Airlines, continuing the privatization agenda. Together with competition for Telstra, it opened big government enterprises to commercial forces, downsizing, and increasing job insecurity.

1993: The National Competition Policy Act (referred to as the *Hilmer Reforms*) bound both state and federal governments to implement comprehensive pro-market reforms leading to the corporatization of government business enterprises and a comprehensive program of competitive tendering and contracting for publicly provided services.

1994: Australia supported the creation of the World Trade Organization (WTO), formerly GATT (Uruguay Round), that aimed to broaden the global move to free trade. It became the focal point for international protests against the dismantling of protection policies in developed countries.

1996–1998: Election of the Howard Coalition (Liberal and National Parties) Government:

- Further privatization of national-owned companies such as Telstra, and the Commonwealth Bank, and further outsourcing of government services.
- Further deregulation of industrial relations and vigorous pursuit of workplace reforms with the aim of reducing the power of unions; attempts to break some powerful unions like the

- Maritime Union with scab labor, but with only limited success.
- Cuts of 25 percent to Commonwealth Public Service; loss of 100,000 jobs.
- Privatization of the Commonwealth Employment Service.
- Cuts to social welfare programs; more stringent tests for access to social welfare benefits and unemployment benefits; Work for the Dole programs.
- Unemployment rose from around 8 percent to 8.7 percent.
- Election policy to reduce Australia's foreign debt which stood at $A280 billion (by 2000, debt ballooned to $A380 billion).
- Reduced capital gains tax rate to half the income tax rate.
- Reduced R&D tax concession from 150 percent to 125 percent.
- Private health insurance rebate of 30 percent.

1999–2001: Reelection of Howard Coalition Government, moving toward greater free trade agreements.

- Privatization of Refugee Detention Centers.
- Introduction of Goods and Services Tax (GST), a regressive tax, and reduction in personal income tax, a progressive tax.
- Ralph Review—Business Tax Reform.
- Telstra reorganized into two divisions, Telstra Country Wide and the rest of the company, designed to allow the Howard Coalition Government to privatize the rest of Telstra.
- Crackdown on welfare, saving taxpayers over $A2 million per day.
- Many bank closures, especially in suburbs and rural towns.
- Petrol prices pegged to world prices.
- Compulsory unionism outlawed producing lowest level of strikes since 1913.

This catalogue covers the policies and practices of both Labor and Coalition governments. These governments would argue that their programs have delivered benefits to many Australians. A well-versed contention is that there has been a reduction in the unemployment rate. However, while the official rate may have fallen, the number of discouraged and underemployed workers has grown steadily since the late 1980s. On this, Denniss (2001: 2) notes that the "burgeoning problem of overwork" now takes its place alongside underemployment as a serious problem.

More generally, the evidence points to a growing divide between the rich and poor. Saunders (2001) estimates that over the past two decades, the incomes of low-income families have declined not only relative to the incomes of other

families, but also relative to consumer prices. Similarly, a report on welfare reform commissioned by the government found that there was a growing divide
between the work rich and the work poor since the early 1980s, with employment and unemployment becoming more unequally distributed between regions
and localities (McClure 2000). These inequities have been exacerbated by other
aspects of government policy. While subsidies have been cut to welfare recipi-
ents and assets tests made stricter, the Industry Commission in 1996 estimated
that Federal, State, and Territory governments provided more than $A16 billion
each year in financial and other assistance to industry (Baragwanath and Howe
2000). To take one example: the Commonwealth government's subsidies to the
health insurance industry through tax concessions (initiated in 1997) have operated to the greatest advantage of the wealthiest third of taxpayers, with well over
a billion dollars of public money underwriting their health care (Smith 2000).

It is perhaps not surprising, then, that a quality of life study commissioned
by the Australia Institute (1999) found that only 24 percent of Australians think
that their quality of life is getting better, while 36 percent think it is getting
worse. There are also worries that workplace reforms have damaged public
service professionalism. The Australia Institute (2001a) found that the system of
specific and narrow contracts, performance measures, and a general culture of
mistrust and short-term relationships had increasingly made Commonwealth
public servants "dispirited, fearful and lack[ing] in self-confidence."

It is against this uneven and problematic background that we set developments in higher education.

Creating Universities as Enterprising Institutions

In considering the particular impact of globalization on universities, we need to
start with the transformation of the nation-state into a competitive player in a
web of international relations. Above all, this new competitive state moves to
create markets where none existed before and encourages public institutions to
behave in market rational ways (Lingard and Rizvi 1998; Sassen 2000). This has
had a significant impact on higher education in Australia. Over the past two
decades, governments have been involved in a concerted attempt to get universities to act in a more competitive and enterprising way. These changes have
affected the ways in which institutions are funded and managed, the kind of research that is undertaken, the student profile, the teaching loads, and the collegial relations.

In 1988, the binary divide (that is, the distinction between universities and
other tertiary institutions, such as institutes of technology and colleges of advanced education, which were not similarly funded for research purposes) was
abolished. In its place the government created the Unified National System
(UNS). This was to "encourage an environment of productive competition between higher education institutions" and allow institutions to "compete for

teaching and research resources on the basis of institutional merit and capacity" (Dawkins 1988: 10-11, 28). The Relative Funding Model (RFM), introduced in August 1990, was designed to equalize the allocation of resources and create a *level playing field* for institutional competition. Under the RFM the operating grant is separated into teaching and research components and a set of discipline indices produced, encouraging comparisons both between and within institutions.

As part of this strategy, new funding systems were evolved, with grants made subject to competitive performance. This includes both research (infrastructure and research quantum funds) and teaching initiative grants. The research allocations have consistently favored the older established universities with greater financial reserves and longer research traditions. Indeed, the idea behind the reforms is that the already strong should be rewarded, ensuring that "research funds go to those best able to make most effective use of them" (DEET 1993, cited in Marginson 1996: 30). Over and above this, academic areas seen as serving the economic needs of the nation were given priority. Defined priority areas were established as part of Dawkins' (the then Labor Minister of Education) planning for what became known as the *clever country*. These represented programs considered best able to meet the future needs of the economy and the labor market. They included Asian studies, business administration, engineering, information technology, and management.

A quantitative model of performance indicators was canvassed as part of the so-called Dawkins reforms. His proposed plan was later abandoned by Peter Baldwin (as Labor Minister for Education) in favor of a quality assurance approach where university participation was to be invited rather than compelled, qualitative measures included, and rewards provided in the shape of funds additional to the operating grant (Vidovich and Currie 1998: 193). Under the three-year quality assurance rounds, universities were allocated to different bands according to their institutional profiles and national data. Alongside these measures, publications such as the *Course Experience Questionnaire* (CEQ), the *Graduate Destinations Survey*, and the *Good Universities Guide* contributed to a consumer ethos whereby students were expected to make informed choices about their place of study.

Significant changes have also occurred in relation to fees, all designed to encourage user-pays principles. Fees, in some form or another, were traditionally paid by Australian students until they were abolished by a Labor government under Prime Minister Whitlam in 1974. Attending universities then remained free until an upfront higher education administration charge (HEAC) of $A250 was introduced by Labor in 1987. In 1989 this was abandoned in favor of the more far-reaching Higher Education Contribution Scheme (HECS) that brought about student contributions or deferred fees, payable through the tax system. In 1997 the Coalition government lowered the income threshold at which repayments commenced, changed other thresholds so that repayments had to be made more quickly, and introduced three different levels of liability based on the estimated costs of course provision and the expected financial benefit of different programs of study.

Other consequential initiatives came into play, all working to privatize the costs of education. In 1985 Labor ended the Overseas Student Program. This was a free scholarship program for foreign students from neighboring Third World countries to study in Australia. Ending this program permitted universities to charge full-cost fees to overseas students. In contrast to the Overseas Student Contribution (OSC) that was paid into consolidated revenue, these fees went directly to the institutions concerned (Marginson 1997a). In 1989 certain postgraduate courses were made liable to fees. In 1994 the restrictions surrounding these courses were almost entirely removed, effectively leaving postgraduate coursework a fee-paying domain. Then, from 1998, the Coalition permitted universities to enroll a proportion of private Australian undergraduate students. While many restrictions applied, Nicholls (1996: 43) notes that this decision signaled the government's commitment to a deregulated and commercially oriented system of higher education. Crucially, these measures were accompanied by falling levels of government support for individual students, with the grants given to students reduced and the income tests tightened. Between 1984 and 1996, the proportion of students unable to obtain government support almost doubled, increasing from 35.1 percent to 61.9 percent (Marginson 1997a: 241).

As a result of such measures, the proportion of higher education income contributed by students (through HECS, fees, and other charges) rose from 3 percent to over 24 percent in the decade following the Dawkins' 1988 reforms, while the proportion coming from government sources fell from 91 percent to 62 percent (Marginson 1997a: 236). Allied to this, public funding declined relative to the increase in student enrollments. Between 1988 and 1998, student enrollments increased by over 45 percent while the real value of operating funds per full-time student fell by around 15 percent (Marginson 1997a: 220).

At a managerial level, universities have experienced changes in the style, structure, and nomenclature of management directed toward more streamlined administration, greater control over spending, and more flexible staffing practices. In line with this, there has been an explicit attempt to move universities from collegial to executive decision making. The new management practices have led to the decentralized committee system being replaced by a centralized executive management system, with devolved budgetary control. The official reports of both Hoare (1995) and West (1998) have criticized universities for their slowness in adopting these forms of practice.

A detailed summary of these and other events follows. Most changes occurred over one decade, although the impetus for further privatization continued into the next decade.

Events in Australian Higher Education
Illustrating Globalization 1975–2001

1975–2001: Overall growth in enrollments coupled with funding reductions and reduction in staff numbers.

1982–1992: Development of Special Research Centers, Key Centers of Teaching and Research, Cooperative Research Centers, and Advanced Engineering Centers. There were ninety-four centers funded during this period.

1985–1986: The Hawke Labor Government deregulated the model of recruitment of overseas students. The government introduced an Administrative Fee of $A250, when higher education in the decade prior to 1985 was free.

1986–1991: Recruitment of overseas students accelerated and shifted from "aid" to "trade" students: 20,000 aid students and 200 trade students from overseas in 1986; by 1991, 6,000 aid students and 48,000 trade students.

1987–1989: The Dawkins' 1988 White Paper promoted active steering of universities by the newly formed superministry that combined education, training, and employment. The most important developments were:

- Creation of the Unified National System through mergers and transformations of colleges of advanced education and institutes of technology into universities.
- Introduction of the Higher Education Contribution Scheme (HECS)—fees for undergraduate students—following the Wran Report in 1988. Fixed HECS at $A1,800 for all courses.
- Payment by results, clawback of funds to be redistributed by research performance, targeted grants for certain research areas, creation of key centers in teaching and research, special grants for staff development and teaching innovations.
- Educational profiling began in 1988 where institutions had to negotiate their profiles with the Commonwealth government and begin bidding for extra funds. Equity programs were part of the profiling process.

1991: Open Learning Australia began as a television-based open learning program coordinated by Monash University and later developed as a private company.

1993:   Deakin Australia formed as a private company within Deakin University to provide short courses for large government and private employers. Later began training for Coles Australia.

1993–1995: Quality Audits

- Committee for Quality Assurance reviewed each institution in its research, teaching, and community service (quality assessment) and reviewed their internal procedures for monitoring and improving quality (quality audit).
- It ranked the universities into six groups, later reduced to three, allocating $A75 million, with the highest ranking rewarded with the most money.

1995:   The Hoare Report on University Management focused on smaller governing councils and more streamlined decision making.

1996–1998: Under the Coalition Government, Higher Education Ministers Vanstone and Kemp introduced greater competition and privatization through reduced funding and extended the user-pays philosophy.

- Increase in HECS fees in 1997, three tiers: $A5,600, $A4,700, and $A3,300. Repayments began at a lower threshold of $A20,701.
- An Efficiency Dividend was demanded from the sector from 1997–1998, which reduced funding of operating grants by 4.9 percent.
- Increased funding for targeted research ($A112.4 million over three years).
- Voluntary unionism, to break control by so-called left-wing Student Guilds.
- Universities were allowed to charge fees for Australian students who did not gain entry into university under university admissions quotas of government-funded places.
- Fees were charged for postgraduate coursework degrees.
- West Report into financing of higher education, *Learning for Life* (1998), argued for more reliance on market forces and student vouchers.

1999–2001: Dr. Kemp's, Minister for Education, Training and Youth Affairs, preferred reform options were leaked to the press. They included fees and admissions deregulation and workplace agreements for staff to create more staffing flexibility. Cabinet decided not to im-

plement most of his reform policies, with the exception of workplace agreements, due to an outcry in the press against them.

- Government continued to reduce funding.
- Eight universities began operating at a deficit.
- *New Knowledge, New Opportunities*, a discussion paper on
  higher education research and research training by Dr. Kemp
  (1999: 6) pointed to greater commercialization of research:
  "Institutions need to create a more entrepreneurial culture . . .
  and need to recognize the importance of commercialization to
  our national economic and social interest, and to value effective linkages with the business sector. The other, related challenge is to put in place the structures and internal management
  arrangements which can give effect to a set of cultural objectives along these lines."
- Melbourne University Private launched as a full-fee-paying
  private extension of the public university.
- *Universitas 21* formed as a global network of seventeen research universities from Australia, North America, and Europe
  (National University of Singapore, Universities of Hong
  Kong, Fudan, Peking, Melbourne, NSW, Queensland, Auckland, McGill, British Columbia, Michigan, Birmingham, Ed-
  inburgh, Glasgow, Nottingham, Albert-Ludwigs-Freiburg, and
  Lund) with Thomson Publishing as a media partner. (Several
  have since dropped out due to disagreements about the alli-
  ance.)
- Enterprise Agreements negotiated. Many strikes by staff and
  students (at least ten universities went on strike in 2000). Federal government made industrial relations measures, such as
  the Australian Workplace Agreements, a condition for re-
  ceiving a portion of $A259 million for salary supplementation
  (contingent on genuine workplace reforms).
- Movement toward smaller boards. For an extreme example,
  the University of Adelaide appointed businessman Robert
  Champion de Crespigny as its new chancellor. Within months,
  he succeeded in having the council powers delegated to him
  and formed a small committee of eight to operate *in cabinet*
  (in secret).
- Budget 2000 keeps strategic partnerships with industry at current levels of $A62.9 million; $A4m per annum for the next
  four years for research infrastructure equipment; and bonded
  scholarships for rural doctors.
- Whistle-blowers alleged that standards had been lowered for
  overseas students. At least six cases of academics being

sacked, contracts not renewed or suspended, and disciplinary action taken against these whistle-blowers (Australia Institute 2001b).

- *The Virtuous Cycle,* the report of the Health and Medical Research Strategic Review, boosted funding by $A32 million for 2000 and a further $614 million over six years from 1999-2005.
- Innovation Statement, *Backing Australia's Ability* (Howard 2001), represented an additional Government investment of $A2.9 billion over five years, with $A159 million in the first year growing to $A947 million in 2005-2006.
- Competitive bidding for new places in certain high-technology fields (government added funds for new enrollments, but universities then had to bid for the places, based on criteria).

Parallel British Developments

Strikingly similar developments began transforming British higher education in the mid-1980s, and within a decade, a major restructuring had occurred. The Jarratt Report (1985) recommended that vice-chancellors become chief executives and governing bodies perform as boards of directors, while the Croham Report (1987) established performance indicators for universities' finance, management, teaching, and research. This form of assessment was backed by teaching quality audits and research assessment exercises (Morley 1995). This resulted in competitive league tables based on formula funding. Another major change came in the early 1990s when tenure was eliminated—even though there had already been a 71 percent increase in the number of academic staff on part time pro rata contracts (Hearn 1999: 137). These changes gave employers more flexibility in their staffing profiles. This was necessary, vice-chancellors argued, because direct public funding for teaching fell to about 25 percent by 1995. As a result, there was an increase of 64 percent in overall student numbers and a rise of only 11 percent in staff in British universities during the 1990s (Morley 1999: 34).

Edwards (2000: 325) gives a good description of the new British system:

The system is now replete with corporate identities and mission statements; competitive hierarchies between old and new universities, between departments within universities and between individuals within departments, for scarce resources; market mechanisms drive the funding of research; there are external teaching and quality assessments with graded departments; and discourses of inputs and outputs, and of individualistic student consumer rights, have come to the fore.

Developments at the Coal Face

Marginson and Considine (2000) surveyed a representative group of Australian universities to find out how these global practices were affecting them. While some of the seventeen institutions in their study had been more successful than others in competing on the new level playing field, and while some had reformed their institutions to a greater extent than others, they had all experienced certain critical changes in common. Marginson and Considine (2000: 10-11) identify five principal trends that characterized Australian universities across the board in the mid-1990s:

- A new kind of executive power, including a will to manage and to manage according to *good practice*.
- Structural changes, including the replacement of collegial forms of governance with senior executive groups moving from more formal to semiformal types of power.
- A move to produce flexibility of personnel and resources through industrial deregulation, and the use of soft money and commercial companies outside of the main legislative rules of the university.
- A decline in the role of academic disciplines as a result of new super deans or executive deans who control several disciplines and are often drawn from outside of academic disciplines.
- A pattern of devolution supporting centralized control and increased line management authority. They noted a decline in the role of academic boards as management either bypassed them altogether or reduced their powers. In relation to this, Marginson and Considine (2000: 10-11) found that university leaders often saw collegial forms of decision making as "a nuisance" and as "obstacles" to managerial imperatives.

Because of competition pressures, Australian universities have experienced closures and amalgamations; elimination of jobs; threats to certain disciplines which do not generate the income required under the new funding formula; the replacement of the old collegial committee structure with executive boards; and new performance measures, penetrating to the level of the individual staff member. Alongside these developments, university administrators have promoted various forms of entrepreneurial activity such as commercial land development, forging profitable links with industry, and outsourcing activities such as childcare, counseling, and security. In cases where the entrepreneurial ethos has been adopted most enthusiastically, the new mission statements come to rest on market attractiveness, income diversity, and management efficiency.

Marginson and Considine (2000: 39) suggest that as a result of these developments, universities in Australia have changed "more in the 1990s than in the previous 40 years." They also argue that "neo-liberal policies have been enforced with greater rigor in Australia than in the USA. Fiscal constraints have been tighter and competition reform has been harder" (Marginson and Considine 2000: 54). In line with this, many academics believe that intellectual traditions are being *forcibly* displaced by market directives. Coady, professor of philosophy at Melbourne, thus speaks of the threat that the new practices pose to "intellectual virtues such as honesty, intellectual courtesy, indifference to the mere fashion in ideas, and a dedication to the regulative ideal of truth" (Coady 1996: 51).

These views are echoed in other parts of the world, particularly the Anglo-American countries. In discussing the impact of corporatization on public universities in Canada, Polster (2000) proposes that academics may become complicit in advancing profitable links with industry, at the expense of their real interests, because of the incentives and penalties involved. Moreover, she warns:

> As for corporate links, they are not an add-on to the university, such that after their establishment one has the old university plus these links. Corporate links are an add-into the university, which produce the qualitative changes that pervade its multiple and interacting aspects and dimensions including its culture, operating practices, funding systems, reward structures, etc. (Polster 2000: 183)

Another Canadian academic, Tudiver (1999: 168), suggests that

> Operating universities like businesses changes their essence. Gearing to the market means redefining relevance. Social values that have shaped higher education are replaced by measures of financial viability. Research and teaching are assessed in narrow market terms. Profit becomes the guiding principle for deciding which services and products to offer. . . . Corporations draw faculty into a search for sales rather than truth, favouring projects with strong market potential over theoretical or basic research. Inherent value of the work is less important than its potential to generate revenue.

Similarly, in the United States, as Press and Washburn (2000) contend, commercially sponsored research is putting disinterested inquiry at risk. They describe university administration as "co-capitalist" and say that it is systematically downgrading arts faculties where, for the most part, staff are not engaging with market values. The humanities, they say, have been "neglected, downgraded, and forced to retrench" due to the market-model university which gives priority to those subjects which "make money, study money, or attract money" (Press and Washburn 2000: 52). In the same vein, Miyoshi (1998: 263) describes how the function of the university has become industrial management with, he says, an "unmistakable reduction of its public and critical role." Reflecting on this endangered tradition, he comments that

From Fichte and von Humboldt, through Newman and Arnold or even Thor-
stein Veblen, the university was thought of as a part of national culture, national history, national identity, and national governance. The construction and
maintenance of the coherent nation-state was at the core of its agenda. (Miyoshi
1998: 262)

More pragmatically, one of the well-documented consequences of the corporatization of universities is the increase in working loads. A study conducted by the
National Tertiary Education Union (2000), *Unhealthy Places of Learning,* found that
the majority of staff worked above a 40-hour week and the average for full-time
academic staff was 52.8 hours per week. Some 83 percent of all academics and 77
percent of general staff reported increases in workload since 1996, with a majority
working in departments that have lost staff. In another national study of Australian
academics, McInnis (1999) reports that the great majority of academics talked about
loss of morale and the deterioration of overall quality and working conditions.

The Challenge to Traditional University Values

At this stage, we bring together much of what we have said so far by reflecting
on the impact of change on traditional university values. In 1997 we asked senior managers and those just retired from their positions: "Which university practices and traditions would you like to retain for the future?" We report the responses of four managers from three different Australian universities (one of the
oldest universities, one established in the early 1970s, and one of the newest
universities). Their answers are remarkably similar:

I think the practice that is most important is the recognition that academic excellence comes from individuals and their self-motivation. . . . I don't think you
motivate them through quality control or performance indicators or distant bureaucratic measurement or outcomes analysis. (Former vice-chancellor)

Robert Menzies [former Liberal Prime Minister] once said that universities
were guardians of the soul of Australia. In a funny sort of way, I still believe
that. Where else is culture going to be defended and retained? It also seems to
me that universities are for encouraging that spark of curiosity when a faculty
member gets turned on by an idea. (Former vice-chancellor)

I think we need to retain the sense that individual academics are valued for their
individuality. Their individual research, their spin on the world, if you like, . . .
you can't tinker too much with that sense of academic autonomy and individuality without risking the sense of what makes a university valued in the community. (Pro vice-chancellor)

I think the university is a place that encourages freedom of thought and expression, which encourages people of all ages to develop their talents, irrespective
of the current prevailing orthodoxy. (Pro vice-chancellor)

The responses of these senior managers point to three traditional values believed to be under threat: professional autonomy and integrity, critical dissent and academic freedom, and the public interest value of universities. To this we add a fourth: democratic collegiality. We start with it.

Madden (1999) suggests that the new forms of directive leadership in many liberal arts colleges in the United States are insulting to academics and contribute to adversarial relationships between administrators and faculty members. From her experience, "participatory and consensus-based decision making is far more satisfying for participants and produces results and plans that people can buy into more readily" (Madden 1999: 2). Others have voiced similar concerns about authoritarian models of management in universities. Lafferty and Fleming (2000) maintain that that they are inappropriate to the organization of academic work. They comment on the intrinsic motivation academics have for their work and the value they place on autonomy to perform it. They urge academics to retain the better aspects of collegiality (such as peer review and a respect for scholarship) in the face of intensified managerial control and top-down decision making.

Marginson (1997b: 364) suggests that in the "current period of the 'managed university,' institutional autonomy and academic freedom are being quite substantially reworked." He sees a transition toward market forms of autonomy and freedom where the ambition of (New Right) governments is "to implicate the individual citizen, as player and partner, into this market game as autonomous chooser" (Marginson 1997b: 365, quoting Gordon, C. 1991: 36). Drawing on Foucault, he notes that "people are nudged in the right direction, 'caused to behave' in the required manner" (Marginson 1997b: 363). It is tremendously difficult for institutions and individual academics to reject the market game given that their survival depends precisely on becoming more competitive in terms of the parameters set by government policy makers. The reliance on performance indicators as a funding carrot means that those who play the game reap the benefits; those who do not, risk going to the wall. Shore and Roberts (1993) make a similar analysis of the British Quality Audit exercises, which, they argue, will have devastating consequences for intellectual freedom.

The erosion of academic freedom is graphically illustrated in the case of the University of Toronto. On October 15, 1992, the Governing Council of the University of Toronto passed the following statement regarding academic freedom:

> Within the unique university context, the most crucial of all human rights are the rights of freedom of speech, academic freedom, and freedom of research. And we affirm that these rights are meaningless unless they entail the right to raise deeply disturbing questions and provocative challenges to the cherished beliefs of society at large and of the university itself. It is this human right to radical, critical teaching and research with which the university has a duty above all to be concerned; for there is no one else, no other institution and no other office, in our modern liberal democracy, which is the custodian of this most precious and vulnerable right of the liberated human spirit. (Cited in Graham 2000: 23-24)

Despite the passage of this statement into the university's statutes, the University of Toronto has allegedly attempted to restrict academic freedom in several cases. Olivieri (2000) describes her battle with the university when she stood up for patient protection and scientific integrity. Her trial results about a particular drug's negative effects on sick children were eventually published in *The New England Journal of Medicine* in 1998. Prior to that, the drug company in question (which had partially supported the work) allegedly sought to suppress the findings. Moreover, the university did not support her when the hospital at which she worked sought to remove her from her position. It was only through the efforts of family, friends, prominent researchers, and the University of Toronto Faculty Association that her dismissal was reversed. Her case is one of many that have been documented by staff unions and professional associations around the world. Graham (2000: 23) states the dilemma involved when "money and truth collide":

> The scholar and the scientist pursue knowledge, faithful to the drive of their discipline; and they must preserve academic freedom and scholarly/scientific integrity. The entrepreneur knows no equivalent freedom. . . . Scholarship and entrepreneurship are two different cultures, two different kinds of life: the life of the mind as opposed to the life of the bottom line.

In short, when universities become increasingly dependent on corporate donations (in the Toronto case, the drug company is said to have offered a donation of $C25 million to the university), it is easy for conflicts of this nature to arise. With the increase in university–industry partnerships in which knowledge is patented and profits shared between universities and industries, there tends to be less concern for the public good. Another implication of these partnerships is secrecy, with Delanty (2001) noting that there have been several cases where academics were punished for breaching agreements in disclosing sensitive information they felt to be in the public interest.

Patterns of Control and Resistance

The issue of academic freedom is central to this narrative. There is tension between the political claims of right-wing governments and university administrators and the experiences of faculty and students. Neoliberalism claims to wind the state back in order to set the people free. However, universities commonly report a distinct increase in official interventions over recent years. Currie and Vidovich (1998) found that more than half of the respondents from Australian universities thought that control had become more centralized and intrusive over the past five years. Davis (1996: 10) points out that the "freedom to act and deregulation are not the same thing . . . indeed, greater freedom and more intensive accountability measures may go hand in hand." Similarly, Clarke (1998) argues that new forms of audit and performance appraisal allow authority to be more effectively spread throughout the organization.

We suggest that three forms of interlocking control have come to bear on university staff and students in the neoliberal epoch (Harris 1999). The first operates through indirect strategies. It appeals to self-interest—or, more fundamentally, survival—through a series of incentive/penalty systems. Examples include the quality assurance measures formulated by Baldwin, the protocols and discourses surrounding managed competition, and the measures whereby students are encouraged to think and act as consumers. The second form bears more directly and immediately on its staff and students, involving the application of detailed assessments at both an individual and organizational level. The tuition fee system, or HECS, for example, gives rise to a legal obligation by each student to the Taxation Office, requiring "suites of software to track every subject taken by every individual and to assign to this a price based on the specific course of study of that student" (Davis 1996: 17-18). Other examples include the Relative Funding Model with its capacity to turn global categories into small sets of indices and the research quantum with its complex calculations relating to different types of publications, grant monies, and research completions. Third, there is coercion, manifest in forced amalgamations, job losses, funding decline, and program closures.

These forms of control have an intersecting and triangular relationship, one with another, commonly directed toward the promotion of competition and private enterprise. Each, however, carries its own language and set of justifications. The *indirect, incentive-based* group speaks about choice, productivity, and motivation, the *direct* or *regulatory-calculative* group about measurement and assessment, and the *coercive* group about the need for governments to take command. There is also a distinctive idiom attached to each group. The catchword as far as incentives are concerned is *personal choice*, camouflaging how far choices are purposefully structured by government, ruling out options such as scholarly, noncommercial research and collegial decision making. In the case of the regulatory-calculative strategies, the appeal is to "rigor" and "bearing the pain," masking the fact that governments have, as a matter of political choice, introduced regulations that steer universities toward becoming more commercial enterprises. The intersecting and obfuscating nature of these claims makes the composite whole hard to challenge, the more so as they engender a climate of divide and rule and personal alienation. The main patterns are set out in table 1.1.

Although these claims are self-supporting, they are not invincible. Neither is globalization. Not all nations respond in the same way with specific historical, political, cultural, and economic contexts influencing the types of programs to emerge. There is no essential determinacy to the ways in which globalizing processes work. There are also important sites of resistance.

Table 1.1 Patterns of Regulation and Their Associated Rationalities

Form of Control	Epistemology and Justification	Idiom
Indirect—incentive and penalty based	Private enterprise, competition, and personal independence are in the national interest as they enhance productivity. Incentives are needed to promote these qualities.	Personal choice
Direct and regulatory calculative—based on detailed assessments and calculations	Output, productivity, and quality can be measured and made transparent. Official assessments are required to compare and improve individual and organizational output.	Rigor
Coercive	Democratic governments have a mandate to rule. It is necessary to enforce certain decisions or compel people to act in a certain way in the interests of the nation.	Bearing the pain

In Australian universities, both staff unions (academic and general) and student guilds have protested the changes commonly associated with globalization and corporatization. In some institutions, there have been demonstrations, votes of no confidence in management, appeals to the media, occupations, and sit-ins. In one Australian university, for example, the students reclaimed the senate building as the Student Embassy and made certain demands on the vice-chancellor. They requested that

> In determining the future academic profile of the university, at all times the basic ethos under which this university was founded should be its primary concern. In this instance, the basic ethos is defined as remaining an alternative institution to other universities; promoting and maintaining interdisciplinarity of offerings and flexible degree structures; encouraging, maintaining and strengthening research in all disciplines; maintaining and fortifying a commitment to a student-centered university community; restoring a commitment to quality teaching and research over market principles; and sustaining a commitment to courses for the non-traditional, non-mainstream student population. (Education Action Group, May 30, 2000)

During the same period, an academic at this university argued that:

> We need to remain a university in the full sense of the term, dedicated to critical examination and dissemination of the spectrum of knowledge that is significant to Australian society and a globalizing world. This must not only include those dimensions which are "marketable." (Submission to Working Party on Academic/Qualitative Principles for Refocusing the University, March 2000)

These voices are important reminders that individuals and groups help shape their institutions, even if both the external and internal pressures are strong and difficult to resist. The alternative vision for Australian universities is actually a conservative one: conserving the best values that have shaped the university tradition over the last century. This hinges on independent critical inquiry and forms of knowledge that inquire, rather than dictate. By recognizing those values, the university could chart a different course that would serve its students and the community in the public interest.

Looking Ahead: Globalization, Universities, and Gender

The next chapter discusses how women have fared in the globalized university. Following that, the rest of the book reports on our findings about gender and organizational culture in the universities participating in our research. There are chapters on power, success, failure, sacrifice, and the worldview of managers. Underlying each is the process whereby the male culture becomes normalized, invisible, and everyday. In concluding this chapter, we provide a few pointers to the broad relationship between globalization and gender, linking what has been said so far with what lies ahead.

Just as capitalism and patriarchy interlocked to produce a particular gender order in the national era, so it does in the new globalized epoch. One of the marked differences between the two periods relates to women's work. The old tradition was based on a domestic division of labor that relied on women's unpaid work to support male breadwinners and, hence, the national economy. The current era continues to rely on women's unpaid domestic work, but it also requires extensive female labor force participation to support the national economy in its newly competitive, globalized role. There is mounting evidence that work demands on women, relative both to men and to what went before, have increased. The implications of this are voiced by female participants throughout this book.

This intensification of work is not only damaging to those directly affected but also to family, friendship, and community. This unfriendliness is exacerbated by globalization's central characteristic—its restless search for new markets—that percolates down to staff incited to go when and where opportunity knocks. Such a pattern is gendered, rewarding the roving strategist, rather than the person *in situ*. Many women participating in our research recognized this tension but spoke, nevertheless, of their decision to stay with local and familial commitments, rather than further their career. So, too, did those men who wished to participate more fully in child rearing and family life.

In tandem with this, the changing countenance of capitalism brings about new representations of the successful persona. In universities, there is a shift from the independent, quasi-monastic scholar who produces the outstanding paper to the strategic entrepreneur who knows how to obtain grants. Both are coded masculine. The scholar was always supported by a wife who saw to his needs and took care of his children. The entrepreneur (who still has a wife) stands as the new version of economic man. He is footloose and fancy-free, owing allegiance to no particular locality, collegial network, or intellectual frame. He goes where he must. He also thinks what he must, accommodating research projects to suit the call of industry. Put another way, and relating this to the previous point, we suggest that global pressures produce a *disconnectedness* in academic life and intellectual commitments, which sits at distinct odds with women's traditional *connectedness* to family, community, and research inquiry.

Perhaps the most marked characteristic of the corporatized university is its downgrading of collegiality. As a result, success is tenuous, individualized, and highly tailored to the needs of the entrepreneurial institution. Importantly, this does not mean that women do not get to high-ranking positions. Indeed, an important corporate expectation is that talented females should be actively sought out. What it does mean is that the (few) women who are selected have little room to maneuver and high pressures to conform. The difficulties facing them are greater because the peak culture operates by stealth. It is invisible, because it is rendered *normal*. Such is the main theme of this book.

Chapter 2

Gendered Universities

Introduction

Historically, universities have long been recognized as male institutions into which females have been admitted. First, they admitted female students, and then they began to hire female academics. Now female students predominate in many universities around the world with women constituting more than 50 percent of the enrollment. However, female academics have not fared so well. In most universities, they are less than a third of academics. Females are also less likely to reach the higher levels of administration or become professors at the top of the academic hierarchy.

This chapter explores why there are still relatively few women in academia despite decades of affirmative action and equal opportunity legislation. The underrepresentation of women in academia seems to be a persistent and global phenomenon (O'Connor 2000). Lund (1998) discovered no real differences between high-income countries and low- and middle-income countries in the percentages of males and females among full-time academic staff. She also found few differences at the top of the hierarchy. There appear to be few countries where women are gaining senior positions at an equal rate with men.

In this chapter, we start with some general comments on global practices and gendered work patterns. We then summarize the overall pattern of gender discrimination in western universities and outline the findings of a study investigating the treatment of men and women in three American and three Australian universities. Following this, we turn to the theoretical framework informing our understanding of these differences.

Global Practices and Gendered Work Cultures

Our general proposition is that the more competitive environment ushered in by globalization practices makes the position of women in universities more tenuous. Restructuring in England has reduced the number of women in senior positions (Lie, Malik, and Harris 1994). More generally, since the majority of women are at the bottom of the hierarchy, they are disproportionately affected in a negative way by the neoliberal reforms bringing universities closer to market forces. As the last ones hired, women are the first to lose their jobs when money becomes tighter.

Economic globalization has created the situation in which the most valued activities in universities reflect individualist rather than collective values and competitive rather than cooperative practices. Alongside this, universities are rapidly losing their ethos as collegial communities. Scholars are competing against each other in a *performativity* culture that tends to benefit men more than women. This competitive atmosphere reduces the sense of community within institutions and is likely to emphasize those aspects of the male culture that are seen as most hostile to women (Currie 1998).

Competition takes its toll on all areas of the university, but some areas are more vulnerable than others. Universities favor those areas that lead directly to jobs. Following from this, students begin to take a more instrumental view of their university studies, and governments direct their higher education policies toward achieving greater competitiveness in global markets. Both the students' choices and government policies favor information technology, commerce/economics/business areas, biotechnology, and, to a lesser extent, the hard sciences (favored more by governments than by students). Within universities there are battles to save areas such as women's studies, ethnic studies, philosophy, and the classics, which are either seen as too radical or irrelevant. If these struggles are lost, academics in such disciplines lose their jobs or have to retrain to teach in more favored areas. Some choose to orient their discipline toward the more popular areas and teach courses like Ethics in Biotechnology, Managing Diversity, or Women and Management. Generally, though, the pure, more critical studies of philosophy and women's studies are losing ground to the more practical and job-oriented subjects.

Not all universities have adopted the new ethos, and there are pockets of resistance to this dominant trend. Nevertheless, in most Anglo-American universities (and their derivatives in Australia, Canada, and New Zealand, for example) global practices have been adopted by managers bent on restructuring their universities to be more competitive in the global economies.

Overview of Gendered Universities

Universities are segregated both horizontally and vertically. Women are more often found in certain jobs and certain disciplines and are more often located at the bottom of the hierarchy at entry-level positions. Park (1996) studied the gender roles and gender hierarchies implicit in university tenure and promotion policies in the United States. She noted the revolving door phenomenon where junior faculty are rotated through entry-level positions and rarely given tenure. More of these revolving scholars are female.

Despite the fact that women are matching men in some disciplines in obtaining Ph.D.'s, something seems to happen to them when they enter into universities. Husu (1999) cites a study suggesting that after finishing their Ph.D.'s, Finnish academic women fall into a black hole. Her own findings are not quite so dramatic. She concludes that the exclusion of female scholars does not start immediately after women obtain their Ph.D.'s, but accumulates gradually. Even in a society that some would depict as a paradise of gender equality, Husu (1999) reports that women continue to be in a minority position (about one-third of academics) and in the lower levels of the hierarchy.

Finland, nevertheless, boasts the highest proportion of women among professors (18.4 percent) of fifteen European Union countries (Osborne 1998). In contrast, Ireland has just over 5 percent of women in the professoriate and the United Kingdom 7-8 percent (O'Connor 2000). Not only are women fewer in number in senior positions in British universities, but they are paid on average 18 percent less than their male counterparts (Association of University Teachers 2001).

In the two countries that are studied more intensely in this chapter, namely Australia and the United States, a similar pattern exists. Kolodny (1998) notes that women are still predominantly clustered in the untenured ranks of assistant professor in American universities. She concludes that women continue to hit the proverbial *glass ceiling* at two crucial points: in the initial promotion and tenure review and then, again, in advancement to full professor. O'Connor (2000) reports that women are approximately 16 percent of those with full professorial status in the United States. In Australia, as Ward (2000) records, females made up only 11 percent of professors in 1998, whereas at the base level women were 51 percent. Illing (1999) also notes Australian universities' poor record in employing women at senior levels. In 1995 there were only two women vice-chancellors out of thirty-eight, although this increased to six (or 16 percent) by 1999. After her retirement, one of these pioneering vice-chancellors, Fay Gale, was asked to address a gathering of 100 females who were all senior executives in Australian universities. She gave an account of the dirty tricks that dogged her all the way to the top of the university (Illing 1999; Eveline 2000).

Rai and Critzer (2000), two male political scientists in the United States, argue that affirmative action has had only a minimal impact on academe. Here it is important to note that the Equal Employment Opportunity Act has been in exis-

tence since 1972. The legislation was followed by universities establishing
Commissions on the Status of Women (Glazer 1997). But despite three decades
of work by feminist activists, supportive presidents, and the appointment of affirmative action/equal opportunity officers, little has changed in American universities, with Rai saying that "white males still dominate academia. Period"
(Schneider 2000: 20).

Moses (1997) reports that the financial gender gap persists in American
academic salaries with women earning 85 to 96 cents for every dollar earned by
their male counterparts. The record is even worse for administrators. Female
administrators earn up to 39 cents less for every dollar earned by male administrators. In a careful study, which successfully untangles the variables that might
predict this difference in pay, Bellas (1994) found that differences remained,
even after controlling for labor-market conditions for different disciplines and
the characteristics of individual faculty and their work. She concludes that the
market was operating imperfectly and having a detrimental effect on women's
salaries.

The story is much the same in Australian universities where concerns for efficiency and accountability have resulted in equity issues moving down, rather
than up, the policy agenda (Farish, et al. 1995; Blackmore 1992). One measure
of this is that the number of women in senior management positions within
Australian universities, and more generally within government and the private
sector, appears to have fallen (Still, Guerin, and Chia 1992). Despite Sex Discrimination Legislation (1984) and Affirmative Action Legislation (1986), only
2.4 percent of senior management positions in the nation were held by women in
1994 (Australian Bureau of Statistics 1994). Even though there has been some
movement into middle-level positions, Australian statistics on women in management reveal a systematic decrease in representation with each step up the
hierarchy (Schneider 1993). Alongside this, Ramsay (2000) notes that in Australian universities female administrative staff are consistently several classifi-
cation levels lower than male administrative staff with identical qualifications
and years of experience. She concludes, "Neither qualifications nor years of
experience working in higher education provide the same rewards or professional recognition for women general staff as those which their male colleagues
enjoy" (Ramsay 2000: 5).

A study of 3872 academic and general staff in Australia found substantial
gaps between the earnings of men and women (Probert, Ewer, and Whiting
1998). Male academics earn $439 biweekly more than women academics, and
male general staff earn $265 more than female general staff. The report states
that the differences can be attributed to employment level, full time status, qualifications, and the number of years worked. The report also warned of the potential discriminatory effect of cuts because of the concentration of women in lower
employment levels and in temporary positions (Illing 1998). Probert, when interviewed by Illing, said that changes over the past ten years in universities
mean that things will get worse. "With their managerial overlay, high-level jobs
have become much more demanding. Long hours, and late and early meetings,

make these jobs unfriendly to good parents" (Illing 1999: 42).

Another factor affecting male and female financial parity is the growing practice of negotiating individual salary packages. This is well established in American universities and beginning to infiltrate Australian universities where managers have moved to negotiate salaries within an enterprise agreement framework, thus breaking down the common national salary levels. Within particular disciplines, there is a handful of professors who have negotiated their own salary packages. These moves are often depicted as the thin edge of the wedge toward individual salary negotiations, which in most countries disadvantage women. In 1999-2000, the Australian Federal Government (Liberal-National Coalition parties, on the Right side of the political spectrum) awarded universities extra funding if their administrators could include individual workplace agreements in their Enterprise Bargaining (Collective Bargaining) Agreements, even though the academic unions opposed these.

To compete for higher salaries, women are being asked to get tougher, be more productive, and become more competitive in attracting grants. There is a lack of recognition that women do not have the same material conditions and freedom as men. Fay Gale (1997: 2), in searching for strategies to redress gender imbalance in numbers of senior academic women in Australia, commented that "there is an expectation in universities that unlimited time will be devoted to academic work, and as women often have significant domestic responsibilities, they find it difficult, if not impossible, to meet this unrealistic expectation" (Gale 1997: 2).

In our introduction to this book, we made reference to the MIT (1999) study on the status of women faculty in science. This suggested that

> Each generation of young women, including those who are currently senior faculty, began by believing that gender discrimination was "solved" in the previous generation and would not touch them. Gradually, however, their eyes were opened to the realization that the playing field is not level after all and that they had paid a high price both personally and professionally as a result. (MIT 1999: 9)

Another important finding of the MIT study was that "problems appear to increase progressively as women approach the same age as their administrators" (MIT 1999: 13). A similar conclusion was reached by Spurling (1997) in a study on women and change in British higher education: "Senior men get Brownie points for encouraging the careers of junior women, but it's different when you're on a level with them" (Spurling 1997: 45). According to the MIT study, these problems are exacerbated by nondemocratic practices and departments:

> The committee believes that problems flourish in departments where nondemocratic practices, including administrative procedures whose basis is known only to a few, lead inevitably to cronyism and unequal access to the substantial resources of MIT. (MIT 1999: 13)

In sum, despite the increase of women in the workplace and in higher education over the last twenty-five years, their continuing underrepresentation in senior management and the senior levels of academia remains marked (Burton 1997). Studies of women in corporate and higher education management consistently point to the significance of patriarchal power structures and informal cultures that construct visible and invisible career impediments termed glass ceilings (Heward 1994). A major UNESCO report, *Women in Higher Education Management,* states that "with hardly an exception, the global picture is one of men outnumbering women at about five to one at middle management level and at about twenty or more to one at senior management level" (Dines 1993: 11). That study found cultural attitudes and practices to be the key impediments to women's equal access to education and, consequently, to academic career mobility.

Morley (1999) suggests that under the new managerialism, three "Es" are promoted: economy, efficiency, and effectiveness, with a fourth "E"—equity—absent. Like Ball (1994, cited in Morley 1999: 29), she believes that "equity is off the agenda, inequality is a cornerstone of the market." Under the new conditions, she says, feminist demands for educational equality are perceived as "ideological extravagances" (Morley 1999: 40). Newman (1995) likewise identifies a number of dangers for women in the new managerialist culture. In particular, she suggests that when women argue for special interests such as gender and ethnicity, they are told that this would be diversionary to the larger mission of the university and that women and men should be seen as equal partners in pursuing the university's goals. In sum, the new model of leadership offers few points of identification for women in general and even fewer for Black women, older women, or women with disabilities.

What such arguments do not reveal is how male and female academics respond to the unequal position of men and women within universities. We turn to a study that directly bears on this question.

The Study

The data we discuss here comes from a study investigating the way men and women are treated in three American and three Australian universities (see Currie and Newson 1998). (This formed part of a larger project studying the impact of globalization on the work culture of academics.) Our discussion relates to one question in this study. The question varied slightly depending upon the interview, but the gist of it was, "Is there any marked differences between the treatment of men and women?" Objectively, we knew that female academics were more often in junior positions and more often teaching in areas distant from the market. What we wanted to probe was male and female academics' subjective assessment of this situation.

The Australian universities chosen for this study represent a range of different contexts (old, traditional; small, alternative; and new, amalgamated) in the higher education sector. The universities from the United States represent state universities in different geographical locations as well as different strata within the ranking of what are termed the 100 research universities. In discussing the study's findings, we collapsed the three universities in each country and made comparisons between the total samples in Australia and the United States. There were 154 Australian and 100 American respondents.[1] About 37 percent of the combined sample were females and 63 percent were males.

We found that four types of explanations were given in answer to the question about the differences between the treatment of men and women. We named these the *structural, denial, historical,* and *positive action* responses.

Structural Responses (35 percent of responses)

Structural responses concentrated on the patriarchal nature of the institutions and the male culture in which women worked. They included comments on overt hostility and sexual harassment as well as the more subtle aspects of working in a male culture. Of all those who gave structural responses, females were proportionately overrepresented (56 percent of structural responses, with females representing 37 percent of the sample). Characteristic responses ran as follows:

> I think there is a systematic bias [against women], given that in our faculty, more than 50 percent of the staff are women, and fewer than 10 percent are in very senior positions. The sorts of tasks and responsibilities expected of women are different. I think a lot of the administrative tasks and the tidying-up is given to women, it's the housework, it's the nurturing—all those things that are traditionally expected of women tend to be reflected in the workplace as well. This institution is a very male orientated, hierarchical place and the way things are done is very much from a male point of view. (Female, Education, Australian University)

> I think our department is definitely male dominated so I think it is very difficult for women to get through the system. Some of the characteristics that the males have in this department tend to be a lot of drinking, male-based activities that naturally exclude females. We have had a few instances where females have been completely excluded. (Male, Social Sciences, Australian University)

> The culture here is very definitely male and your views are not necessarily welcome because you're a woman. I think the record of promotion just indicates very plainly that there is a great difference in treatment between the genders. (Female, Education, Australian University)

> Women and minorities suffer discrimination in this institution across the board—they are paid less, they are less well regarded, they are not seen; there are few women in high administrative positions—isn't it amazing; there is

strong faculty sentiment to change that. There's less than three percent of Afro-Americans in the College of Arts and Sciences—it's shocking. I believe the reason is an ante-bellum mentality. (Male, Biology, American University)

Denial Responses (30 percent of responses)

Denial responses were characterized by the suggestion that there was no difference in the treatment of male and female staff. Women were said to be treated the same as men, hired and promoted on merit, and given the same opportunity to succeed. Of all those who gave denial responses, males were proportionately overrepresented (76 percent of all responses, with men representing 63 percent of the sample). The kinds of things said here were

> No, women are not treated differently, [even if] the number of women on the staff in the school is small. . . I don't think the women, all at senior lecturer level, are treated any differently. (Male, Sciences, Australian University)

> I think all the female staff is treated the same way as the male staff. I think one should take the best person for a job and the gender doesn't matter. (Male, Sciences, Australian University)

> I don't think we treat women any different from men. The female faculty wants to be taken on their own terms and not treated differently. (Male, Sciences, American University)

> I am sure years ago there were differences but in today's world, you know the affirmative action world, there is a great rise of women in the work force, so they are exactly like men, so there is no public explicit difference. I am sure someone will say there are but by and large no one discriminates. It doesn't happen any more. (Male, Social Sciences, American University)

Historical Responses (19 percent of responses)

Historical responses suggested that the male/female imbalance was due to past situations that were discriminatory or to a previous lack of qualified women (pipeline effect). Of all those who gave historical responses, females and males were almost proportionately represented (35 percent and 65 percent, respectively). Under this heading, we also included responses focusing on socio-biological reasons (women as mothers or carers). The important element here is that these responses blamed events or processes remote from present members of the university (in the past or outside in society). Thus, for example:

> I do know that in the past there has been women faculty in this department, none of whom has survived the tenure process. Whereas I know of no males

who have not survived the tenure process. Now I don't know if that relates to their being women or to their family situations, perhaps, where women are expected to be child rearers and researchers, and can't do both at the same time, whereas men are not expected to do that in most cases. (Male, Sciences, American University)

Because of the inherent differences in lifestyles between women and men—we are the ones who have babies—women are generally more interested in quality of life issues than their male colleagues; mostly men make these decisions in the sciences; they are judging you by their standards; in the past this has been a problem. I have not seen any evidence of bias in my unit that I would view as such; I'm not saying that they don't have these opinions but at a professional level I don't see any evidence of it and I am fairly sensitive about these things as you can imagine. (Female, Sciences, American University)

Positive Action Responses (16 percent of responses)

Positive action responses were provided by those who maintained that the university was using affirmative action to improve the position of women and/or that heads of departments or other managers were implementing policies or programs to make the culture more supportive of women. Of all those who gave positive action responses, males were overrepresented (76 percent). Under this rubric, responses could be positive when interviewees were in favor of affirmative action or negative when they were against the idea. Some respondents commented that women could suffer from a backlash against the notion of equal opportunity programs and find themselves in hostile environments.

I think there has been a real attempt to be fair, sometimes silly, sometimes misguided but I even think there's been some desire—without going overboard—to hire and to try to get women moving into Economics because there was an embarrassment of the lack of numbers involved. (Male, Social Sciences, Australian University)

This department has historically been very bad in terms of having a representation of women. In August, we had one woman on the faculty out of about sixteen people that are here. But we've hired two now and that brings us up to three . . . and I might add that all of the women hired in this department, I hired. I told the search committees in advance: "Make certain that we have a woman who is interviewed." (Male, Sciences, American University)

I think women in the past five years have certainly been favored over comparable men leading to some animosity on the part of some men. The number of women on the faculty has increased because specifically they have said you may have this position if you can hire a woman or a minority person. (Male, Sciences, American University)

The Quantitative Data

Turning now to the quantitative data. Table 2.1 groups all the universities together for each country and looks at the responses by males and females. In both
countries, the largest response for females was structural. In contrast, males
more often gave denial responses. These two categories, structural and denial,
made up almost two-thirds of the responses.

Table 2.2 shows the pattern by discipline for each country. In the Australian
universities, the majority of responses in education and social sciences were in
the structural category. This was the same for education in American universities, whereas in the social sciences the majority of responses were in the category of denial. In the case of science, the majority of responses in the American
universities were in denial, whereas in Australia they were equally in the denial
and historical categories. It is, of course, significant that the majority of respondents in the sciences were males.

How might one go about explaining these different interpretations as well as
the unequal patterns that underlie them?

Our Theoretical Frame

Gherardi (1994: 592) writes, "Our direct experience tells us that organizational
cultures—as holistic phenomena—are strongly 'gendered.'" This gendering of
organizational culture is not just tacked on to a previously neutral organizational
structure, but enters the very logic of the organization and its processes (Burton
1987; Acker 1990). It structures the artifacts, values, and assumptions of which
organizational culture is composed (Diamond 1991; Hatch 1993). Universities,
for all they are widely (mis)perceived as neutral, are gendered organizations
(Wilson and Byrne 1987; Wieneke 1988; Poiner 1991). Acker (1990: 146) suggests that

> to say that an organization is gendered means that advantage and disadvantage,
> exploitation and control, action and emotion, meaning and identity, are pat-
> terned through and in terms of a distinction between male and female, mascu-
> line and feminine. Gender is not an addition to ongoing processes, conceived as
> gender neutral. Rather it is an integral part of those processes that cannot prop-
> erly be understood without an analysis of gender.

She (Acker 1990: 146-147) maintains that this structuring pervades at least
five interacting processes that relate to

- the construction of divisions along the lines of gender—divisions of labor,
  of allowed behaviors . . . of power;
- the construction of symbols and images that explain, express, reinforce, or

Table 2.1 Treatment of Women in Australian and American Universities (by gender) 1994–1995 Percentages and (numbers)*

Treatment of Women	Australian		American		
	Male	Female	Male	Female	Total
Structural	22 (25)	53 (35)	28 (17)	51 (18)	35 (95)
Denial	32 (35)	20 (13)	44 (27)	17 (6)	30 (81)
Historical	24 (27)	18 (12)	12 (7)	17 (6)	19 (52)
Positive Action	22 (24)	9 (6)	16 (10)	14 (5)	16 (45)
Total	100 (111)	100 (66)	100 (61)	99 (35)	100 (273)

* Numbers represent responses, not respondents (see note 1 at end of chapter).

Table 2.2 Treatment of Women in Australian and American Universities (by discipline areas) 1994–1995 Percentages and (numbers)

Treatment of Women	Australian			American		
	Education	Social Sciences	Sciences	Education	Social Sciences	Sciences
Structural	41 (26)	41 (29)	12 (5)	60 (21)	23 (9)	18 (4)
Denial	29 (18)	20 (14)	37 (16)	23 (8)	38 (15)	50 (11)
Historical	16 (10)	17 (12)	37 (16)	11 (4)	13 (5)	18 (4)
Positive Action	14 (9)	21 (15)	14 (6)	6 (2)	26 (10)	14 (3)
Total	100 (63)	99 (70)	100 (43)	100 (35)	100 (39)	100 (22)

- sometimes oppose those divisions;
- interactions between women and men, women and women, men and men, including all those patterns that enact dominance and submission;
- consciousness of the existence of the other three aspects of gender;
- the fundamental, ongoing processes of creating and conceptualizing social structures.

It is evident that the gendering of organizations draws from wider social norms concerning the proper relations between men and women (Acker and van Houten 1974). Organizational members manage their behavior "in the light of the normative conceptions of attitudes and activities appropriate for (their) sex category" (West and Zimmerman 1987: 126). Within any particular organization, this produces a certain "politics of speech and silence" (Luke 1994: 211. See also: Johnsrud 1993; Spender 1980), a politics of who is allowed to say what, when, how often, and in what way. Within the academy this dictates not only women's experiences of organizational culture but also their relationships with knowledge production, setting the terms on which they enter particular knowledge domains (Tancred-Sheriff 1985).

The work of a number of organizational theorists suggests that the suppositions which form and sustain organizational logic are produced at an unconscious or symbolic level (Diamond 1991; Hatch 1993; Gherardi 1994). In this context, Gherardi (1994: 595) argues that "gender is not just located at the level of interactional and institutional behavior (the gender we do) but at the level of deep and trans-psychic symbolic structures (the gender we think)." She says that at the second level of gendering the suppositions have stability "to the point where we conceive of them as universal and ahistorical concepts" (Gherardi 1994: 595).

Critically, then, the gendering of organizations enters people's conceptual apparatus, forming and sustaining the way in which they think about organizations and their own part within them. Gendering informs suppositions about what is fair and unfair, and about what is natural, normal, or right. It pervades perceptions of merit, successful performance, career choice, and authority (Burton 1987). Central to Gherardi's *gender we think* is the establishment of men as the primary referent.

In line with this, much of the work on why there are so few women in management positions in universities and other public and private corporations focuses on the masculinist assumptions underlying management structures and practices (Cockburn 1990; Burton 1991; Blackmore 1993; Lingard and Limerick 1995; Smith and Hutchinson 1995; Barraclough and Company 1995). Moore and Sagaria (1993: 16) describe the origins and current forms of US universities as "deeply imbued with patriarchal ideology." They also point to the invisibility of this ideology: "This male-defined culture and its ideology are so profound that most writers have been unaware of its existence or have not found it troubling" (Moore and Sagaria 1993: 233). Of the Australian academy, Allport (1996: 8) says that "our universities remain highly gendered workplaces for all staff, and male culture based on male experience continues to affect the way women's work is valued in higher education." Thornton described the exclusionist male culture within Australian higher education in these terms:

> Within the university, the key decision makers, or gatekeepers, . . . are invariably men—white Anglo-Celtic, heterosexual, able-bodied, middle class men. I term them Benchmark Men because they constitute the standard against which women and others are measured. In determining who should occupy positions of authority, Benchmark Men tend to favor those who most look like themselves. That is, they have historically constituted themselves as the standard. (Thornton, cited in White 2000: 14)

Grant and Porter (1994) suggest that the lack of a critical mass of women in educational management both reflect and reproduce its masculinist orientation. The women in their study had the experience of being the first woman in a job, often feeling that they did not fit in with the management styles of their organizations which, in many cases, they attempted to challenge. Castleman, Allen, Bastalich, and Wright (1994) reach a similar conclusion in their report for the National Tertiary Education Union on the position of women within the sector. They conclude that the major factor accounting for the paucity of women in senior positions is management's own masculine styles and practices. They quite specifically discount factors like the domestic and family responsibilities of women, merit, or women's disinclination to advance their careers.

These differences in the cultural expectations of a workplace are well depicted by a female academic describing the way men work in her department:

> I think men just work differently together and older men work differently together than women. The culture, the expectations, everything is a very different kind of working relationship. Every department has its own particular culture. Here I work mainly with men. The men are more aloof and share very little about their personal lives. They seem less detail-oriented, in terms of making sure the job gets done. Sometimes it appears that things are thrown together at the last minute. Whereas, the women I have worked with previously, if there was a problem, they would roll up their sleeves, figure out what the problem was and they would find a solution. In this department where there are mostly men, problems get glossed over and we don't really deal with them. I think they think if you ignore a problem long enough, it will go away. (Female, Education, American University)

University cultures around the world value and reproduce concepts of career, academic achievement, and institutional and intellectual work based on male life trajectories (Itzin and Newman 1995), and the pathways to success are built upon dominant male traits and characteristics (Izraeli and Adler 1994). The often-understated power of the male norm is that it works to men's advantage and makes its own operations invisible. Another woman interviewed picked up on just this point:

There's not anything that's done officially or overtly. I think many stereotypes
are still with us. I think male bonding is real (laughter!). I think they take care
of each other. I don't think they take care of the women in the same way. It
came home to me during the preparation for this tenure process. As a brand
new faculty member, I needed someone to start me on a course of publishing. I
didn't get that help from anyone. (Female, Education, American University)

Women are beginning to learn about the invisible operations of mentoring
and networking, but despite their knowledge of these processes, they still seem
to find the path to success a more torturous one than men. This is revealed in
their material status as well as their subjective reading of how they are treated
within universities (Brooks 1997). There are studies that report that academic
women are still the objects of both overt and covert acts of discrimination (Ward
2000; White 2000; Husu 1999).

Conclusion

How universities respond to market forces will make a difference to how wel-
coming and supportive they are of female academics. Universities do not have to
respond in a uniform way to the impact of globalization (Newson 1998). There
are many examples of different organizations resisting globalization practices.
This suggests that universities can decide on local practices that will not necessarily imitate the neoliberal reforms that are considered best practice in some
parts of the world.

However, having said that, we are aware that it is not easy to change organizations into places where women can feel comfortable and be supported.
We are also aware that the *gender we do* may be easier to change than *the gender we think* (Gherardi 1994). It is often the case that even when certain gendered practices have been challenged and changed, there is a residue of thinking
about gender which retains its potency within institutions that are still inhabited
disproportionately by males in the more powerful positions.

At the same time, we can be somewhat optimistic that our knowledge about
achieving gender equity goals has increased, allowing us to be more critical of
simple procedural changes, and we can prompt management to adopt a deeper
conception of gender equity. There have been writers calling for nonpatriarchal
and postcolonial management practices and values (Yeatman 1993); for participatory and flatter organizational structures (Limerick and Cunnington 1993); for
a multidimensional and multidirectional view of power (Blackmore 1989); and
for accessible and supportive management styles (Barsoux 1987). In short, there
is agreement that there is both scope and need for redistributive agendas aimed
at reducing inequality and promoting fairness (Yeatman 1990; Flynn 1990;
Bottery 1992; Hearn 1992; Olsson 1992).

These feminist researchers were writing in an optimistic tone in the early

1990s. As we enter the twenty first century, that optimism has considerably diminished. Books discussing the impact of globalization on universities toward the end of the twentieth century were much more pessimistic as some of their titles illustrate: *The University in Ruins* (Readings 1996), *Chalk Lines: The Politics of Work in the Managed University* (Martin 1998), *Universities and Globalization: Critical Perspectives* (Currie and Newson 1998), *Universities for Sale* (Tudiver 1999), and *Burning Down the House: The Bonfire of the Universities* (James 2000). Other titles illustrate the growing concern about preserving the fundamental values that universities represent, as depicted in these volumes: *The Future of Academic Freedom* (Menard 1996), *Challenges Facing Higher Education at the Millennium* (Hirsch and Weber 1999), and *Why Universities Matter* (Coady 2000).

That so much has been written is the good news. To understand what is going on is the first step toward changing the institutions. Part 2 takes us into a closer analysis of how gendered universities work.

Notes

1. Numbers represent responses, not respondents because, in some instances, there were more responses coded per person since they gave several explanations and a few people did not answer the question at all or gave an answer that could not be easily coded. We ended up with 177 responses for the Australian universities and 96 for the American universities. Respondents represented a range of discipline areas across Education, Social Sciences, and the Sciences, and a range of academic ranks from professor to associate lecturer, assistant professor, and adjunct.

PART 2

THE AUSTRALIAN STUDY

Chapter 3

Context of the Australian Study

Introduction

In this book we argue that gender constructs patterns of academic and managerial success. For almost all women some kind of trade-off has to be made between their lives and success. Conversely, for most men masculinity and patterns of university prowess more closely correspond. Taking these as givens, we began this study with particular objectives in mind. The main objective was to examine the current gendered nature of universities, and we did so with an eye on the rapidly changing environment that was confronting Australian universities at the time and the different and particular organizational cultures of the institutions we studied. We wondered whether women would fare better in different kinds of organizational culture or would survive the restructuring of the higher education sector better in one than the other. In any event, there were not such substantial differences between women's experience of the two institutions, and the national and international forces driving the changes to university culture were such a dominant force that they overshadowed the experience of women in both institutions.

Setting for the Research

The research we report on in the following chapters was conducted in two public Australian universities with very different traditions. The smaller university was established in the early 1970s, offering a style of governance and an academic orientation that was an alternative to that of traditional Australian universities. Its ethos was defined as participatory, collaborative, egalitarian, and interdisciplinary. Overall, the stage appeared to be set for a situation that was conducive to the development of a culture congruent with, and supportive of, women— perhaps even supportive of the advancement of women. The larger university was established initially in the mid-1960s as a diverse institute of technology and converted to a university by a State Act in the late 1980s. Despite its broad interpretation of technology as involving almost all areas of human endeavor, it inherited a strongly masculinist culture in which considerable value was set on high technology and technology transfer, with explicit links to industry and to practical professions. Overall, the situation was not necessarily one in which women would be expected to flourish, although the inclusion of female-dominated professions in the health sciences provided enclaves in which women might be expected to do better. (As noted above, despite these differences in culture, the actual representation of women was similar across these two institutions, with very few women in senior academic positions in either university, and the managerial elite was exclusively male in both universities.) Although now there are a few more women in the managerial elite in both institutions, the working conditions and the general atmosphere of these universities have altered to become even less conducive to women. Globalization practices, such as privatization, increased competition, managerialism, and accountability, have penetrated these universities, turning them into entrepreneurial institutions (Currie and Newson 1998).

In 1997, as part of the overall study, we undertook a survey of post-secondary institutions in the State (four public universities and two Technical and Further Education colleges) in order to ascertain how staff described their actual and ideal organization.[1] Our respondents saw the smaller university as more entrepreneurial, and the larger university as more bureaucratic, than the other institutions surveyed (see Hall, Parker, Currie, and Pears 1998; Currie, Pears, and Thiele 1998). In both universities, there was a wide discrepancy between their ideal of a clan-oriented culture and their actual rating of their universities in this characteristic.[2] This clan characteristic was defined as "a personal place where commitment is high and morale is important and the head is like a facilitator or team leader and the working environment is like being in an extended community." In contrast, the entrepreneurial culture was described as "a dynamic and entrepreneurial place run by an innovator and risk taker whose emphasis is on being first, growing bigger, and acquiring new resources." The smaller university desired a rating of 20 for entrepreneurial culture and actually rated it 32. The bureaucratic culture was described as "a formal and structured place where the head is an administrator and the emphasis is on running smoothly, following rules and procedures, and maintaining stability." Respondents from the larger university desired a rating of 16, but actually rated it 34 on bureaucratic culture.

The changes emanating from globalization have led to a reduction in collegiality and a greater distancing between academics and management. They have also led to greater conflicts within the institution, among departments, between general and academic staff, and between *high-profile* research academics and those who have to do the bulk of the teaching. Studies (Moodie 1994; McInnis 1997) have found that general staff often feel as though they are treated as *second-class* citizens in Australian universities. This is one of the factors that have created divisions among staff. Another factor is the increased workloads resulting from a series of restructuring measures that have reduced the number of staff across Australian universities, both academic and general. This has led to divisions among academic staff in their fight to retain positions or gain new positions in a time of reduced funding. In turn, all these factors have led to greater demoralization among staff (McInnis 1997; Currie 1996).

Our own investment in the research, in understanding the gendered nature of our working environment, was about gaining some appreciation of how, in this roller-coaster ride of change, we might be able to continue to promote equity and equal opportunity between women and men. In this way, our research has a political agenda. It is clearly feminist in its motivation. Like other feminist researchers, we want our research findings to be transformative. Thus, with the goal that the officers would use our research findings to dislodge preconceived ideas about the gender neutrality of the universities, we made our research available to the Equity Offices of the institutions involved in the study.

We recognize, as other feminist researchers before us have (Morley 1999), that to change the established order we have to destabilize the current culture. We believe this is possible because, as Morley (1999: 6) points out, "the academy, like any other organization, is full of contradictions—structures are both fixed and volatile, enabling and constraining." We are aware as well that we are building our research upon the foundation of feminist research that has tried to understand organizational culture and the gendered nature of institutions. We developed our research methods at a particular political and historical moment and were influenced by other feminist academics working on similar topics around the world. Thus our choice of methods was not made in a vacuum.

Methods

In designing the project we chose qualitative research methods, focusing on interviewing and drawing on our knowledge as participant observers of the institutions concerned. The material discussed in the following chapters was collected between 1995 and 1998 in in-depth interviews. The sample was selected to obtain a cross section of the university by rank (senior and junior academics; senior and junior administrators), by position (secretaries, technicians, administrators, academics, and librarians), and by areas (faculties, units, and chancellery). At the time of interviewing, the institutions were not structured in the same way. The larger institution had fewer and larger organizational units and, in particular, the managers of academic units in that institution were more closely integrated with senior university management, whereas in the smaller institutions, the deans of faculties were more allied to academic than management culture. The structural differences between the two institutions meant that the sample could not be strictly comparable. In all, the views of 202 individuals, 111 from the smaller university and 91 from the larger, were gathered. Table 3.1 sets out the distribution of the sample by gender and rank. Managers included both the senior executive managers of the universities as well as managers of administrative and academic units (deans) within the organization. Senior general staff were those who held significant administrative or technical responsibilities and were in positions classified at the higher public service levels, in contrast to secretarial and clerical staff, administrative assistants, and technical support staff. We did not interview maintenance staff, gardeners, or catering staff. Junior academics held the ranks of lecturer A (tutor/senior tutor) or B, while senior academics were senior lecturers, associate professors, and professors (lecturers C-E). In keeping with our interest in women's experience within the institution, the overall sample is weighted toward women.

Table 3.1 Sample (by rank and gender)

	Males	Females	Total
Managers	20	5	25
Senior General Staff	13	24	37
General Staff	9	32	41
Subtotal	22	56	78
Senior Academic Staff	32	23	55
Junior Academic Staff	15	29	44
Subtotal	47	52	99
Total Numbers	89	113	202

Two interview protocols were used, one for the managers and another for academic and general staff. They differed only in that the management interview protocol asked interviewees to reflect on the changes taking place in universities, the part they played in them, and their experience of life at the top. Both protocols have been reproduced in the appendix. The managers were generally interviewed singly (occasionally in pairs). In contrast, most of the academic and general staff interviews took place in small focus groups of between two and four people (occasionally a staff member was interviewed individually). Overall, there were fifty-nine focus group and thirty-four individual interviews. The interviews generally lasted between one hour and one-and-a-half hours. They covered participants' perception of their careers and career planning, who they saw as successful within their institutions and the attributes for success, the distribution of power and influence, the barriers that were placed in the way of individuals, networks, job satisfaction, and male and female styles of working. We tested the interview protocol on ourselves by having one of the interviewers interview us as a focus group, and in that process, we revealed aspects of the organization to each other. At that point, we decided to insert ourselves into the data and added that transcript to the database for future analysis. In essence, the methods we used combined case studies, in-depth interviewing of individuals and focus groups, and participant observation.

Because we were aware of the particular feminist orientation that we brought to this research and our agenda of political action, we also took a number of precautions to produce reliable and valid research findings. Our research process was a collaborative one among the principal researchers and those employed to assist in the interviews. For example, we had a male interviewer interviewing groups of male academics. We had a technical research assistant interviewing technicians. As the principal researchers, we interviewed the managers because we often knew them personally and felt we were closer in social status to them. Sometimes we interviewed individuals alone because we felt we might derive more honest answers from them. At other times, we arranged for all females to be together or all males to be together. Sometimes a mixed group worked better. We thought about the research process as a social process to gain a deeper understanding of the organization. We wanted informants to feel comfortable and rearranged focus groups to achieve a greater feeling of spontaneity and ease of revealing information in the groups. We also interviewed the interviewers halfway through the process to gain their insights into, and impressions of, the story emerging from the interviews and to enrich our understanding of the focus groups and the interview process.

The interviews were taped, transcribed, and entered into a computer software package, NUD.IST, for analysis. As a group of researchers, we coded each question to gain a greater understanding of the themes emerging from the focus groups. This was a team effort. We brought together all those who were involved in the interviewing for the coding process, and as we developed the codes out of the data and coded the transcripts, we discussed them at length as a group. We tried to be *true* to our data, at the same time recognizing that all the members in the group were feminist in orientation and that our codes would be derived with a gendered lens. We also decided that while sometimes we would use NUD.IST to quantify the responses and give a more detailed analysis of the data in tables, the general approach was to interpret the transcripts in a more narrative fashion to tell a story about the institutions and the way they are organized. Unless otherwise indicated, where we have quantified responses the data provided is aggregated for the two universities. We have only provided institution-specific data where there is a significant difference in the pattern of responses between the two institutions or where, in special circumstances, data was collated only for one institution. It is also important to note that the quantified data represents *responses* not *respondents*. It was common for our respondents to offer several explanations or point to a combination of characteristics in answering our questions, and in coding the transcripts, we endeavored to capture the range of responses, rather than oversimplify the answer given by an individual respondent. The quantified data provide a sense of the overall pattern of responses, but without the added explanations and rationales, expression, and nuances, it remains relatively impoverished data. It is the textual material that really opens a window onto the experience of staff in the workplace of the university.

In using qualitative, in-depth interview material to unveil the current organizational culture of two universities, we wanted to develop a narrative of how gender manifested itself in accounts of our respondents, how power was used in the institutions, and who was seen as successful and why. We realize that any narrative is likely to be biased depending upon the theoretical position of the researchers, those interviewed, and the type of questions asked. We did not go into this study believing that we were politically neutral or that we were going to find some kind of *objective* truth about these institutions. As feminists, we were aware that no study could be politically neutral and that all work is theoretically grounded. Along with Maynard (1994), Kelly, Regan, and Burton (1992), and Morley (1999), we do not believe that research predates theory. Rather, we believe that individuals begin with a particular theoretical perspective and that this informs the type of questions asked, the methodology used, and even the interpretation that creates the narrative. We are aware that our research method involves "carving out pieces of narrative evidence that we select, edit, and deploy to border our arguments" (Fine 1994: 22). We took gender as a fundamental organizer of these universities and of the lives of the workers in them. Like Morley, we see our workplaces as sites of gender politics. We employed a similar methodology to Morley's micropolitics of universities. She describes the way conflicts and competing interests influence everyday transactions in institutions. "Micropolitics is about influence, networks, coalitions, political and personal strategies to effect or resist change. It involves rumour, gossip, sarcasm, humour, denial, 'throwaway remarks,' alliance-building" (Morley 1999: 4-5).

In this book, we have not used all the findings produced by this research. The following chapters concentrate on a subset of the questions that allow us to address our central concerns about the manifestations and experience of gender in the working environment of the universities. These questions covered respondents' reasons for the paucity of senior women in the institution, their views on the characteristics of those with power and the different working styles of men and women, and their accounts on what they sacrifice to work in the university, who gets rewarded, and who does not. In exploring these questions, we have quoted extensively from our respondents, allowing their words to tell their story. Each quote carries with it a code that identifies the respondent by their rank and gender. All respondents are also numbered consecutively within each category and in order of their appearance in the text. The codes are set out in table 3.2.

Table 3.2 Identifying Codes for Respondents Quoted in Part 2

Rank	Male	Female
Manager	1–18 MAN/M	1–4 MAN/F
Senior General Staff	1–9 S.GEN/M	1–16 S.GEN/F
General Staff	1–3 GEN/M	1–13 GEN/F
Senior Academic	1–21 SAC/M	1–14 SAC/F
Junior Academic	1–12 JAC/M	1–21 JAC/F

Notes

1. In developing the organizational culture questions and in assessing the other aspects of the institutions, we have drawn items from the survey instrument, Institutional Performance Survey (IPS), developed at the National Centre for Higher Education Management Systems (Krakower and Niwa 1985). The organizational culture typology that this research drew on was based on a fourfold typology proposed by Cameron and Ettington (1988).

2. For example, respondents from the smaller university considered their university to be rated as 22 in clan characteristics, but desired a rating of 58. The respondents from the larger university considered their university to be rated 27, but desired a rating of 52 on the clan characteristic.

Chapter 4

Normalization of Male Working Styles

"Are there few women? I guess there are. I guess . . .
they don't fit into men's culture so well."
(Senior member of the general staff: 1 S.GEN/M)

Introduction

Feminists recognize that men are often constituted as the standard against which women are measured and women are understood to be different and lacking. In this chapter, the practices that establish and preserve this *male norm* are explored through the responses given by general and academic staff at the two universities when questioned about the relative absence of women from the senior ranks of their institution. The positioning of men's lives as normative, the invisibility of that norm in the everyday discourse of our respondents, and the obfuscation of male advantage thereby accomplished are demonstrated in the answers given both by those who regard the number of senior women as unproblematic and by those far less sanguine with the employment profile of their university.

When we undertook the study of our first institution in 1995, there were no women among its top management. Two years later, this university had one woman at pro-vice-chancellor level and at the time of writing, and after restructuring into divisions, also has women in two of the five executive dean positions. At the second and larger institution, the senior management team consisted of eleven males at the time of interviews. It recently appointed its first female deputy vice-chancellor and currently has a number of women in middle management positions. In exploring the way staff in these two universities account for the relative absence of women from the ranks of management, this chapter points to their heavy reliance upon a notion that the masculine tenor of the work culture is a given. Our analysis focuses on the operations of a male norm and the way it serves effectively to marginalize women within universities. The normalization of male culture is not restricted to the peak management culture, although it is strongest there.[1] Rather, it pervades the organization and can be detected in the responses of those content with the gendered status quo and those seeking to challenge it.

There has been considerable work on why there have been so few women in management positions in both the public and private sector. Much of the work has focused on the masculinist assumptions underlying management structures and practices. At its most general level then, a *masculine* or *male* culture refers both to the style of workplaces and the deep structural logic underpinning them. The term invokes a general *blokiness* (or chumminess)[2] in the day-to-day practices of organizations whereby men are made to feel, and express, their sense of being comfortable as members of the workplace. Women, in contrast, may understand themselves to be tolerated or peripheral or temporary members of the work culture. More than this, the notion of a masculine culture highlights the profound ways in which this *style* of workplace is accomplished. Here the deep logic of the way work itself is organized in our culture (the gendered division of labor between paid and unpaid work) and how this logic is carried forward into the structures, practices, and organization of paid work is understood to be aligned with men's lived experience and understanding of the world. It is here that the power of normalization processes really emerges.

Normalizing Male Culture

Feminist writers are familiar with the way in which men and their lived experience are constituted as *the norm* and how this has particular ramifications for the lives of women. With relation to the experience and organization of paid work, Acker (1990) and Cockburn (1990), among others, have offered powerful accounts of how constituting *work* in western industrialized nations as normatively male causes distinctive patterns of disadvantage for women entering that particular realm of activity. The positioning of men's lives as normal and women's as otherwise is especially prominent as far as sexuality, reproduction, and emotions are concerned. On the face of it, such things are controlled or ruled out of paid work and bureaucratic organizations as they disrupt normal and orderly functioning. In fact, though, it is *women's* sexuality and their responsibilities (pregnancy, breast-feeding, childcare, menstruation) which are ruled out; and "*men's* sexuality and their minimal responsibilities in procreation which are ruled in" (Acker 1990: 152). Acker goes on to argue that "male sexual imagery—including notions relating to emotion, abstract thought and control—pervades organizational metaphors and language" (Acker 1990: 152; see also Wieneke 1995).

At its most basic level, as Acker (1990) argues, the organizational logic which presents the notion of "a job" as gender neutral is flawed. The concept of a job is fundamentally gendered because "it already contains the gender-based division of labor and the separation between the public and the private sphere. The concept of 'a job' assumes a particular gendered organization of domestic life and social production" (Acker 1990: 149). The primary effect of this, as Dines (1993: 22) notes in a UNESCO report on *Women in Higher Education Management*, is that women are disadvantaged by the fact that they are not men.

Positing male participation in work as normal also constructs men as the standard against which women as workers are to be judged (and are frequently found wanting). As Bacchi (1990) argues in her analysis of the *EEOC v. Sears Roebuck and Co.* case in the United States, among other examples, the imperative for women to choose between being treated as the *same as* men or *different from* men leaves unchallenged and unquestioned what men are like and how they live their lives. Those women who succeed in work are likely to be those who are most like men, at least in their material circumstances, while those least able to organize their lives that way are likely to be the most disadvantaged.

Eveline (1994) has further deepened our understanding of the operations of the male norm in respect to paid work by asking, in a simple, but important, reversal, how the male norm operates to *advantage* men. She points out that there is more to the power of the male norm than the constitution of man as the reference point and woman as falling short of the standard. This becomes very evident when posing the question in terms of male advantage, rather than women's disadvantage. Indeed, as Eveline (1994: 129) points out, although "as knowledge and as struggle the politics of advantage is remarkably familiar to feminists, [as] rhetoric it is often strange. . . . The discourse of women's disadvantage reinforces an assumption that processes advantaging men are immutable, indeed normative."

So it is not just that the male norm constitutes men's lives as *normal* vis-à-vis women's lives but that it constitutes men as normal, rather than *advantaged*. The often-understated power of the male norm is that it works to make men's advantage and its own operations invisible. Eveline (1994) goes on to argue that some of the political import of the feminist project is lost if the acknowledgment of women's disadvantage is content to point to a *relative* disadvantage—relative to the accepted (male) norm—rather than a *relational* disadvantage. The former tends to result in disadvantage being seen as *women's problem*, whether in the sense of *having a problem* or of *being the problem*. What is missed, in the absence of an explicit attention to the relational nature of advantage and disadvantage, is the way that men are advantaged *by* women's disadvantage. As Eveline's (1994) analysis of equal employment opportunity policies and procedures shows, positioning women as relatively disadvantaged focuses attention on measures that redress or compensate women for their *apparent disability*, rather than singling out men for some kind of remedial treatment which will rid them of those benefits. When translated into concerns about gender, the everyday spectrum of privileges that accrue to men are taken as unremarkable, and instead attention is directed to any instances where the situation seems to be reversed. Hence not only the ways in which men are implicated in sustaining that sexual ordering is obfuscated; the material advantages, and the dynamics by which they are accorded, also remain unspoken (Eveline 1994: 130).

In the analysis that follows, we want to demonstrate these elements of the male norm: the positioning of men's lived experience as normative, the invisibility of that norm in the everyday discourse of our respondents, and the obfuscation of male advantage in the articulation of women's disadvantage. We do so because, as well as being "something we do and something we think," gender is also something *"we make accountable to others"* (Gherardi 1994: 593, emphasis added). Organizational patterns relating to seniority and the exercise of authority, for example, are rationalized and defended in line with wider notions of masculinity and femininity (Acker and van Houten 1974; Burton 1987; Acker 1990; Hatch 1993). So while the gendering of organizations may originate from unconscious relational patterns between organizational members, it is actively and purposefully played out in day-to-day relations. Gender is a primary way of *justifying*—as well as signifying—relationships of power.

The Pattern of Responses

In the remainder of this chapter we explore the normalization of male culture and its invisibility in our respondents' answers to a single question: "Why do you think there are so few women in senior positions?" The pattern of responses by gender and rank that emerged across the combined institutions is summarized in table 4.1. Four broad kinds of responses or explanations were forthcoming in response to our question, and these are presented in the table in a rank order of decreasing frequency, which holds for all of our analytical categories except managers. In contrast to the results of the Australian/American comparative study reported in chapter two, and despite the slightly different analytic categories generated in that study, there were some differences in the general pattern of responses between it and the present case study. In particular, the overall denial responses were much smaller in the Australian case study. Nonetheless, the gendered distribution of responses remains similar between the two studies.

To pursue our detailed analysis of the male norm, we have collapsed these four kinds of responses into three by grouping together those explanations that blame women and those that blame historical or traditional factors. What connects these two responses is that their acknowledgment of a problem with the number of senior women is undercut in a similar way. Both kinds of explanations direct attention *away from* men and male culture, either by blaming women themselves for their underrepresentation in senior ranks or by offering a historical/traditional explanation which blames events and processes remote from present members of the university. We begin our analysis with this combined group (explanations which blame women or blame historical/traditional factors) because it is these responses that most clearly demonstrate the positioning of men's lives as normative. An analysis of the nuances in such accounts reveals a variety of ways in which male advantage is neutralized, normalized, and obscured. Not surprisingly, this grouping contains more male (50 percent) than female (33 percent) responses. More significantly, management, in particular, favors this kind of response (57 percent). Thus it may well be indicative of the dominant, and male, culture.[3]

Table 4.1 Why So Few? Percentages and (numbers)
Why do you think there are so few senior women?

	Gender		Rank/Position			
	Men	Women	Ac.	Man.	Gen.	Total
Structural Explanations The culture is hostile to women; they carry extra burdens.	38 (68)	64 (122)	49 (75)	31 (18)	62 (97)	52 (190)
Explanations Which Blame Women Women choose not to or their personality is such that they don't want to or can't do it.	26 (46)	18 (35)	25 (38)	19 (11)	20 (32)	22 (81)
Historical/Traditional Explanations Pipeline effect; no, or small pool of, women to draw on; sociobiological reasons.	24 (42)	15 (29)	18 (28)	38 (22)	13 (21)	19 (71)
Denial There is no problem; it is a small and improving problem; there is no room at the top; have no idea.	12 (22)	3 (5)	8 (12)	12 (7)	5 (8)	7 (27)
Total Percentages	100	100	100	100	100	100
Total Responses	(178)	(191)	(153)	(58)	(158)	(369)
Total Respondents	89	113	99	25	78	202

Having illustrated the normalization of male culture, we then turn to the group of responses that deny there is a problem with the number of senior women. While nominally our smallest group, the denial responses could be regarded as a strong version of the above in that the male norm has become thoroughly invisible. Our analysis focuses on some examples of how this disappearance is accomplished. Overall, only 7 percent of aggregated responses argued there was no problem with the number of senior women. There appears to be a significant difference between the proportion of responses at the two institutions: 13 percent of the smaller university, compared with 3 percent of the larger university. Notably, fully one-quarter of the responses given by the managers at the smaller university fell into this category, whereas none of the managers at our second institution expressed the view that there was simply no problem. Several factors may account for this difference,[4] but for the purposes of the case we make in this chapter, it is the way in which this group phrases their answers and the style of argument they adopt, which is of interest here.

Our final group of responses is those that point to structural factors discriminating against women. It is clear from table 4.1 that more responses by women (64 percent) than men (38 percent) fell into this category. Women are far less likely to deny there is a problem with their representation in senior ranks, and their responses are almost twice as likely to attribute their underrepresentation to systemic structural factors discriminating against them. In stark contrast, male responses are just over one-and-a-half times as likely to make some other answer to the question about senior women, that is, to deny there is a problem or to offer nonstructural explanations for it. Overall, the structural response is the most common one but, as mentioned, because our sample is unrepresentative of the staffing profile at either university (we have biased it toward women), this response cannot be taken as an accurate indication of a predominant university view. What it does allow us to demonstrate, however, is the subtle ways in which the normalization of male culture pervades and can subvert explanations which otherwise challenge that culture. In particular, we point to some of the difficulties that arise for our respondents because of the disadvantages they experienced as women.

While we have organized our analysis around these three groups of responses, there are intersections and recurrent themes that belie the tidiness of our categories. For example, women as childbearers and rearers are invoked by respondents of all persuasions in their explanations for why women are differently involved in paid work. Where these are important, we have raised them, out of place if need be, so as to highlight the differing treatments similar themes are given or a perception common to respondents of otherwise differing persuasions.

Normal Men Can Explain the Problem Away

Explanations for women's underrepresentation at senior levels, which having acknowledged the problem, proceed to *explain it away*, are deeply expressive of the male norm. The following quote, which is typical of the subset we have characterized as *blaming women*, is from an administrative officer:

> Are there few women? I guess there are. I guess—I suspect they tend to interrupt their careers for bearing children or following their spouse around. Women are not quite as driven. They don't fit into men's culture so well. (1 S.GEN/M)

Men's culture is a given which women fail to fit into; women follow their spouses, spouses don't move and make women follow; and men's contribution to procreation is elided by women bearing children. The imputation is clearly that women's poor showing at senior levels is, in various ways, women's own fault and, more importantly, that men's lives and *men's culture* are simply as given. Women fail because their lives are not conducted like men's lives, and, crucially, that is not men's responsibility, men have nothing to do with the problem. That this orientation toward women and away from men is not solely the preserve of those who fall into this category illustrates the pervasiveness of the male norm. A woman academic, for example, spoke of the structural problems which disadvantage women as "women move in and out of the workforce, women move with families, women do a whole range of things, women tend to service the organization somewhat more than men" (1 SAC/F). Eveline (1994) has pointed out that the rhetorical focus on women and women's disadvantage, at best, leaves the male advantage implied and, at worst, deleted. The similarity between these two responses suggests there is only a slight shift between implied and lost.

The first kind of response in this combined grouping, *blaming women*, itself comes in two forms which constantly reinforce each other: attributing it to (what are assumed to be) women's gendered qualities and characteristics, or, more simply, their choices (see table 4.2). Men are equally likely to ascribe it to the first as to the second, whereas women's responses which fit this category are far more likely to argue that, more than just choice, women's personalities keep them out of senior positions. General staff overwhelmingly blame women's qualities, academics are more evenly divided, while managers and deans make fewer (and at the smaller university, no) explicit references to women's qualities—*in management speak*, the rhetoric of choice is paramount.[5]

Respondents understood women to have a number of personal qualities that made it unlikely that they would succeed in senior positions. These included being unwilling to sacrifice themselves or work hard; being unprepared to take on responsibility or to engage in the politicking associated with managerial positions; lacking confidence; being reluctant to take risks or to promote themselves; and as lacking the aggressiveness, the hardness, or the ambition to succeed. Often these characteristics are explicitly presented as failings, as in these blunt words by a senior academic and a secretary:

> It would be easier to generalize and say many of the ladies I know are not ag-
> gressive enough and ambitious enough and nasty enough to be good heads of
> schools or good deputy vice-chancellors. That's a gut feeling. I don't have a lot
> of evidence to base that on. (1 SAC/M)

> Maybe it is because they are just not prepared to make the sacrifices. (1
> GEN/F)

For some respondents, the qualities and sacrifices required of a successful or
good manager were viewed somewhat ambivalently, and so their accounts of
women's personality *failings* were almost inclined to *damn with faint praise.*

> It is difficult for me to say this because some may feel that I'm being somewhat
> patronizing, but I do think . . . that women can feel quite happily fulfilled doing
> a number of roles or functions within society. Whereas men may find that their
> sort of fulfillment and the way they are judged by society is more unique in the
> sense that there is one role that you are expected to fulfill, and that is to try and
> get to the top. Maybe women are slightly more mature . . . that they feel that
> that is not the be all and end all. I think they're right. (2 SAC/M)

Table 4.2 Blaming Women Percentages and (numbers)
Why do you think there are so few senior women?

Explanations Which Blame Women Women choose not to or their personality is such that they do not want to or can not do it.	Gender		Rank/Position			
	Men	Women	Ac.	Man.	Gen.	Total
It is women's personality	52	69	58	36	69	59
It is women's choice	48	31	42	64	31	41
Total Responses	(46)	(35)	(38)	(11)	(32)	(81)
Total Percentages	100	100	100	100	100	100

The apparent approval of women's maturity, however, is contradicted by the
logic of *success* within the university. Questioned about success, our respondents
identified a single-minded, dedicated pursuit of the career and an exclusive
commitment to the university as likely to produce success and as deserving of
reward (see chapter 7). By this logic, men's success is naturalized and women, if

women have multiple or divided commitments, are disadvantaging themselves.

The proposition that women are quite happy with their lot is even more apparent when the rhetoric of women's choices is invoked in place of, or in addition to, women's qualities. At its simplest, the rhetoric of choice that operates is that women make different choices than men and that they are quite comfortable with their choices. One senior male academic answered our question with, "Could it be a case of, in fact, and this I suppose at the risk of being politically incorrect, that maybe women don't want it?" (3 SAC/M). He directed this remark toward a junior male in the same focus group whose answer had been "patriarchy. . . . Direct subversion of women by men" (1 JAC/M). Whether women lack ambition or choose not to pursue more senior positions, their contentment endorses the status quo. It normalizes men's possession of senior positions and obscures their privileged access to such positions.

Significantly, women's choices were often discussed as though the demands of the workplace and the levels of commitment and sacrifice required of senior posts are givens. Women are represented as unwilling, rather than unable, and the conditions which make it possible for men to make such commitments to their jobs (supportive wives who will free men of domestic and family responsibilities) are invisible and, thus, placed beyond challenge. A male manager commented:

> It's also conditioned by how far people want to go. . . . I think "x" has gotten as far as she wants to go, judging from the comments she makes about the hours that I work . . . saying how silly I am to work such horrendous hours. (1 MAN/M)

Similarly, a senior general staff member observed: "Probably a lot of women who would be good in senior positions, and could probably get there, can't be bothered, are just not willing to pay the price" (1 S.GEN/F). That the hours are horrendous, that a price is exacted, is not being critically scrutinized, unlike women's *choices*.

These responses give us a strong indication of the normalization of male culture. They reflect a lack of consciousness of Acker's (1990: 149) point that a job is always underwritten by the gendered division of unpaid domestic labor. The organization of paid labor presumes the normal worker is a male with a wife at home relieving him of considerable amounts of unpaid maintenance work in order that he can prioritize his job and his career. This assumption was never applicable to women workers and is increasingly inappropriate for male workers, as the following two women make very clear:

> Over the years I have always felt at such an incredible disadvantage when I see their little packed lunches and their nicely pressed shirts and all of this. And they have one whole person, very often, devoted to looking after their needs. (2 S.GEN/F)

A lot of the males who are currently in the senior positions had had partners who have stayed at home and played that traditional role, so everything in the career game went into their career, and they had not only their own efforts but also the support of their partner behind them. That is not the deal for us or our partners and it completely changes what you are able to achieve. You cannot work twelve hours a day, you cannot produce however many papers or whatever is required. (3 S.GEN/F)

That the wife at home taking care of her husband and their children is an outmoded assumption, however, has not changed its cogency for some of our respondents, and, in keeping with it, what the rhetoric of choice does is establish women's role in this system as neither coerced nor problematic for them. It is freely chosen, their support is freely gifted to men.

The status of childbearing and rearing is illuminating in this respect. It was a recurrent theme, mentioned with the greatest frequency by those who talked about women's *choices* in order to lay the blame on women, but also frequently cited as evidence of structural discrimination and used as an explanation for why the numbers of women in senior levels was, in fact, not a problem at all, but the natural outcome of women's other roles. We discuss it here in order to highlight the difference between the rhetoric of *choice* (women choose to bear and rear their children) and *responsibility* (women are responsible for childbearing and rearing). The following conversation is drawn from a focus group of senior male academics:

If I were to drop out of academia for five years and then attempt to get back in, I think I'd have just as much difficulty as some of the women are having now. The women who graduated with me, they did exactly that, they took time out to rear a family and made that choice. My wife went out of the workforce for fifteen years. She made a decision that she wanted to be home during the early childhood years of our kids. But I said to her, I personally couldn't make that decision myself, and I don't expect you to. You have to make that decision because you want to do it, I mean, I'm not demanding it, if you want to go back to work we'll work through it, but she chose to remain home. So in a sense then, because of her choice, I was advantaged, and she was very much disadvantaged in terms of her career development. (4 SAC/M)

I think the important thing is that there is, there has to be, an active choice. . . . The only person who can physically bear that child is the woman and quite often also they feel that they really want to bring up these children they [produced so perfectly]. So they take the time off and then, yes, that will disadvantage them. But, it's not a disadvantage, it's a choice in career paths, and it's just an alternative. The alternatives are either you have the kids or you don't have the kids. . . . Granted it's a very, very difficult choice, but it is a choice. (5 SAC/M)

It *is* a choice. And it's a career choice. So a lot of women who've made that choice do not see themselves as disadvantaged, they see themselves as having established a very appropriate career as, you know, a homemaker and mother and support for the broader network of the family. (6 SAC/M)

For these men, choice offsets the disadvantage experienced by women when they take time away from paid work to rear children. It also offsets the advantage men gain from having their partners stay home: only one of these senior academic men actually acknowledges that advantage. More commonly, male responses about childcare would applaud the choice and accept the consequence: "I am overjoyed my wife does not wish to work full-time anymore. But I am sure that is a very serious setback to [her] career" (1 SAC/M).

Also noteworthy about these responses, and a hallmark principle of male culture, is the complete failure to connect fathers with children. Women have children, women choose to have children, and men do not. This was most forcefully put by one male general staff respondent who completely fails to conceive of any obligations that he could have to care for his children:

> I have a few hobbyhorses. One of them is a disliking of women who demand as a right that somebody else raises their kids while they go and do what they want to do. If you want kids, if you want to have kids, then you look after them until they are reasonably self-sufficient, and then you can go back into the workforce if you want to. (2 S.GEN/M)

One is strongly reminded of Acker's point that while women's responsibilities for reproduction are ruled out of paid work, men's "minimal responsibilities in procreation" are ruled in (Acker 1990: 152).

The obligation to care for children, which is delegated to women, and the costs it extracts, gives rise to a sense that women must make a choice between family and career. We were explicitly told (and it was generally implied) that successful women did not have children. Children's absence from the male/work culture constrains women's ability to succeed, the most successful women are those who are as like men as possible—that is, free of responsibilities for children. That most women are not like men in this respect will handicap them, but not through any fault of men. Consider the layers of defense and blame in this comment from a male manager:

> It is difficult to catch up all those years. Scholarship if it is to mean anything, it has got to be fairly equal so that the opportunity to have the same scholarly track record is made more difficult, but there is certainly enough here that have shown that it can easily be done, but no where in the same numbers. (2 MAN/M)

This brings us to a second set of arguments within this first group of responses: those who understand women to lack the qualifications or experience to make them competitive against men but relate this back to various historical or traditional factors. This was a favored response of management, from the vice-chancellors down. They typically complained that there was little they could do about the problem because there were "so few women [with] adequate experience" (3 MAN/M) suitable for senior posts, and these women were highly sought after.

This small pool of suitable academic women is attributed to past practices, be those discriminatory acts or the effects of more traditional or more conventional roles. Time, it is said, will resolve the problem[6] by allowing the new generation of educated and ambitious women to move through the system. This increases the pool and, thus, the number in senior posts, and has been termed the *pipeline* effect. The argument is put forth by a senior male academic:

> One of the reasons why there are so few women in senior positions is the time axis there. Women have to make the decisions to go in that career path, and to go for a senior position they would have had to make that decision twenty years ago. So we have to look at the conditions that were prevailing twenty years ago and it will take twenty years for any change to happen, if it happens in an appropriate manner. So yes, there is a slow increase in women which reflects the increase in women graduating from universities, the increase in women entering management areas and so on, and taking that as a career and working their way up to that. So there is an increase in women in senior positions, and . . . I don't think it's due to any discrimination at this point, there may have been some discrimination earlier, and so on, which meant that at that stage fewer women started on that career path, or were stopped from going beyond the particular level. But at this stage there are very few areas where there are major barriers if they make the choice. (5 SAC/M)

Just who prevented or discouraged women in the past is not named, nor is it thought to matter if women are no longer prevented from achieving senior positions should they want them. Neither the present system nor the behavior of the men who predominate within it needs to change.

In pipeline arguments the same displacement is achieved as before, but with a more explicit defense of the neutrality and normality of the present system. Here are two instances where this becomes evident. In the first, a woman manager, even while irritated with present practices, understands the institution to be operating in a self-evidently rational and blameless way:

> Most of the instances where women haven't got up have been because the men were patently better qualified, because they had much longer experience, they didn't necessarily have more future potential, and we are looking at past experience rather than future potential because it is easier to measure. (1 MAN/F)

In the second example, from a male manager, the presumed blamelessness of the present system underwrites the explicit rejection of affirmative action.

I don't believe in social engineering to the point that you should deliberately decide that the next head of [department] is going to be a female for example. I think there is something fundamentally wrong about that. . . . I think that we just have to keep on [trying to attract women into the jobs]. (4 MAN/M)

The possibility of speeding up the pipeline did not have particular appeal to those who made this argument because it offends against the asserted neutrality of the present system.

Underpinning both these accounts is a merit argument which asserts that the playing field is, and must remain, level. It claims that "women in senior positions . . . have gotten there on their abilities . . . on the same criteria as anybody else who has gotten there" (7 SAC/M) and that the selection process does actually "select the best person for the job" (1 GEN/F and 2 GEN/F). The unstated, or understated, corollary of the merit argument is that if women are not prevented from achieving to the same level as men, their failure to do so is because of something particular to them. Thus the merit argument leaves women as the problem, or as having a problem, and men as achieving success in a neutral system through no fault of their own.[7]

Of course, the system is not neutral. As we have already seen in this chapter, and we will explore further in chapter 7, the capacity to put in long hours, to totally dedicate oneself to the institution, was repeatedly emphasized by respondents. In the words of one male academic: "If I'm going to get on at this university, the first thing I'm going to have to do is to give up all my weekends, and most of my holidays" (2 JAC/M). Underpinning the apparent neutrality of the rhetoric of merit is the blunt fact that the *ability to comply* with these institutional expectations—and thus the distribution of success and failure—is unequivocally gendered. The implications of this point are taken up by the following two respondents reflecting on who gets rewarded in their institutions:

Institutions are prepared to reward those people who are prepared to devote a large part of their energy and life to their job. So, if you are prepared to work twice as long and twice as hard as anyone else it is likely that, having put most of your energy into that aspect of your life, that is where you would tend to dominate and where you would be most successful. (4 SAC/M)

The person who is not going to get ahead is the person who is not willing to devote almost all their being to the place. This person is not willing to sell his soul to the institution. I mean, I have a young family and my career is going to have to slide along because I am not willing to sell my soul to this place. (3 JAC/M)

Women, because of their pivotal position in the family, are less likely to be able to meet the exclusive demands of the university than are most men. And in many cases, men's capacity to work long hours hinges on the familial support offered by their female partners (Finch 1983:24-31). In this context, a senior academic argued that those who got ahead were

Very clearly, males, largely between the ages of 40 and 60. They are people who don't have major family responsibilities. If they have families, the wife would be taking the substantial load of raising the children. They are people who can afford 60 plus hours because they don't have outside responsibilities. They are normally males in that age range who have obsessional characteristics who are willing to put in high workload time, that includes both research and career advancement. (8 SAC/M)

Throughout the argument to date, we have revealed the ways in which the normalization of male culture and men's lives is achieved in the accounts of our respondents through a persistent location of women as the category needing explanation, as the problem, and a concomitant assertion that men, and the system which advantages them, is *normal*. This is not achieved in a seamless way. These arguments are both contested within the universities' communities and, more subtly, are themselves framed as refutations of the possibility of discrimination or men's culpability. In an irresistible example, one senior member of the general staff protested at the push to increase the number of senior women:

You can't do everything in one or two years. This is ridiculous. It takes a hundred years for males to dominate the top. You can't expect to change the world around in the next hundred years. It will come. It is phasing in. I would say it is phasing in at incredible speed now. . . . But it is very, very wrong to totally blame the male for not allowing the female to get to the top. I don't think that's ever been an issue at all. (3 S.GEN/M)

While not seamless, it is, however, very easy to slip from an account which deflects attention from men and the system which privileges them into an account where the effects are not even hinted at and the male norm is rendered, powerfully, invisible. The small group of responses that denied that there is a problem with the number of women in senior positions provides the clearest illustration of this. Those offering denial responses are endorsing the status quo, but more than that, they are simply taking the present situation as a simple, unproblematic given. There is really nothing to defend, it is simply normal that few women will achieve senior positions.

What Problem!?

Most of those who responded to the first question by denying that there was a problem actually said that *if* there was a problem, it was either a small one that was improving because of affirmative action or that it wasn't a problem at their university which was generally better than others. Here these points are made by two male academics, one from each institution:

Is it true that within [the university] there are relatively fewer women in senior positions than one would anticipate? . . . I mean the chair of the promotions committee is a woman, two of the last deans were women, and two out of six of the academic members of the research board are women. So if you exclude the chancellery for the moment, I would have thought, relatively, women were very well represented in the university. I accept, of course, that the ratio of women to men is low, but . . . I don't believe within [the university] women are in any way prevented from obtaining senior positions. And in fact, demonstrably they've done very well in this regard. (9 SAC/M)

I don't know. . . . In our profession [information systems] there are more women taking over the senior roles. . . . It is swinging the other way. It is even happening in the universities now where a lot of the vice-chancellors now are becoming women. So I don't think you could say there are few women. . . . There is quite a few. Let me think. One, two—there are four heads of school here on our campus if I remember rightly. Is it four or two? (10 SAC/M)

In these accounts, the achievement of a select few women is taken as evidence that the general body of women is not disadvantaged. This is particularly clear in the above quotes where the low ratio of women to men is accepted and, in this way, is read as given and placed beyond question: that senior women exist makes their small numbers irrelevant, and so the relative numbers of senior men and women is never made an issue.

A similar occlusion is achieved in the response of a senior manager by individualizing and psychologizing the problem:

Well, I think that you would have to say that *prima facie* there seems to be a problem because you couldn't say *a priori* that men are, by nature of their gender, better suited to university work, so *prima facie* there has to be a problem. Whether or not there *is* a problem would have to require a lot more investigation and evidence. Now in my view the ideal would be where both genders feel quite happy and contented with whatever the balance is, their needs and aspirations are being met, whether that's been met at a 50-50 balance or a 60-40 or a 70-30, I don't think matters, the important thing is, are people able to fulfill their potential or are they being frustrated by that, and I think that's what we've got to get at. Now I don't really have a definitive answer on that although I am well aware that some people feel that their potential is not being met. (5 MAN/M)

By this account, *the problem* is made more apparent than real and, more importantly, is no longer gendered—it is simply a matter of individual *people* not feeling as if they are fulfilling their potential. The neutralizing of gender accomplished here is clearly a key ploy in rendering the male norm invisible. Another ploy used to the same effect is evident in the following style of argument. A senior male academic, in conversation with the first of the two academics quoted at the beginning of this section, said:

Gosh, I mean that's a big issue isn't it? How far back do you go? I guess I mean you'd have to look at the whole social structure I guess, and the traditional roles of women. That has obviously had an effect on how many women see academia as a career, and how that's going to fit in with motherhood and all that sort of stuff. But, it's interesting, I mean I can get myself into all sorts of hot water here, but I really don't hold very strongly to the view that women have been grossly disadvantaged in the professional area. My mother-in-law is seventy-six years of age, she's a dentist, now that's fairly unusual for her to be a dentist from that time, but in talking to her about it she strongly believes that she's suffered absolutely no discrimination, there were no fewer opportunities for her than any of the males that went through with her at that time. She reckons it's a whole lot of bunkum. Women are making the decision that they want to go in a particular direction and the decision they are making is that they don't want to go into academia. (6 SAC/M)

Here, not only is there is no problem, but a *woman* (his mother-in-law) says there is no problem. This was by no means an uncommon device in the arguments put to us by our male colleagues. Men offering *denial* responses often referred to their wives or other female relatives for supportive anecdotal evidence or endorsement of their views. Curiously, they rarely deferred to the experiences or opinions of their female colleagues. The power of this device, like blaming women beforehand, is that it keeps the dispute about opportunity and discrimination between women, and this helps maintain the invisibility of the male norm and of men's investment in it.

The male norm is at its most powerful when invisible and perhaps especially so when the masculinity of the culture is invisible to those within it and, arguably, the beneficiaries of it. As Eveline (1994: 134) notes, citing Maud Eduards, "The most effective opposition to change is one that is kept intangible." Our study produced one very clear expression of this in a forcefully expressed critique of feminists generally, and of our project specifically, driven by the intangibility of operations of the male norm. A senior male academic argued:

One of the things that gender and organizational culture, at its roots presumes, is that various organizational cultures have been set up in various ways for men. One of the problems women have here, is that they even think that. They tend to propose, therefore, that this boys' network works in a sort of a highly connected way, which it doesn't; that there are these sorts of solidarities and mateships, which there aren't. . . . there is a situation in fact of very isolated, highly mobile networks in the university that are highly contingent, that are not based on playing golf together, or any of these kinds of things. But it's presumed that that's the way it is. One of the ways that women react to this often is to build their own networks and act in ways that are just sheer bastardry, but not be able to recognize this because their kind of critique of the culture is impoverished. Their understanding of organizational culture is so impoverished that they don't understand the ways in which it's literally working. (7 SAC/M)

The normalization of male culture is denied because of the absence of specific organizational practices like tangible male networking, practices which are arguably obsolete where male culture *is* effectively normalized. Neither the manifest advantage held by men within the organization nor that women are regularly ruled out of succeeding within the system is admissible to this account. The very invisibility of that culture rebounds on women's disjunctive experience of it, allowing this male academic to dismiss women's accounts as mistaken and impoverished.

Pointing the Finger: The System and Male Advantage

There is a different interpretation proffered of the issues that have been woven through the responses we have cited so far. It is an account that is clearly informed by feminist analyses, whether or not respondents would self-identify with feminism. In this alternative account, the normalization of male culture is challenged to the extent that the social structure, the organization, and men's investments in them are scrutinized and named as discriminatory rather than neutral. This group of broadly *structural* responses, was, in fact, the most common response (see table 4.1). Half of all responses to our question about why there were so few senior women proffered explanations that pointed to structural factors. Women (64 percent) were more likely than men (38 percent), by a factor of 1:8, to offer a structural account of women's disadvantage. This should not detract from the fact that a large group of male responses also fell into this category. It is gratifying to see the extent to which the broad outlines of a feminist account have entered into the university communities' explanations of themselves, even if the extent to which it has done so must be qualified by the bias toward women in our sample and by the fact that it is not as popular an explanation among management as it is for other sectors of the university community.

Notwithstanding its apparent popularity, there are ways in which *structural* responses are still caught up in the male norm and struggle to displace it within the institutions' rhetoric and practice. In part, we are mindful here of Eveline's argument that there are strategic costs, as well as benefits, in the preoccupation with women's disadvantage. As pointed out earlier, structural responses were as likely to be expressed in language that normalized men's lives, even when explicitly critical. One female manager, for example, refutes the concept of a pipeline as follows:

> The profiles are changing but whether . . . it's just a matter of time, I don't believe that. I believe women will drop out, I think the ratios will improve but not much in the next 20 years. . . . Women will drop out and some of that will be voluntary, as life cycle choices or personality choices mean that women will self- select to leave, but others will be forced to leave, or pressured into it—pressured because conditions at home or because conditions at work simply mean that it is too hard. (2 MAN/F)

The problem is rhetorically constructed as one women face. While that may also be practically true, the rhetoric ensures that it is routinely left to women to resolve.

But there are other difficulties arising from the operations of the male norm for those making structural responses, and it is with these that we conclude our analysis. Structural responses were critical of the normalization of male culture at two levels (see table 4.3): first, in accounts of the institutional culture as sexist and hostile to women, and second, in accounts that treat the social structure itself as a particular construct which systematically disadvantages women and advantages men. With respect to the first, difficulties arose in making tangible to the community at large the covert nature of discrimination. That is, the invisibility of the norm was difficult to counter. The problem with the second arose from the intimate connection between the normalization of male culture within the organization and that which operates in society at large. Those critiquing the male norm within the university find negotiating the two strategically difficult, just as those defending the male norm find it strategically convenient.

Table 4.3 Blaming Women Percentages and (numbers)
Why do you think there are so few senior women?

Structural Explanations						
The culture is hostile to women;	Gender		Rank/Position			
they carry extra burdens.	Men	Women	Ac.	Man.	Gen.	Total
Sexism, Hostile Culture	66	70	75	72	63	68
Women's Domestic/Family Burdens	34	30	25	28	37	32
Total Responses	(68)	(122)	(75)	(18)	(97)	(190)
Total Percentages	100	100	100	100	100	100

Women were far clearer that they were faced with a hostile environment than were their male counterparts. In response to our question, women would often produce a list of sexist acts and events. The following montage from several women respondents collates these accounts:

> Women are not fostered except in exceptional circumstances and may be per-
> ceived as a threat. . . . For a woman to get on she has to be much better than the
> majority of men. . . . They've got to be super, super good, do so many things
> much better. They've got to play the power game in the male way . . . and
> they've really got to be all the time promoting themselves and all the rest of it.
> Women in non-traditional areas may have to survive in a hostile environment
> for years. This "tempering of their steel" makes them an obvious threat to

the men around. . . . Women are often given insignificant tasks to keep them occupied while the men get on with what matters, e.g., Finance and Policy. . . . Men are very comfortable with women until it gets to the very senior positions. . . . Sometimes [a senior woman's] life is made so difficult that . . . it is not worth it. They don't want to be a spearhead for sisterhood any more.[8]

This sexist culture was understood to mean that women had to perform better than men in order to mark time with them, that they had to become like men in order to succeed, and that even then the price exacted for their success would make it unrewarding. In other words, it was understood that men were normatively advantaged and women normatively disadvantaged by the culture.

Although many women were clear about sexism, they found it difficult to point to specific practices or policies that discriminated against them. For example, generally, women staff regarded the procedures for appointment, probation, and promotion as *fair* and as improving, but they were just as convinced that in practice they were subtly subverted. On the issue of selection, for example, women at both universities spoke of the problems generated by the definition of *merit*; "what referees and assessors say about women and men" (2 SAC/F); "the way that males will portray themselves plus a bit [while] women will undersell themselves" (3 S.GEN/F). Regarding promotions, they spoke of the glass ceiling:

But I do really believe in the glass ceiling. To be counted as an equal you have to be better than your counterpart. And then there is a barrier where . . . it's not a conscious thing, it is an unconscious thing that you are just not quite suitable. I don't think they do it intentionally, but it's the white male stereotype. (4 S.GEN/F)

I've struggled with this one in my own mind, I believe there probably is a glass ceiling. My ability to actually detect it whenever I sit in a selection committee is not particularly sensitive. . . . in other words I have difficulty in saying that at this point somebody was blocked or at that point somebody was blocked because it is managed, whatever biases exist are managed, and clouded in such sophisticated ways, consciously or unconsciously, that it is extremely deep rooted and endemic and for that reason invisible. (2 MAN/F)

Male respondents who identified sexism found it even more difficult to articulate the more intangible aspects of sexist practice. They spoke much more tentatively, in more general terms, about the consequences for women of working in a predominantly male workforce. Here, two male respondents, the first an academic, the second a member of the general staff, speak of the existence of such a culture almost as a self-evident by-product of the greater number of men:

I'm not sure I have any particular insights into why that is the case, or whether it's really just the dominant male culture which was simply being expressed and reinforced without any affirmative action, from the people in that culture, to kind of look at what they were and who they are and, you know, where are our values. It kind of sort of happens, it's not quite inevitable, but almost, at least from my perspective, just by the fact that people tend to appoint the people like themselves. . . . I'm not sure whether that's too glib, or if there are other structural things in there, but that would be one comment I'd make. (11 SAC/M)

I have a perception, but I might be totally wrong, my perception is that the senior management right at that top level are not particularly pro-woman, that is my perception. I can't even tell you why that is my perception, but if enough people have it that is a problem in itself. But I would say in the vice-chancellery they would find it difficult having a woman in there. And you know, we are changing vice-chancellors so maybe that will change things as well. But I would have thought that certain people at fairly high levels, and I am talking administratively now . . . would have difficulty [with women in those positions]. (4 S.GEN/M)

The culture is passively, almost accidentally, hostile to women, rather than actively so. The difficulties being experienced here, both in articulating the subtleties of sexism and in understanding it as something actively produced, rather than almost inconsequential, owe much to the continued operations of the male norm. While a male culture is understood to exist, it, itself, is not being directly challenged, certainly not by the men's accounts, and even the women are struggling to say it is deliberate or that those privileged by it have a responsibility for it.

The second kind of general structural response was to point to women's disproportionate share of unpaid (domestic/family) work as a reason why women could not compete fairly with men in paid work. Rather than the rhetoric of choice, which operated within earlier accounts, in structural accounts, women are understood to be burdened by their wider social roles and responsibilities. Here a male academic sums it up:

The problem is first of all structural. For women to meet the criteria of a 60 hour week to have a significant research reputation established, it means essentially they have to give up a commitment to a family and a personal life or make a series of compromises which delay their advancement to senior positions; it's partly economic; she has to be able to employ part-time work at home to be able to put in the hours in meetings and preparations that are required at the senior levels. (8 SAC/M)

While this is a more sympathetic account of the bind women find themselves in,[9] the difficulty which arises is of the extent to which these problems are external to the university itself. The disadvantage experienced by women because of the social practices operating in the wider society is understood to be somewhat beyond the scope of the university to address. As one male academic put it, "I think that some things may be reflecting outside structures rather than the inside structures" (12 SAC/M). In general, the institution would be regarded as being very generous if it were to take measures within its organization to redress the effects of those outside structures. One small measure of this was the degree to which responses were self-editing with regards to the larger structural questions: more than twice as many responses identified the work culture as male and sexist, rather than the wider social structure as fundamentally problematic for women as workers.

The focus for the most intense comments on the broader structural issues was the specific management of child work and university work. Many responses from junior women, and some from male academics with young children, were acutely expressive of the "incredible juggling act" (4 GEN/F) required to manage both tasks, and the commitments and costs exacted. Here are the combined voices of several junior academic women on why there are so few senior women, followed by a junior male academic responding to a later question on what a predominantly female workplace might look like:

> Well . . . I took 10 years out raising children and even when I did sort of return to my career, I still had other commitments that I could not neglect. . . . I too would like a wife, so I think that it is the personal dimension, the other call on your time . . . the expectations on you . . . And the fact that most of us believe that those things are worth doing, and that a life that is narrowing, career, is a life that is impoverished. (3 JAC/F and 4 JAC/F)

> I really don't think high level men here understand what it is like for younger academics with families who are trying to run partnerships and not traditional old style family relationships, they don't understand what that's like because they have never had to do it. That really frustrates me. That frustrates me when a senior academic will make a joke when I leave at 4:30 because I have to pick up my son from child care, he just doesn't understand that someone has to pick up their kids from child care because his wife does it and always has done it. Those sorts of things annoy the hell out of me. (4 JAC/M)

Indeed, the shift in expectation of some men regarding active parenting led to a shift of emphasis of their analysis:

> I would probably see now family status as being even more important than gender. The people I see rising are the ones who are either DINKS [Double Income No Kids] of either gender, or single people of either gender. If you are trying to raise a family, whether you're a father or a mother, . . . all I [you] can do at this stage is cruise and try and get a life in a broader context. (13 SAC/M)

It was a simple matter for our respondents to excuse the university from responsibility for acting in regard to this structural factor: in part it requires broader social change, in part it is up to the individuals involved to resolve, and in part the university is understood to already be a flexible working environment (at least for academic staff) and, therefore, already accommodates the domestic commitments of its employees. For one male dean, these perceptions led him to discount the costliness of the juggling act completely:

> I can think of at least three very young women in my school who have had children over the last five years without seriously interrupting their career, without doing their career any harm in the long run at all. . . . Again, they look single-minded because they have chosen to have families. I think the university is much more relaxed about allowing women to juggle family and academic responsibilities than it used to be. I think the home environment is much more supportive than it used to be, but these kind of tough-minded, intelligent women don't put up with partners who won't cooperate. (6 MAN/M)

Again, it is clear that the male norm subverts the challenge to it. The organization of paid work and the operating practices of the university as an organization are taken as givens. In this way, even people who recognize these as structural problems are at a loss to know whether, and how, to make the university responsive to the problem or responsible for its alleviation. The funding of universities, the intensification of academic work, the levels of commitment demanded of general staff, have all created a climate where hard work and long hours are made a virtue, deemed to be a part of the job, and rewarded through career advancement. Again it is important to recall the normalization of the worker as male discussed earlier, and note here that there is no sustained challenge to the notion that a *good* academic or a "good member of the general staff" is one committed to the job and prepared to put in long hours.

> The level of commitment that is required is total and there are very few role models I think for women. . . . Where are the role models for women who want everything, and have everything. Who want a family and want children; who want a professional life but also want to have a creative life and do their own work. . . . the models are normally women who have given up everything, sacrificed everything, either for an academic life or for a creative life. (14 SAC/M)

Conclusion

All these considerations have implications for organizational change. They suggest that the gender that is "thought" by "hegemonic masculinity" (Connell 1987, 1995) may retain its potency even when certain gendered practices have been challenged and are changing in the lives of employees and at lower levels of organizational hierarchies.

It is clear that the normalization of male culture is under challenge and that one brake on the challenge translating to changed working cultures is the fact that managers, the peak male culture, constitute an exception to the majority view. They remain unconvinced of the intangible nature of discrimination, putting their faith in policy and procedures that create the appearance of equity.

They are less enamored of structural explanations, preferring those that blame the past or blame women and preserve the illusion that men are not actively advantaged by the system. Where they do concede structural accounts, administrators are disinclined to think through ways in which they could intervene to address those issues for themselves and their workers. The joint effect, as one woman manager put it, is that "there isn't a genuine commitment to change the situation" (3 MAN/F) among those with the power to introduce such changes. Power and influence is the focus of our next chapter.

This perpetuation of masculine management styles and values—alongside their normalization—poses a real dilemma for women in senior positions if they wish to manage in a more cooperative or nurturing way (Wieneke 1995). Alleviating this dilemma and achieving more fundamental change depend upon disrupting the often unconscious, and widely supported, ways of thinking which produce particular patterns of male advantage (Blackmore and Kenway 1993; Blackmore 1993).

More optimistically, and as this chapter has suggested, there is sufficient critical knowledge within at least some quarters to challenge current directions and prompt management to adopt a style more reflective of gender equity goals. Opposition and critical understanding are growing and must continue to be refined. The arguments advanced in this chapter point to the need for a practical program of reform that would identify the means of translating perceptions of unfairness and structural disadvantage into concrete and positive benefits. Crucially, given Acker's (1990) analysis of the interconnected gendering of paid and unpaid work and Eveline's (1994) observations about how the normalization of male culture renders male advantage invisible, practical change within the organization must acknowledge and encourage changes taking place outside the organization. For example, men and women need to renegotiate men's traditional freedom from responsibilities for family care. If such changes are not accommodated in the way the organization orders its work, the pressures on women employees will remain intense, and those on males taking childcare responsibilities will also increase.

Notes

1. We return to an examination of the peak management culture in chapter 6.

2. Sinclair's (1994: 7) research describes the Australian executive culture in two ways: "clubby" masculinism, "an older patrician elitism and a more youthful locker room and larrikin-like boyishness." Mant (1994: 3) identifies a "sloppy, club-like rugby-scrum mentality" that pervades Australian boardrooms, making it difficult for women to fit in. Sinclair (1994: 8) also notes that some men welcome women putting "a brake on the rampant masculine excess."

3. The commonness of this response among management may be partly attributable to their age. Some younger, more junior men were well able to articulate the alternative response (blaming structures) and understand the difficulties such structures posed for themselves as fathers of young children wanting to be more actively involved in parenting. They were, nonetheless, a minority among their peers.

4. It is possible, for example, that the responses of management at the larger university were influenced by a mentoring program which members of the research team implemented at both institutions in 1995, the year before interviews with the larger university staff. The mentoring program included some educative work with senior management and may well have resulted in the managers being more aware of *acceptable* responses. It is also possible that the views of key members of the management team set the tenor of the group's view. The larger university had an advantage over the smaller university in that one of its management team was understood, by the university community at large, to be very supportive of the promotion of women into senior positions.

5. Only four of the eleven comments made by this group mentioned anything other than women's choices. The lack of explicit commentary does not mean that it is not there, however. In managers' responses to other questions, there was ample commentary on the differences in men and women's qualities. But in responding to the direct question about why so few women, it is *choice* that predominates.

6. A degree of complacency is evident in the estimates male respondents offered for how long it would be before the pipeline took effect. Despite the fact that the event or practices which generated *the problem* are seen to have been thoroughly *past*, estimates of the time it would take to be free of their effects are still in the mid- to long-term future. Twenty to twenty-five years was a popular time frame, the shortest suggested was five to ten years. Some thought even this was "incredibly fast."

7. The fact that there hasn't been any significant shift in the dominance of men at the senior levels of organizations, despite the introduction of affirmative action and merit principles (Affirmative Action Agency 1993), suggests that merit is defined by the profile of the current incumbents and, consequently, based on the values and behaviors of men (Smith and Hutchinson 1995: 78).

8. Senior Academics: 2 SAC/F, 3 SAC/F, 4 SAC/F, 5 SAC/F. Junior Academics: 1 JAC/F, 2 JAC/F. General Staff: 3 GEN/F.

9. Although sympathetic to women's position, this quote exhibits the same normalizing tendencies described above: "*women* [must] meet the criteria," "*they* have to give up" family and so on, and "*she* has to be able to employ" help at home.

Chapter 5

Anatomy of Power in Universities

"It's very difficult not to be crude here isn't it [and] go for anatomical features."
(Female junior academic: 5 JAC/F)

Introduction

In the previous chapter we mapped the relative absence of women from positions of seniority within the university and the range of explanations offered for that absence. The extent to which male culture was *normalized* and the invisibility of that normalization were both evident and were posited as an explanation of the persistent absence of senior women. Normalization and its invisibility operate to enhance male privilege and, in this way, contribute to both men's *right* to exert power (their sense of themselves as powerful) and their tenure in powerful positions. We interviewed general and academic staff about power within their organizations. Interviewees were asked to describe the characteristics of those who are and are not rewarded in their universities and the attributes of those who are seen to have power. In this chapter we look at the different ways in which academics and general staff, men and women, view power and the attributes of the powerful.

Power, of course, is seen differently depending upon one's position in an organization. In particular, a discussion of the language of power and its gendered patterns has to be set against the reality of where women were located within these two universities. At the time of the study, both universities had few women above the level of senior lecturer (16 percent), an underrepresentation of women in senior positions that, as we have already noted, is consistent across universities in Australia (Ward 2000) and other countries (Osborne 1998; O'Connor 2000). General staff hierarchies reproduced the same pattern of men bubbling to the top and women mired in the lower echelons of the hierarchy. Men's and women's accounts of power and the powerful and their accounts of powerful women are shaped by the absence of women from powerful positions. This chapter seeks to extend our appreciation of some of the underlying reasons for this lack of female power within academic settings.

Literature on Power in Organizations

DuBrin (1994: 264) describes power as "the ability to influence decisions and control resources." To this, Lakoff and Johnson (1980: 158) add the ability to shape how we think about and understand the world or influence how we must speak about it. Noting that "we define our reality in terms of metaphors and then proceed to act on the basis of the metaphors," Lakoff and Johnson (1980: 157) point out that "whether in national politics or in everyday interaction, people in power get to impose their metaphors." Much of the literature is cast in an essentialist way, blurring the distinction between natural and derived behaviors in ascribing gender differences in, for example, how power is perceived. Probyn (2002: 35) describes two types of thinking about power: "power over versus power to," with women more associated with the power to achieve a goal rather than the *power over* or domination of others. Similarly, Schaef (1985: 124) describes men's concept of power as based upon a scarcity model, in contrast to women who view power as something that increases when given away: "In the . . . Male System, power is conceived in a zero-sum fashion. In the Female System, power is seen as limitless." It is suggested that women and men communicate differently when engaged in the exercise of power. Samovar and Porter (1995) suggest that women try to elicit cooperation or create rapport, whereas men use conversation to negotiate status and often engage in verbal competition in which points of discussion are made in a definitive and forceful fashion.

Some authors relate differences in how men and women *do* power to men's dominance of powerful positions and, thus, to the masculinist styles that underlie management practices in both the public and private sector (Tancred-Sheriff 1988; Cockburn 1990; Blackmore 1993; Lingard and Limerick 1995; Smith and Hutchinson 1995; Mitchell 1996; McKenna 1997). Acknowledging women in higher education as "marginals or outsiders to the male world of academe"

(Clark and Corcoran 1986: 38) enables academic women to be represented as "initiates who wandered into a ritual designed for men" (Beaman-Smith and Placier 1996: 3). As a result, McKenna (1997: 76), quoting Albert, argues that the "successful woman is required to repudiate most of what makes her a woman: her feminine viewpoint, her feminine values of nurturing and caring. In order to succeed she develops a strongly male-oriented bias and a tendency to uphold and defend the masculine culture of ideas and ideals."

More specifically in regard to universities, Kuh and Whitt (1988: 43) claim that higher education in the United States is a "product of western society in which masculine attributes like an orientation toward achievement and objectivity are valued over cooperation, connectedness and subjectivity." And more recently, Chliwniak (1997), analyzing the gender gap in American higher education, noted that historical cultural norming often dictates an image of successful leadership that includes assertiveness, decisiveness, and authority. As a consequence, such authors suggest, women must choose whether to challenge these social norms or become socialized to fit the traditional, masculinized, organizational expectations of leaders. Some choose to leave (McKenna 1997; Wenzel, Blackburn and Hollenshead, 1997; Tancred 1998).

Halford and Leonard (1998: 2) are critical of these perspectives which they summarize in the following way: "It is argued that male behavior, values and attitudes have been hegemonic in organizations because men have historically had more power than women and have built organizations in their image. Thus women find it difficult to thrive in organizations because their behavior, values and attitudes are 'other' and therefore not valued or rewarded by men." In moving beyond this essentialist, categorical perspective, Halford and Leonard suggest that gender should not be seen in such oppositional, fixed categories, but rather as relational and sustained by prevailing discourses in both organizational and wider social cultures. They suggest that an organization should be understood as "a discourse through which individual subjectivities are constructed" (Halford and Leonard 1998: 2). They also suggest that organizations are "not homogeneous spaces" and that there are "multiple mappings of organizations" (Halford and Leonard 1998: 3).

The latter view of organizations is derived from a postmodern analysis in which organizations are seen as fluid and in process. Annandale, Clark, and Allen (1998) discuss the need to look at organizations from a critical postmodern perspective that sees aspects of modernity persisting as new social forms emerge. They argue, "We are witnessing not the demise of 'deep structures' (such as the operation of capitalism or patriarchy in the organization) but their articulation in new forms" (Annandale, Clark, and Allen 1998: 3). Of course, these new forms are influenced by the prevailing culture of economic rationality, which is seen by many writers as affecting the chances that women will gain the more powerful positions in any organization. In the following discussion, we draw on the views of respondents who are situated in positions below the university executive to see how gendered relations of power are created and sustained.

Power in Universities

Power in universities has to be seen as diffuse and complex and, while we are interested in who has power, how the powerful are characterized, and the gendering of power, we first have to explore how respondents understood power to operate within universities. We asked our academic and general staff respondents: "How would you describe those who have power and what attributes do they have?" Their responses were colored by their understanding that universities are not simple hierarchical organizations, but combine both academic/professional status hierarchies and bureaucratic structures which intersect in complex ways. Our respondents understood their universities to be unlike other organizations in that very different kinds of power resided in different sorts of positions and different status/power groups had to negotiate with each other and seek each other's cooperation, thus limiting the scope for even the most senior officers of the university to have clear untrammeled *power*. As a senior administrator said:

> I think a university is more complex than other organizations. . . . academics individually have power . . . a certain amount of freedom; there is not the accountability that you would have in commercial organizations. So power is more diffuse I imagine. I suppose if you asked the VC or the DVC they would say they don't feel very powerful at all, because lots of things they try and do they can't because they can't really direct people to do things. I think the power is different. (5 S.GEN/F)

Table 5.1 summarizes the results as far as they relate to the location of power (who has power) in the universities.

Responses between the two universities were reasonably consistent, as were the responses from men and women and, with one exception, those between academic and general staff. The exception relates to the relative power of each group to the other and will be discussed shortly. Before going on to flesh out staff responses, the extent to which the gender of the powerful was acknowledged is worth noting: fully two-thirds of our respondents did *not* find the gender of those in positions of power remarkable. In general, our respondents focus-

Table 5.1 Who Has Power? (by gender and position) Percentages and (numbers)

	Gender		Position		
	Male	Female	Academic	General	Total
The Executive (VC, DVC, Senior Executive Group)	17.3 (9)	9.3 (5)	17.7 (11)	6.8 (3)	13.2 (14)
Deans/ Heads of Schools	9.6 (5)	9.3 (5)	11.3 (7)	6.8 (3)	9.4 (10)
Professors	1.9 (1)	3.7 (2)	3.2 (2)	2.3 (1)	2.8 (3)
Central admin. has power over the periphery	30.8 (16)	40.7 (22)	32.3 (20)	40.9 (18)	35.8 (38)
Senior staff have power over junior staff	3.8 (2)	3.7 (2)	4.9 (3)	2.3 (1)	3.8 (4)
Administration has power over academics	13.5 (7)	1.8 (1)	9.7 (6)	4.5 (2)	7.6 (8)
Academics have power over general staff	5.8 (3)	14.8 (8)	3.2 (2)	20.5 (9)	10.4 (11)
Power lies in particular jobs (position/ tenure/ responsibility)	17.3 (9)	16.7 (9)	17.7 (11)	15.9 (7)	17.0 (18)
Total Responses	100 (52)	100 (54)	100 (62)	100 (44)	100 (106)

ed on positions and individuals, and the gender of the incumbents or of powerful individuals was not commented upon, especially if they were male. The other third of our respondents did describe the powerful as men, either as one among a series of defining characteristics or as the single most obvious feature:

> Those who have power, positions of seniority within the university from [the] dean upwards within our hierarchy, who can make executive decisions, can exercise power; those people are almost exclusively males; normally careerist; normally in the age range of 40s to 60s; they are married with families and their wives take the major responsibility for family labor; people who have been ruthless in relation to themselves as well as others in ensuring that they are able to build up a research reputation in the first 20 years of their university employment; there is a strong correlation between those who have power and those who are rewarded within the university system. (8 SAC/M)

I guess a more facetious way of putting it is that they are fat and they are fifty and they are male. (5 JAC/M)

Those who singled out maleness as the single most significant feature of the powerful often did so with laughter and as an immediate, up-front response to the question:

Well, men. And they increasingly wear suits and ties. (5 GEN/F)

Male, relatively out of condition, wears a suit and tie most of the time and walks around with an extremely snobbish attitude towards people at the coal-face doing the teaching. (15 SAC/M)

I was about to say testicles. (6 S.GEN/F)

Women were especially quick to acknowledge this characteristic of male-ness with power; men, more reluctant to do so (although as the above quotes indicate, not exclusively so). The majority (65 percent) of such responses came from women, with about a third (35 percent) from men. The spontaneous laughter that accompanied particularly the women's responses to this question had an interesting echo in the observation one of our interviewers made about how the focus groups dealt with the question on working styles which will be discussed toward the end of this chapter. He noted that when the men he inter-viewed talked about women (and the majority of men commented positively on women), they tended to lower their voices almost to a whisper! This was nicely contrasted by our women respondents who, particularly when talking about men in a negative way, did so with much laughter.

Formal Power

The people who were most readily named as powerful were so by virtue of the senior positions they held—what we might call formal power. They were the vice-chancellors, deputy and pro vice-chancellors, business managers, and the small management team surrounding these key positions, and, within the aca-demic structures of the university, the deans. While the former have institutional leadership and the latter academic leadership, what marked their power was control over the budget. As one senior academic said:

Those who control budgets are the ones who have the power, so in the university there are very many powerful people because they have control over the purse strings. (10 SAC/M)

Thus deans, as the line managers and devolved budget holders for academic groupings, were more often (3:1) mentioned as having power than professors, the most senior status position in the academic hierarchy (see table 5.1). Interestingly, one of the managers, reflecting on the changes wrought by recent reforms in Australian higher education, suggested that it would become increasingly difficult for women to gain a foothold in management positions. These reforms, he suggested, emphasized "a managerial approach which puts more stress on numerical, budgeting, and planning skills," which "I would suspect males [to] have more than females." While not endorsing his suggestion that women cannot add up, we follow Yeatman (1990) in arguing that the technocratic elements of the new managerialism are antithetical to a cooperative style of management, and we agree with our respondents that budgetary control is an important component of formal power.

The other marked response about formal, positional power came from general staff who understood very clearly that academic staff had power both over, and relative to, general staff. The following quotes are from women, one a technician and the other a dean's secretary:

Academic staff can have power over general staff. It's assumed that they know more, which can be quite frustrating. (6 GEN/F)

Power is still in the hands of the academics. General staff are relatively powerless and not well represented. They are left out of where the university is going. They are treated as the "hands and feet" of the institution, certainly not regarded as its "heart and soul." They "almost don't exist." (7 S.GEN/F)

These general staff were usually located away from the central administrative structures, either out in academic areas or in the service units, and were mostly women. Academic staff did not generally recognize their power over general staff explicitly (seven times as many general as academic staff made this distinction) and, in stark contrast, were more likely to offer an account of the illegitimate power of the more senior general staff positions—the (central) administrators. Three-quarters of the responses pointing to administration having power over academics came from academics, and mostly male academics. The gulf, so acutely felt by the general staff cited above, is reflected and reversed in the following comment from a senior academic:

You get the impression quite often that a lot of the administrators and the people with administrative powers seem to think that the university is there as an administrative organization. They seem to forget that it's really the administration's role to be supporting research and teaching, rather than being an end in itself. (6 SAC/M)

Although identifying positions with formal power, our respondents also commented on the extent to which that power could be exercised. The deans, for example, understood that in financially stringent times their discretionary power was severely limited. Their view of themselves was that they administered budgets decided by the central university hierarchy, which were largely allocated to salaries, and thus yielded very limited discretionary funds.

The constrained nature of power within the universities led several respondents to observe that there was a reluctance to use power blatantly. Despite real and explicit formal power, most people in positions of power acted in a kind of benevolent dictatorship. Here are the views of three senior male academics:

Look I think that some people have power and don't use it. They almost seem to be apologetic and uncomfortable with power. Others exercise it as much as they can and probably will try and go beyond the jurisdiction that they have. If I have to generalize at all, I would say that the people "in power" in [this university] are very reluctantly so. They have not been particularly tyrannical or thirsty for power. (16 SAC/M)

Well, it's like it is several little totalitarian states all in one. As head of school, I basically have a lot of power, which in most cases I choose not to use. But if I wanted to be a total autocrat, I could be because everything has to be signed by me. Everything has to be approved by me. I am ultimately responsible for everything that happens so basically I am a little Hitler or potentially so. Above me is the deputy vice-chancellor of the division who has exactly the same role that I have, but of course is senior to me. So he has to sign everything, he has ultimate control over whether you can do this or not. And then over him is the vice-chancellor who has the same sorts of powers. So it is a ridiculous hierarchy where at every level you have these little potentates who have life and death control over everything that those under them have to do. That actually just describes the system not those who have power. (14 SAC/M)

It's very, very much a collegial model in the faculty, apart from the dean who has, as head, total absolute power of decision making, use of resources etc. It's a benevolent dictatorship, and a good one. (17 SAC/M)

This coyness about exercising formal power could be a gesture toward an older model of collegiality or another normalizing strategy whereby the formal power invested in positions is trivialized or denied. Certainly the constrained nature of formal power was acknowledged by those who spoke of the diffusion of power throughout the institution and argued that the diffused nature of power constrained the power of the formally powerful and/or bequeathed to the relatively powerless the power to resist. As a junior academic put it:

> I think there are many of us who have power; that the more it becomes centralized, the harder it is for the central agenda to actually be achieved because power actually resides all over the place and the more people feel dissatisfied and put upon and not appreciated, and [the greater the] lack of good faith between them and their employer, [the more likely] they are to [use their] power to make [this university] not achieve its mission goals and statement. (6 JAC/F)

Nonetheless, the power vested in the position was very evident in the level of acquiescence to the position, even when the person occupying the position was considered incompetent. As one senior woman pointed out:

> The closer you are to the pinnacle of the hierarchy, the more people will be absolutely silent about some absolutely absurd statement because there is some notion that, well, I can't really understand it, that one doesn't say certain things or deal in certain ways with the misuse of that position. People expect to have that kind of authority when they enter those positions and they deeply resent it if you contest the actual grounds on which decisions have been made. (6 SAC/F)

Informal Power

In addition to the formal power bequeathed by position and diffused throughout the institution, our respondents also spoke of informal power. As one senior administrator put it, what underlies the formal responsibilities and lines of management, the decision-making structures, and committee system "is the informal culture and the informal structure" which "runs the system" (3 S.GEN/F). This structure ran parallel to the power bequeathed by position. Staff at both universities spoke of how the vice-chancellors were supported by an informal group of senior advisers (the senior executive group or senior executive management group that met independently of the more formal university committee structure). This made power more secretive and less transparent, and decision making more mysterious.

For a third of our respondents, formal and informal power came together in the discussion on the powerful as largely White, middle-aged, middle-class, and male, in that many of their responses drew the link between male power and the informal power structures of the old boys' network.

> I don't know if they're all Masons or what. (8 S.GEN/F)

> That particular way of operating through networking and informal decision making clearly favors the man because they are in close contact with each other and the women are inclined to operate through proper channels. (2 SAC/F)

> The boys' club type of thing is quite important. You know, the standing at the bar having a beer is quite important at this university, and those people who don't do that I think may find it a disadvantage. (2 SAC/M)

One of the managers was also quite open about the exclusionary practices of the men networking when he argued:

> There are ways in which men network. For example, there aren't many women who go to watch the rugby. Several of the senior managers catch up with some of the academic staff who are watching the rugby. I wouldn't expect to see any of the senior women there. (1 MAN/M)

This nexus of informal and formal power also marked a difference in how powerful women and powerful men were perceived. In sharp contrast to the acknowledgment that men had power, or the powerful were men, very few of our respondents (7) spoke of powerful women in their answers to this question. Moreover, when they did so, it was mainly to speak of women's power as even more constrained than men's.

> Why people get ahead is the boys' club or the girls' club. And the girls' club works well but it is a much more limited power within the broader structures of the university. (1 JAC/M)

> They wear ties! They're men. Some women have some power, but it's usually compromised power—power that operates in certain spheres but not in others. I think those that have power—not absolute power, but are pretty damn self-satisfied with the amount of power they've got. . . . they're all men. (5 SAC/F)

Women were thought to operate through the proper channels, to not be able to wield power in the same way as men, and to wield power by virtue of their association with powerful positions (as in the notion that the dean's secretary had power in relation to general staff, or as "The power behind the throne").

We suspect that, at a more subtle level, there is a difference in male and female conversations about power in that women talk of power as somehow external, disconnected from themselves, whereas men, even very junior men, seem to express a sense of power as something they might expect to come into, in due course. Among one focus group of men, for example, this emerged from an account of their own power to "get what they want." Even though the two junior staff who dominated this conversation portray themselves as radicals, that is, as working the system for the advantage of their students, their account of their activities and their self-perception reads like a tale of powerful men in training:

How would you describe those who have power? What attributes do they have? (Interviewer)

They want it. Simple as that. (3 SAC/M)

Yeah . . . I have got power inherent in my position, but I know other people who have power inherent in their position who can't get much done. I can get a lot done. . . . I get done what I need to get done through fair or foul. (6 JAC/M)

Yeah [and] the club of interpersonal connections works fantastically. If you get on well with someone, and you have got a mentor. I mean that is why you get ahead. You have some tenured, senior tenured member of staff who reckons you are ok. (1 JAC/M)

[We] access that covert culture. . . . it's almost like a black market. We get so much stuff around the university because I infiltrate at low levels. I get all the techo's [technicians] on side. If the heads of school knew the equipment we take away, they'd die. But because we have networked very carefully throughout the university, we get it. (6 JAC/M)

I see this as in fact quite powerful . . . forming those alternative structures that are external or opposed to or different from the hierarchy to get things done that suit you. . . . it's a sort of anarchist position. . . . you take responsibility for what you wish to happen and then you make it happen. (1 JAC/M)

I have got this theory that all the rules are made of rubber and you find out how hard it is to break them by how hard you hit them, or how softly you prod in the right places. Sometimes the rule breaks and you get caught out, but generally they are very flexible in this place. The lecturers are god; you can do anything in terms of admin if you know the right people. (6 JAC/M)

The people who get ahead think about the system that they are in from the perspective of power and politics and interpersonal relations. They think of it as an organization not as a glorious testament to the enlightenment in which, you know, pure thought would make you a god. (1 JAC/M)

Systems are there to be short-circuited as fast as you can. (6 JAC/M)

This conversation speaks not only of a self-confidence to do what one wants, but also expresses an understanding of power consistent with the more negative characterizations of the powerful offered by our respondents. When taken together with the few throwaway comments on powerful women just mentioned, what these negative characterizations of the powerful suggest is that our vision of *the powerful* is underwritten by gender stereotypes which make the powerful woman an oxymoron or turns her into a man!

For the two-thirds of our respondents for whom it was unremarkable that the powerful were men, informal power was often linked to knowledge, personality, and interpersonal power:

I've seen some very influential people who have got themselves very well connected . . . really strong networks around the university and know how the university operates. (9 S.GEN/F)

Acknowledgment of the informal power system reinforced a sense of the multiplicity and diffuseness of power within universities, and fed into a discussion of the attributes of those with power. Here it was clear that it was less where you were positioned than the attributes you possessed which marked out the nature and extent of your power and influence: the use made of one's formal power or the influence one might exert over the formally powerful.

Attributes of Power

As with the discussion on who had power, respondents' comments on the attributes of power tended to be gender neutral. Indeed, even those who immediately identified the powerful as men tended to revert to neutral terms when describing the attributes of the powerful—they speak of powerful people. Despite the gender-neutral account of attributes, our respondents still spoke in ways which passed judgment on various attributes, giving them positive, neutral, or negative overtones (see table 5.2). Responses were fairly evenly divided among these three evaluative categories, but there were differences between men and women,

Table 5.2 What Are the Attributes of Power? Percentages and (numbers)

	Gender		Rank/Position		Total Responses
	Male	Female	Academic	General	
Positive Characteristics:	42.3 (33)	26.5 (30)	27.6 (27)	43.4 (36)	(63)
Toughness, determination	7.6 (6)	3.5 (4)	4.1 (4)	7.2 (6)	(10)
Noble service	2.6 (2)	0.9 (1)	2.0 (2)	1.2 (1)	(3)
Clear thinkers, decisiveness	5.1 (4)	0.9 (1)	1.0 (1)	4.8 (4)	(5)
Good organization, communication skills	14.1 (11)	14.2 (16)	11.2 (11)	19.3 (16)	(28)
Charisma, good leadership	12.8 (10)	7.1 (8)	9.2 (9)	10.8 (9)	(18)
Neutral Characteristics:	34.6 (27)	45.1 (51)	37.8 (37)	37.3 (31)	(68)
People with information	7.6 (6)	7.1 (8)	8.1 (8)	7.2 (6)	(14)
People who network	5.4 (4)	4.4 (5)	4.1 (4)	6.0 (5)	(9)
Strategic thinkers, know the system	11.5 (9)	13.2 (15)	13.3 (13)	13.2 (11)	(24)
Experienced people, longevity	3.8 (3)	5.3 (6)	4.1 (4)	6.0 (5)	(9)
Extrovert	1.2 (1)	2.6 (3)	3.1 (3)	1.2 (1)	(4)
Devoted to administrative career	5.1 (4)	3.5 (4)	5.1 (5)	3.6 (3)	(8)
Negative Characteristics:	23.1 (18)	28.3 (32)	34.7 (34)	19.3 (16)	(50)
Ruthless, self-centered	6.4 (5)	8.0 (9)	8.1 (8)	7.2 (6)	(14)
Dogmatic, insensitive	5.1 (4)	4.4 (5)	8.1 (8)	1.2 (1)	(9)
Members of powerful clique	0.0 (0)	6.2 (7)	5.1 (5)	2.4 (2)	(7)
Manipulative, conniving	5.1 (4)	6.2 (7)	9.2 (9)	2.4 (2)	(11)
Preoccupied with administration	2.6 (2)	0.0 (0)	1.0 (1)	1.2 (1)	(2)
Send problems elsewhere	2.6 (2)	0.9 (1)	1.0 (1)	2.4 (2)	(3)
Smooth, teflon-coated	1.2 (1)	1.8 (2)	1.0 (1)	2.4 (2)	(3)
Power corrupts	0.0 (0)	0.9 (1)	1.0 (1)	0.0 (0)	(1)
Total Percentages and (numbers)	100 (78)	100 (113)	100 (98)	100 (83)	(181)

and academic and general staff responses. Males were more likely than females (1.6:1) to give positive attributes, and females were more likely than males (1.3:1) to give neutral and, to a lesser extent, negative responses.

Academic and general staff responses were equally represented in the neutral category. However, general staff (1.5:1) tended to give more positive attributes, whereas academics (1.8:1) were more likely to give negative attributes.

Our main interest in this chapter is the anatomy of power and its gender. However, before pursuing these, it is worthwhile to flesh out briefly the main attributes of the powerful as discussed by our respondents. The most frequently mentioned responses are set out in table 5.3, rank ordered for each of male, female, academic, and general staff categories.

Among males, females, and general staff, good organization and communication skills were the most frequently, and positively, mentioned attribute of power, and academics had it listed in second place. This included those who were seen as fair and hard working, along with those who had good interpersonal skills.

> I think the person who has power has to have great organizational skills, management skills, otherwise they get conned; they are not on top of the thing. (7 SAC/F)

> I guess the best of them has the capacity to have reasonably good interpersonal skills and to be able to talk to staff individually and not have confrontations. (8 SAC/F)

> They know who to talk to, they know when to speak and when not to speak and they know who to bow to and who to wipe up off the floor. They are very, very skillful. I mean you've got to watch them at some of these big meetings; you've got to admire them. (7 JAC/F)

The next most frequently mentioned attribute was strategic thinker. We categorized this as a neutral attribute even though some did think of it as negative ("They play the game." 10 S.GEN/F). Here, a senior woman administrator speaks of this attribute:

> I've seen some very influential people who . . . spend time finding out, knowledge is power, people who spend their time finding out what's going on, they're the people who have the power. (9 S.GEN/F)

Being charismatic and showing leadership skills was in second place for males, third place for general staff, and fourth place for females and academics.

It included having a forceful personality, being confident, and dealing with problems—all attributes that we classified as positive.

> I believe they have to be decision makers, and have to have a vision. (6 SAC/M)

Table 5. 3 Most Frequently Mentioned Responses*

Males		Females	
1	Good organization and communication skills	1	Good organization and communication skills
2	Charismatic, with leadership skills	2	Strategic thinkers
3	Strategic thinkers	3	Ruthless, self-centered
4	Toughness, determination	4	People with information
4	People with information	4	Charismatic, with leadership skills
Academic		**General**	
1	Strategic thinkers	1	Good organization and communication skills
2	Good organization and communication skills	2	Strategic thinkers
3	Manipulative conniving	3	Charismatic, with leadership skills
4	Charismatic, with leadership skills	4	Toughness, determination
5	Ruthless, self-centered	4	Ruthless, self-centered
5	Dogmatic, insensitive	4	People with information
5	People with information		

* Mentioned by a total of 9 times or higher (the highest response category was mentioned 28 times).

The next group of most commonly mentioned attributes could have been grouped together, but we saw slightly different tones in these responses: ruthless/self-centered, manipulative/conniving, and dogmatic/insensitive (were categorized as negative), and toughness/determination (was categorized as positive). The ruthless attribute included sacrificing everything to get ahead and being a single-minded careerist. The manipulative included being a coercive decision-maker, overriding democratic processes, throwing temper tantrums, and being unpredictable to get your own way. The dogmatic attribute included being autocratic and thick skinned. The following quotes demonstrate these negative attributes:

> Powerful people are the bullying type and are not disposed to listening to others. (9 SAC/F)

> [They like] trampling others, someone who is just ruthless. (8 JAC/F)

> They are manipulative, most of them, single-minded. (1 S.GEN/F)

> They have very small ears because they don't hear anything anyone else says. (7 JAC/M)

The toughness/determination attribute was categorized as positive, as in these two quotes from general staff:

> I think that many people I know who are powerful, they just have the will to get things done, or the will to have a plan succeed. Often they don't look at how it is to be executed. They just say, "Right, we are going to have this happen and then it is your job to make this happen." (7 GEN/F)

> Personalities are important. Powerful people need to be seen to be clear and decisive; to be determined. (1 GEN/M)

One final category noted more frequently than others was people with information. This usually referred to people in certain positions who had access to information, but it also included people with certain expertise skills that were needed by others. We categorized these responses as neutral.

> Those who have information have the power and without certain kinds of information there is no real chance of attaining significant power. When I was chair of the program, I was privy to information that no one else was likely to have. (18 SAC/M)

Gender Attributes and Power

Despite the overt gender neutrality of the above depictions of the attributes of the powerful, we can flesh out these stereotypes, and gender them, with the answers we received to another question which was put to both our management and general university sample. The university management sample was asked, "In your experience do men and women have different styles of working? If so, what's the nature of these differences?" When we put the same question to the first of our general university focus groups, they suggested we rephrase the question as, "What would a predominantly female workplace be like, and what would a predominantly male workplace be like?" which we did.[1] In the context of this analysis, the responses to these questions are useful because of what they tell us about the particular characterization of women as workers, which is both produced by, and reinforcing of, the normalization of male culture (Eveline 1994), a culture in which the powerful are men, and men are powerful. In the discussion that follows, the differences between the responses of men and women and what they think about their own and each other's contribution to the working environment are especially revealing, but differences of position and rank are also commented upon where they are relevant.

Damned if You Do, Damned if You Don't: Women, Working Styles, and Power in a Male Culture

The majority of responses,[2] two-thirds overall, and over three-quarters of the women's responses, identified gender differences between men's and women's working styles (see table 5.4). Only a very small group of women's responses argued that there were no (gender-based) differences. In contrast, a quarter of all male responses denied that women and men were different, and a further small group had difficulty deciding (we will address the question of denial shortly). In the end, just over half of the male responses identified differences.

Responses from the two university communities were remarkably consistent, except for the management group. Managers from the larger university were far more likely to identify gender differences in working styles than were managers at the smaller institution (83 percent and 29 percent, respectively). There are a number of explanations for this discrepancy. At the time of the interviews, the smaller university had no women in executive management positions within the university, and within our management sample (which included deans of schools, the highest academic management position), there was only one woman. In contrast, 30 percent of the management sample from the larger university were women, albeit at middle management level rather than among the senior executive group. As women were more likely than men to acknowledge differences in working style, their presence in the latter management group accounts for some of the discrepancy.

Table 5.4. Workplace/Working Styles Percentages and (numbers)
What would a predominantly female workplace be like, and what would a predominantly male workplace be like?
In your experience, do men and women have different working styles? If so, what is the nature of these differences?

| | Gender | | Rank/Position | | | |
	Men	Women	Ac.	Man.	Gen.	Total
Difficulty Answering Question	11.8 (18)	3.2 (5)	8.9 (14)	12.5 (5)	4.5 (5)	7.5 (23)
No Gender Difference	26.1 (40)	13.6 (21)	15.8 (25)	25.0 (10)	23.4 (26)	19.8 (61)
There Were Gender Differences	56.2 (86)	77.4 (120)	70.3 (111)	60.0 (24)	64.0 (71)	66.9 (206)
Other Comments	5.9 (9)	5.8 (9)	5.0 (8)	2.5 (1)	8.1 (9)	5.8 (18)
Total Percentages	100	100	100	100	100	100
Total Responses	(153)	(155)	(158)	(40)	(111)	(308)
Total Respondents	89	113	99	25	78	202

The most startling feature of the responses to the questions on working styles is that those in the majority grouping who identified gender differences between men's and women's working styles (67 percent of responses) overwhelmingly characterized women's qualities as virtues and commented unfavorably about men. Over three-quarters of this group of responses and a majority in both sexes and each position fell into this category (see table 5.5). Women, managers, and general staff were more positive than men and academics. Among male responses, in particular, neutral comments and some negative comments about women were more forthcoming. Cross tabulations[3] showed that in the majority of cases where women were spoken of positively, it was in the context of direct comparisons with men who were regarded negatively. No respondent singled men out for positive comment, although a few did so in comparison to a negative valuation of women.

Table 5.6 lists, in rank order of frequency of all responses, the kinds of differences identified in answer to our question on gendered working styles/workplaces. There are some minor variations in the rank order of responses when divided by gender and by position, but on the whole, the level of agreement is high. Larger differences are evident between the two universities, and these are highlighted.

The first difference which attaches a negative value to women—"Margaret Thatcherism: women can be horrible too"—is ranked fourth overall, although it was ranked second at the larger, and sixth at the smaller, university. In the latter institution it was mentioned between a quarter and a half as often as the first four differences, but at the larger institution it was mentioned almost as often as the first positive characteristic of women's working styles. Again, the larger university had more women in management positions, and it may be that the explicitly negative accounts of senior women may be connected to their comparative visibility in that institution. Other negative comments about women were ranked seventh and eleventh by overall frequency.

Table 5.5 Valuation of Identified Gender Differences in Workplace/Working Styles Percentages and (numbers)
What would a predominantly female workplace be like and, what would a predominantly male workplace be like?
In your experience, do men and women have different working styles? If so, what is the nature of these differences?

Identified Gender Differences Valued	Gender		Rank/ Position			
	Men	Women	Ac.	Man.	Gen.	Total
Women Positively and Men Negatively	68 (36)	87 (59)	71.4 (50)	80 (4)	89 (41)	78 (95)
Women Negatively and Men Positively	15 (8)	7 (5)	11.4 (8)	0 (0)	11 (5)	11 (13)
The Sexes Neutrally	17 (9)	6 (4)	17.2 (12)	20 (1)	0 (0)	11 (13)
Total Percentages	100	100	100	100	100	100
Total Responses	(53)	(68)	(70)	(5)	(46)	(121)

Of the most frequently mentioned differences, women were valued positively for their sociability and supportiveness (rank 1), their open, democratic, collaborative, and consensual collegiality (rank 2), and men were valued negatively for their combative and competitive style (rank 3).[4] The following collage of women's voices, junior and senior academics, summarizes the positive features of women's working styles:

Table 5.6 Gender Differences in Workplace/Working Styles in Rank Order (by frequency)

What would a predominantly female workplace be like, and what would a predominantly male workplace be like?
In your experience, do men and women have different working styles? If so, what is the nature of these differences?
Do you think men and women have different styles of working and create a different atmosphere in the workplace?

	Combined			Smaller University			Larger University		
	#	Rank	Ratio with rank 1	#	Rank	Ratio with rank 1	#	Rank	Ratio with rank 1
Women are more sociable, more food, oiling of community relations, supportive, caring, sharing, nurturing, motherly, sympathetic, approachable, happier, easier, good humored, more fun, pleasanter vs. male workplace has less social interaction, less friendly, more petulant, individualist, unsympathetic, socially inadequate	50	1	1	32	1	1	18	1	1
Women are more open, communicative, consultative, interactive, interdependent, democratic, collaborative, community-based, collegial, willing to compromise, consensual, attention to group dynamics, more positive feedback vs. men are more reserved, draw boundaries around what can be talked about, more isolated, male workplaces feature homosocial organization (critical mass of chaps), monolithic, happy with authoritarian model, more hierarchical	40	2	.8	29	2	.95	11	3	.61
Women's workplaces have less conflict and competition, are less judgmental, less driven by prestige into conflict resolution (women moderate male macho behavior) vs. men are more combative, competitive, aggressive, hoonish, and macho back-stabbing, egocentric	28	3	.56	19	3	.59	9	5	.5
Margaret Thatcherism: women can be horrible too, senior women absorb male values and display them in their style, senior women are defensively aggressive, often tougher (i.e., ain't sisters), cattiness, bitchiness	24	4	.48	7	6	.22	17	2	.94

(Continued on next page)

Table 5.6 (Continued)

Combined #	Combined Rank	Combined Ratio with rank 1	Description	Smaller University #	Smaller University Rank	Smaller University Ratio with rank 1	Larger University #	Larger University Rank	Larger University Ratio with rank 1
20	5	.4	Women are sensitive to sexual politics, committed (e.g., politically), less sexism, more flexible, humane, understanding of complexities of life, more integration of children into workplace, etc., vs. more sexism and off jokes in male workplaces, a tendency to focus on women's negative qualities, women forced into background, subservient/servant role/minority, men in foreground, neglect of children, less interested in wider social relations and nonwork lives	19	3	.59	1	12	.05
15	6	.3	Women are more conscientious, thorough, harder working, more professional, efficient vs. men try to get out of work, avoid admin or do it poorly	9	5	.28	6	6	.33
11	7	.2	Women are indecisive vs. men are better at leadership, more decisive and capable, have more confidence, and are more prepared to take risks	-	-	-	11	3	.61
9	8	.18	Women are more interested in their work, less instrumental vs. men are more instrumental (focused on productivity, on doing something, use their work rather than do it for interest), careerism more rampant, into game playing	6	7	.19	3	8	.16
8	9	.16	Women are better teachers (listen more, attend to group dynamics, prioritize teaching) vs. men are more research oriented	4	8	.13	4	7	.22
7	10	.14	Women pay attention to detail vs. men see the big picture	4	8	.13	3	8	.16
4	11	.08	Women are less practical/machine skills, perhaps more theoretical skills vs. men seduced by computer/technology, confident in manual skills	3	10	.09	1	11	.05
4	11	.08	Feminist cabal, women's networks worse than men's vs. men have old boys' networks	2	11	.06	2	10	.11
1	13	.02	Some subject areas not taught by women	1	12	.03	-	-	-
1	13	.02	Feminism is women's academic career path, narrow field vs. men define the mainstream of disciplines	1	12	.03	-	-	-
222			Total Responses	136			86		
202			Total Respondents	111			91		

What would [a female only workplace] be like? Just lovely! There would be more democracy, more caring and sharing, less competition, probably more cross-fertilization of ideas. There would be more working together, more women supporting each other. [A female workplace] is more likely to have much more confidence-sharing, much more admission of mistakes and laughing about what a mess you made of something, clearing it out and discussing it, less formality and less fear about losing power or face. But also more precautions about not losing power or face by checking things out more and doing a bit more homework rather than striding it out.[5]

Also at rank 3 for respondents from the smaller institution was the notion that women's workplaces were more sensitive, and committed, to lessening sexism, whereas male workplaces and styles were sexist: places in which women are treated negatively, the butt of jokes, and pushed into the background. This feature did not figure significantly at the other institution at all (rank 12) and almost certainly reflects the different histories and profiles of the two universities (the smaller institution is a younger, more liberal university and includes women's studies in its offering, whereas the larger institution's profile reflects its origins as an institute of technology). In sharp contrast then, responses from the larger university reflect a more conservative view of the virtues of men and women, ranking women's open democratic collegiality an equal third with their greater indecisiveness. This response—that compared with women, men are better leaders, more decisive and capable, more confident, and more prepared to take risks—was a set of comments that simply did not arise in the interviews at the smaller university.

Looking at these qualities in relation to our concerns about who has power in the university and their attributes, the most curious feature is that the very qualities that in one context are regarded as failings of women, for example, when answering the question on why there were so few senior women, are directly contradicted or regarded as virtues in the responses to the questions on gender differences. In chapter 4, for example, we noted that women were criticized for being unwilling to work hard and, therefore, take up senior positions, and yet here, women are spoken of as being more conscientious, harder working, more professional, efficient, and as willing to take on the administrative work as against men's various attempts to get out of it. Two senior academic women recalled:

A lot of men, even the junior [men], regard the management side as lowly work, call it housekeeping. . . . even being a dean, [is] seen as a good housekeeper. They often see all that administrative stuff as trivial, a little bit beneath them—when they are asked to do any admin tasks, the secretary is the one who ends up doing it. . . . they don't feel too embarrassed when things collapse—that's menial work . . . their research is going well. We put pressure on them, we tease them, we tell them off, even bluntly say it—but it doesn't change. (2 SAC/F and 4 SAC/F)

Similarly, men are both rewarded and condemned for being aggressive and competitive. One senior woman administrator put it this way:

> I spent a lot of time in a male only environment and sometimes . . . you can easily feel that you're watching a David Attenborough program, bulls competing for power over a territory of cows (where there were no cows, at least in a male only environment). . . . there is a lot of, I think, power for its own sake, it's something that I see more of among men than among women. (11 S.GEN/F)

More importantly, if we compare our respondents' views on the virtues of women's working styles with the attributes of the powerful just described, two things become evident: One is that the positive attributes of those with power are not entirely inconsistent with, or exclusive of, the virtues of women's working styles. Good interpersonal and communication skills appear in both, for example. And two, even more significantly, is that the negative attributes of the powerful and the negative descriptions of men's working styles bear a marked resemblance to each other. If women's qualities are so highly valued and congruent with the qualities expected of *good* leaders, these results beg the question of why they do not succeed. The responses to our question on power included so few comments about powerful women, and the responses to the working styles questions are clouded by the differences between the two universities (in that only the larger institution provided significantly negative responses to senior women and women as leaders). Nonetheless, we can throw some light on this question if we go back to the responses to the question as to why there were so few women in senior positions in the university.

In chapter 4, we pointed to four main kinds of explanations for women's absence from senior positions: naturalistic (denial of a problem), historical, blaming women, and structural. We correlated (for the smaller university's data only) the responses on working styles with the results to the "why so few senior women" question, thinking that part of the reason for the contradiction may lie in who is valuing women highly. The relationship between the responses to these two questions is intriguing at all kinds of levels, but in the context of this discussion, it is interesting that there is a substantial relationship (83 percent) between those who believe women suffer structural discrimination and those who value women highly and men poorly (see table 5.7). But even among those who blame women for their underrepresentation in senior positions, the relationship is still quite robust (63 percent). In this context, it becomes noteworthy that what women are *most* valued for in their working relations (ranked first by both men and women, at both universities, and overall mentioned 1.25 times more often than the next ranked quality) is also a traditional *feminine* virtue: women are supportive, caring, approachable, and create a pleasant working environment. What this response suggests, then, is that the positive valuation of women does not wholly contradict the normalization of male culture. Rather, it speaks directly to that normalized culture in much the same way as the old gendered trope that "men and women are complementary but equal" marks out male privilege. Women are primarily valued for what they give to men.[6] In this respect, the academic situation mirrors the home-based domestic division of labor, a point that was made by one of our respondents:

> I think males and females get rewarded for different things. If you're a woman you'll be rewarded if you are competent, caring, do all the support labor, pick up the tab and run with it, do all the bolstering up, are efficient, seen to be a good teacher. Boys are rewarded for publishing—they don't have to do all those other things. (5 SAC/F)

Table 5.7 Correlations between Questions (smaller university only)

| | Differences in Workplace/Working Styles | |
Why So Few?	Denied difference/ difficulty with position	Identified difference was positive to women
Denial	83%	
Historical/traditional explanations	59%	
Explanations which blamed women		65%
Structural explanations		83%

Table 5.7 also shows a relationship between the denial responses to both questions. Eighty-three percent of those responses which denied there was a problem with the number of senior women at the university also denied that there were differences in working styles between men and women. About one-third of overall responses argued that there were no differences in working styles between men and women, with men, managers, and general staff more inclined to take this position than women and academics (see table 5.4). For the most part, they expressed the view that men and women have the same range of styles, emotions, behaviors, and attitudes, and there would be no difference between a predominantly male and a predominantly female workplace. The following voices are those of a male dean, a female secretary, and a male senior academic:

> Women on campus probably go through the same range, some are quiet, some are aggressive, and you know, some are bright, some are not. (6 MAN/M)

> I don't think it would really be much different in some respects, because among women you get different personalities, you get those two types, the ruthless and the other type that is into the process of, not conciliation, what's the word, . . .

collaboration, that sort of thing. (2 GEN/F)

I don't think it would look any different whatsoever, because . . . I don't think having an x chromosome or a y chromosome has anything to do with power structures. . . . If you threw all the men out and said it was going to be run by all women you would find that those that would percolate to the top would be prepared to put in the extra hours and the extra energy. They would be close to the top because they would walk over the top of all the others. I don't see it as a gender thing. I see it as a socializing thing. (19 SAC/M)

Some respondents acknowledged that there may be differences in the *expectations* placed on women, but, together with others, generally attributed any differences between men and women to other factors, most commonly individual personality differences. Similarly, a number of those who had difficulty answering this question were trying to sort out whether differences were apparent or real (for example, socialized rather than natural, or a product of how women and men are represented, rather than what they are actually like). One senior manager disassociated management style from gender in this way:

I think in management there is no one style which is the right management style, there are different styles for different management situations, so in the one position, like the position I occupy, there are circumstances when it will be appropriate to have an assertive management style and circumstances where one should have a completely consensus and participatory sort of management style. It would be quite wrong to apply the one management style to every situation. So that's why I was interested in the question do men and women have different styles of working, I think to work effectively both men and women have to have different styles at different times. . . . I guess I don't think of it as being related directly to the individual, I see it as what is required, let's say, to be an effective school dean . . . they have to be a person who is able to vary their management style, knows when to do it, and can have a participatory approach when policy is being formulated but also after having taken a decision can hold to it and not keep changing their mind and when one has to have a difficult decision made is prepared to take the courageous decision, and it can be a female that can do all those things so I don't see it as being a gendered thing. (5 MAN/M)

Curiously, at the same time as individuality (preference and personality) is used to deny gender difference (and thus discrimination), in the context of the working styles question, in the answers to our question on the numbers of senior women, they were brought into play in order to explain women's failure to achieve senior rank. In a rather revealing example of this, the manager quoted above arguing that management styles are *not* gendered had earlier explained women's relative absence from senior ranks by arguing that men and women are fundamentally different:

Why do you think there are so few senior women? (Interviewer)

Hmmmm we get into some very fundamental questions there, I just wonder
whether it isn't related to the differences between the genders more basically
before you can answer all of that. . . . For me, the evidence is overwhelming
that there are fundamental and basic biological and behavioral differences between the genders that affect how they are going to behave in every situation.
But, having said that there are enormous individual differences. . . . so, while
we make these generalizations, there are going to be women who behave, quite
naturally and comfortably, in a pattern that would typically be regarded as male
and vice versa. So I think that underlying what happens in organizations is this
gender difference. So we are not really comfortable unless we behave and operate in tune with our genetic makeup. . . . So in the organization then, how
does this manifest itself, well you know males are more aggressive, you've
only got to look at sports, you've got to look at prisons to see the gender differences of those in prisons. So in the organization there is going to be an element
of that: in management style; in the selection process; in the conduct of work (I
think it's partly why males are going for research so strongly, it suits their egos,
their feeling of importance, there is a certain amount of assertiveness, intellectual assertiveness required for research); affects how they behave on committees; and I think that in that sort of background, where you start off with a pre-
dominance of males, it can be difficult for women to get ahead. . . . what I am
saying is that where the men have set the scene and have set up the process of
how to get ahead then there can be the tendency for that style of management to
be the style which is accepted. (5 MAN/M)

It was rare to find respondents taking the argument back to biology, albeit in
such a subtle blend with conventional management literature,[7] but it was not rare
to find explanations for women's underrepresentation at senior levels which
having acknowledged the problem, proceed to *explain it away* as this manager
does.

This diversion into the staff's view of gendered working styles allows us to
appreciate why the association between men and power is so readily made and
endorsed despite the generally negative description of it. It is not that the women
are lacking these qualities and abilities to hold positions of power and acquit
them well, but rather that power is considered unattractive in a woman and fundamentally disassociated from women. This puts powerful women, and in the
university context this translates as senior women, in a difficult position. They
are somewhat oxymoronic: managers in a management culture which accepts,
expects, and even values masculine behaviors, but unable to adopt such styles to
the same ends as men, and, despite not using them, are at risk of being carica-
tured that way in any case. As two woman deans said:

I think one of the things that perhaps does happen is that you, I don't say that you take on male attributes, but if you are only one or two women in a very male dominated society, you start to learn some of their rules. Some of the rules that they use are that they talk over people in meetings and their body language is different. When they spread, a male really spreads out on the desk. His papers are everywhere. . . . They really use the space, and sometimes I think you have got to be prepared to be almost forceful and aggressive about some other things you do without becoming male. Because I don't think becoming male really does you any good. You are just seen as a tough female then, you are not seen as a female with some [sort of confidence, with good attributes]. (4 MAN/F)

I found it really interesting going into the dean's position. . . . one part of me was an observer sitting back being quite bemused at the way I went around persuading, being very careful with my words, being quite selective in when I spoke and how I spoke, and trying to operate in a quiet and reasoned and somewhat good humored manner, rather than strident and authoritarian, and deliberately doing so. And part of that was a response to men who couldn't cope with anything else. (2 MAN/F)

Concluding Comments

The gender of power in universities is profoundly male. This is self-evident in the language used to describe the powerful. As Lakoff and Johnson (1980: 157) noted, "people in power get to impose their metaphors" and the metaphors used to describe power itself create a nexus between masculinity and the attributes of power, even as they are, paradoxically, neutralized. The latter means that powerful women will be more constrained and more readily condemned than powerful men. Nonetheless, that power within organizations such as universities is diffuse, complex, and multiple in nature suggests possibilities for women to advance into senior and powerful positions and to acquit themselves well. Barriers to their doing so with ease come from the informal power which men more freely wield and which affords men a base from which to resist and subvert women's aspirations and, yet more urgently, the imposition of a new series of metaphors to name the activities of the university.

The new metaphors are being produced by managers embracing the current entrepreneurial climate and translating collegiality into corporatism. The impact of globalization forces on Australian universities has been quite profound, leading toward more competition among institutions and managers rewarding those who are risk takers. Our respondents were well aware that universities in Australia were undergoing a difficult transformation from a more democratic/collegial community of scholars transmitting and expanding knowledge into more corporate business-like organizations delivering education *products*. So, for example, at both universities the central administration was seen to have more power than the periphery (the academic disciplines and their associated services). At the younger institution there was a clear sense of an increasing concentration of power at the center as the new corporate management model favored by the Commonwealth government was taken up by the university's management. This was symbolized by the relocation of the university's administration into a separate chancellery building. At the older institution, overlaid on the established bureaucratic culture was a more entrepreneurial culture that benefited from the centralized control that was already present in the institution. The centralized control became more prominent and began to override the formal collegial bodies. These old and new traditions were often uneasy bedfellows and, again, produced a culture in which power was somewhat constrained. Here are two senior academics:

> I think what has happened in more recent years is that the extent of that power has shifted. In a collegial model of a university, power is constrained by what is acceptable by the majority of colleagues. Within the new administrative model, the senior administrative staff should have executive authority and there is no constraining of that power by collegial values. It can lead to a productivist culture and a narrow set of production parameters as they do in the industrial environment. (8 SAC/M)

> I think that the university has been redesigned over the last few years to make us a corporation and it has been deliberate that the power for the university must be maintained in the management executive and university resources board. The university academic board, which was designed to be the group that made decisions for the university . . . has in fact been emasculated. (10 SAC/F)

The power of these metaphors to shape the institution is nowhere more evident than at one of the universities where the then vice-chancellor announced four pillars to guide the university: all four were centered around economic goals (that is, market attractiveness, diversification of income streams, entrepreneurialism, and efficiency and effectiveness) and did not even mention the core goals of the university (teaching and research). It is important to note that the metaphors we live by can powerfully shape our behavior, as noted by Lakoff and Johnson (1980). These metaphors can be reshaped by those in powerful positions. The current climate of entrepreneurialism is one of those metaphors shaping university behavior. In such a climate, the more aggressive staff members will be rewarded and those who are the *good campus citizens* (many women) will be overlooked. It is more than likely that the entrepreneurial academics will be males and promotion into higher ranks and into the ranks of management will become even more difficult for females. It is also likely, then, that women who do move into those positions are those who take on masculine values to survive in that climate. Therefore, power is likely to become more, rather than less, gendered as Australian universities move into the next century.

Notes

1. Because the management sample is small in comparison to the main group (25 compared with 202), the difference in wording between the two interview protocols has no significant effect on the overall data.

2. Finally, it is important to stress that we are counting *responses*. There is no direct equivalence between the number of responses and the number of people making those responses simply because, on these questions in particular, people were rarely content to offer just one answer.

3. Identified differences were coded not only for their content and tone (that is whether they indicated that women were regarded positively and/or men negatively, women negatively and/or men positively, or whether the comment was phrased neutrally), but also for the object of the comment: whether a direct comparison between the sexes was being made or whether the comment was mainly about men or mainly about women.

4. These results are derived from cross tabulations of identified characteristics against the tone and object of the comment.

5. Senior Academics: 2 SAC/F, 4 SAC/F, 6 SAC/F. Junior Academics: 1 JAC/F, 8 JAC/F.

6. Other indicators of this are the way that, when asked about the characteristics of primarily male and primarily female workplaces, the majority of participants chose not to comment on male workplaces or male working styles, arguably the working environment which most of our respondents are most familiar with. Instead, it is women that are commented upon and predominantly female working environments which are idealized.

7. Gordon, S. (1991) depicts women managers as prisoners of men's dreams, accepting male norms of work behaviors, lifestyle, and success.

Chapter 6

The View from the Top: Captain of the Ship

"It was like I was being carried forward with the
tide and luckily I was at the helm."
(Male manager: 7 MAN/M)

Introduction

Thus far in part 2, we have examined evidence for an entrenched and normalized male culture in these universities, and the benefits this has for men in ensuring that the attributes of power and authority *naturally* acquires a masculine flavor. In this and the next chapter, we turn our focus from how our respondents describe and understand the organizational culture of their respective universities to how they experience it. This chapter is devoted to senior managers, the executive of the two universities. On two counts, they merit a chapter of their own. First, senior executive groups have considerable influence over the direction and pace of university reform. Second, our research suggests that senior managers are perceived, both by staff and themselves, as a distinct cadre separate from the rank and file. In their interviews, many academic staff distinguished between "them" and "us," talking about those "at the top" and the decisions that "come rolling down the hill," distant from the core concerns of the institution. Equally, senior managers often positioned themselves as a distinct "we," charged with securing the fortunes of the university in the face of an unruly and disorganized "them."

But is there, in fact, a single senior management view or does the *we* of the managers mask multiple and, even, inconsistent opinions? And, either way, how far do senior managers voice different views from the rank and file?

Our answers to these questions draw from interviews with thirteen senior managers, five from the smaller university, and eight from the larger one. Only those with senior executive status are included here, that is, vice-chancellors, pro and deputy vice-chancellors, university registrars, business managers, and executive deans.[1] At the time of the interviews all the senior executives were male. (Since then, the senior executive group at the smaller university includes one female pro vice-chancellor and two female executive deans. At the other university there is a female deputy vice-chancellor.)

Our interviews with the senior managers canvassed the political changes affecting universities, the management as a peak activity, the attributes of success, and a number of issues relating to gender. We also asked senior managers how satisfied they felt with their careers and what, if anything, they had to sacrifice in order to achieve success. It is with these latter two questions that the contrast between management and the broader university community begins to click into sharp focus.

We start with the question of political change.

Political Change and Senior Management
(Sailing into Corporate Waters)

From the Dawkins' 1988 reforms on,[2] senior university managers have been charged with promoting the commercial success and national competitiveness of their institutions (Marginson and Considine 2000). The decreasing proportion of the budget covered by the Commonwealth has left them vying for funds from commercial sources and traveling the world to attract fee-paying students. But this entrepreneurial ethos does not mean that Canberra's influence has waned. To the contrary, if universities are to maintain research funding, build student numbers, and secure good rankings in quality audits, they need, in the way of good disciples, to follow the Commonwealth's instructions. So senior managers have to look both ways, to politics and markets, in an increasingly volatile climate.

Against this background, we asked for senior managers' views on the changes affecting their universities over the past decade.

The Components of Change

Their responses carried few surprises and covered the gamut of new forms of accountability and financial management, scarce resources, and interinstitutional competition. Some senior managers contented themselves with a checklist, summarizing the changes as "strategic planning; resource allocation; the move to one-line budgets; devolved financial management; greater emphasis on managing staff and staff development" (5 MAN/M). Others provided more evaluative comments:

> I think it's the measurement of performance and the winning of funds and so on that has really changed the culture of the place. Basically, that, and the institutional competitiveness. (4 MAN/M)

The new forms of accountability attracted the most comment. Here the senior managers drew attention to "a lot of reporting, reviews, submissions to reviews and so forth and . . . the quality assurance movement more generally" (5 MAN/M). These changes, they said, had substantially affected management practices:

> I think (these changes) imposed on managers a sort of extra dimension . . . in handling large amounts of money and applying them in the most effective way . . . and in the end the finger could be pointed at them, because it was how they marshaled their resources, how they best used their human resources and how they used the other resources to . . . put up a program that produced the product. And that was one hell of a responsibility to suddenly come about. (7 MAN/M)

> I think there has been a gradual, but progressive, recognition that accountability at the senior level is important. . . . I think the view now is that if you are running something you are supposed to get results. And you can't come back and say "I couldn't get support from the people I worked with." (8 MAN/M)

Although senior managers talked about the extra work demanded by the new accountability requirements—"we work unconscionable hours, middle level and senior staff" (1 MAN/M)—their comments did not carry the note of political opposition which, as we see in the next chapter, was so often characteristic of academic staff. Standing in a minority of one was the senior manager who spoke about "more accountability and more pressure on people as the screw comes on [with] people having to run faster to stay still basically" (9 MAN/M). In general, the senior managers' tone was depoliticized, rendering the new forms of accountability either as a matter of necessity or benefit. Around half spoke favorably of the new developments:

> Well I think what has happened is that the sector, the higher education sector has become much more competitive and in that sense managers have to look more closely at their areas of operation, so that they are more likely to become client focused and more likely to be looking at the ways they are spending their dollars and effectiveness. And probably for the first time in a number of areas looking at outcomes as a measurable quantifiable parameter. (3 MAN/M)

Most senior managers also endorsed the emergence of corporate structures. Noting that "deans are now major human relations managers and budgetary managers, much more so than before" (1 MAN/M), and that "the place is becoming a lot more corporate" (10 MAN/M), they argued that the new forms of organization led to more efficient decision making and a more proactive style of management. This produced, said one, "a sense that the university has a mission, a set of objectives, and I am part of the structure and I am meant to deliver on these" (8 MAN/M). Against these views, two senior managers expressed a sense of loss for older collegial relations. They spoke about "a hardening of management styles and a more commercial type management" (9 MAN/M), and "the breaking up, if you like, of the sort of collegial approach that is very much a feature of this place" (11 MAN/M).

Feelings about Change

Overall, almost half (six) of the senior managers were positive about change. In the words of one, it was "like I was being carried forward with the tide and luckily I was at the helm" (10 MAN/M). The feeling of being at the forefront of change, or as another senior manager put it, "in the engine room" (8 MAN/M), was often associated with the belief that traditional practices were deficient:

> I think that now . . . there will be certain things done that should have been done fifteen years ago, and people are getting better as a result . . . [so we can be] at the very cutting edge. (4 MAN/M)

> In the dim and bygone days, which were not so long ago, the relative size of institutions and their total budgets was quite small. But now they would have to be counted with any big business in Australia. Consequently they have to be run like a commercial operation. An institution like a university is designed to make a profit. (10 MAN/M)

This senior manager went on to argue that under the old system, "where everybody was asked for input," no decision was made when there was serious disagreement. He also said that while he was "one of those people who believes that the best decisions are probably collegial," this didn't mean that "you can spend as much time widely discussing things as we might have done in the past" (10 MAN/M). Many other senior managers shared his view that the collegial system needed to be reformed. Like him, they said that they weren't antidemocratic or anticollegial; it was simply that the complexity and scale of decision making demanded a more streamlined approach. The implication that academic styles are *not* efficient was elaborated along these lines:

> I think we waste a lot of time. There is a lot of attempt at process but it is far too big. It is absolutely vital that we get streetwise and do things smarter and

get more efficient. . . . Lots of people hold a model of everyone being involved as an ideal model. . . . I would much rather the university chooses a group of people, giving them the responsibility for a certain function. And then the university community saying: we would accept their recommendations unless there are compelling reasons for overturning them. (13 MAN/M)

In contrast to the positive group, six senior managers had more qualified feelings about change. Rather than "going with the tide" and "being at the helm," their comments suggested something more like steering in tricky waters. Above all, this group suggested that external political forces were leaving limited room to maneuver.

In part the change has come from the federal government. I don't know whether that has been a good thing actually in terms of the management, because we are becoming more reactive. I am not quite sure what next year's reap from the federal government will be. (12 MAN/M)

Well there is a degree of conflict in that the external changes force us to make changes a lot quicker than we would feel is necessary or desirable and also require a lot more form filling and accounting than we would want to impose on our staff but we find we have to do it. We do what we can, but governments have four-year time frames and the minister is anxious to make a mark. (5 MAN/M)

As well as being more reserved about their relationship to the new developments, these senior managers were also more critical about the nature of change itself. One, for example, believed that academic standards were being undermined: "I mean," he said, "it used to be that there were classes to be staffed, and classes to be taught well, but now it is very much driven by, I think, your spreadsheet" (4 MAN/M).

Standing outside both groups, one senior manager voiced a clear commitment to support collegiality in the face of competition and commercialization. We quote from various points of his interview:

Well I think my major part [in the new climate] has been trying to encourage people not to go down what I think is an unhealthy route because it [marks] a division, breakdown in collegiality and a gathering of your own turf. . . . One of the particularly unhealthy things would be to do away with the interdisciplinary focus that has always been part of this university. I know it sounds idealistic, but there still remains a lot of good interaction between people across the university and that leads them to a sense of some sort of common purpose in the institution . . . and I'd hate to see that kind of capacity to look at what is in the institution's best interests disappear into a sort of pit of people who are just fighting for their own narrow interests. (11 MAN/M)

Management as a Peak Activity
(Taking Charge in Troubled Times)

We asked the senior managers whether they felt separate from the rest of the university in their peak managerial role. On this, they were virtually united. With only one exception they said, yes, they were, indeed, set apart. In the main, this was seen as an inevitable part of being a senior manager. The view that "as you get to senior management, you are inevitably isolated" was expressed time and again:

> I think inevitably as soon as you become a manager, your colleagues put you into a different light. . . . the change is instantaneous, you go from being one of the lads to being one of them. (1 MAN/M)

Two senior managers punctuated this sense of inevitability with reflections on the physical and cultural artifacts of management. One told us that he behaved and spoke differently toward the senior executive compared with staff and students:

> By instinct, I probably act in different ways. If I pick up the phone and it's the Vice-Chancellor, I'll talk in a different way. I have no trouble managing that split. Dress standards are different too. I don't wear shorts. The vice-chancellor wouldn't take me seriously if I did. That puts me a step removed from other academics and students. (1 MAN/M)

The other remarked on how recent changes in locale had intensified the split between the executive and the rest of the university:

> Previously as you might know we were located down in the Humanities/Education building and so just by virtue of geography, you met with academic and general staff all the time and it's now more of a conscious effort to get out and just meet informally with people and move around. . . . I really have to make an effort, as I said, to go out and talk to people and sort of wander around and meet people and I think also there's a kind of view that the administration is isolated, particularly because the senior ranks are located on the top floor of this building. (11 MAN/M)

Against such reflections, the majority of senior managers put the separation down to the logic of managerial practice. "You need to be detached from the boys and girls as you are making decisions about their careers and they are responsible to you" (1 MAN/M), said one. Many others endorsed the view that management needed to "stand back" in order to be "objective:"

> You have to stand aloof and try and be objective about what is going on. . . . it doesn't worry me. . . . it's part of the game. (9 MAN/M)

It is difficult to make hard decisions that adversely affect people if you are very closely allied to them socially and emotionally and the rest of it, so I think there has to be a certain distance between senior management and the rest. (5 MAN/M)

In reflecting on the separation between themselves and the rest of the staff, senior managers talked about the move to top-down decision making. In the main they argued that this, like the separation between themselves and staff in the first instance, was either unavoidable or beneficial. The need for quick decisions was a common theme. One senior manager argued that "the time constraints, if nothing else, mean that we just can't do that—we can't involve everybody[3] any more" (13 MAN/M). In the same vein, another maintained that "it has been necessary to have a greater emphasis on top-down decision making as changes are being forced on the university in a very short time frame with deadlines and imperatives" (5 MAN/M).

Along with the justification that there is not enough time, some senior managers maintained that the great majority of staff did not actually *want* to be involved in central planning. On this count, matters had become so complicated, and other demands so pressing, that academics and middle management were all too willing to leave decisions to the central executive:

I have found that increasingly . . . most if not all staff . . . don't want to be asked whether we should do this or that, they want someone else to make the decision so that they can get on with doing what they consider to be more worthwhile. (5 MAN/M)

I'm well aware of a watershed decision made last year by the [elected] deans. They basically said there are so many decisions coming down to the schools in this kind of devolved system that we can no longer deal with them. What we should really like is for you to tell us the decisions that we should take back to the schools. (10 MAN/M)

Two senior managers put a different spin on this line of argument by suggesting that most staff were not even *capable* of making decisions in the general interest. Here it was not so much that academics did not wish to be involved (to the annoyance of these senior managers, they frequently did), it was that they had "this total lack of understanding of how a university really operates" (4 MAN/M). "Like spectators in an AFL [Australian Football League] match," one commented, "their goals are so tiny that they can't see the global picture" (10 MAN/M). According to this view, "the biggest obstacle [to change] is the behavior of people themselves" (4 MAN/M).

This level of disdain was uncommon. For despite all they said in defense of separation, the senior managers worried about the possibility of becoming cut off. One told us that "what worries me is the ability to have time to go out and talk with the groups that are important. . . . I think the way that the structures are set up means that they do tend to keep you in your office" (14 MAN/M). Another said that "you have to take steps to ensure that you are not isolated because isolated decision making isn't good" (1 MAN/M).

By what means did the senior managers try to prevent isolation? They described several moves, both monarchial and democratic. The most common entailed going around, being seen, and making contact—a sort *of king-shakes-hands* tactic. This involved such things as an "effort to visit research committees in the schools," "meeting fortnightly with researchers having drinks," "going round to common rooms," and "trying to go out and have lunch and mix with people" (13 MAN/M and 5 MAN/M). In partial contrast, three managers described a more active attempt to minimize the differences between themselves and others as far as dress, friendships, and/or common interests were concerned.

> My general work style is very informal. If anyone calls me mister, I find that hard to accept. This is the style of this university and one of the desirable things about working here. (1 MAN/M)

> I would never allow the group of friends that I have had over the years to change. Even though, as it has been pointed out to me at times, it is probably not the right thing to do. (2 MAN/M)

> I, for example, spend a lot of time with students and I regularly go to student events, sporting events, these sorts of things. (11 MAN/M)

At the more democratic end of the spectrum, two senior managers described a conscious attempt to sustain collegial links. One told us he went to his staff saying, "Look I need your support on this issue to help me work it through." He identified this as "the positive aspect of the way women do business," emphasizing that he "chose not to operate in the male macho way" (12 MAN/M). The other reversed an earlier senior manager's view of staff as "spectators with tiny goals" by arguing:

> You've simply got to acknowledge and respect academic mores and the culture of the academic community and understand that the angles from which they come to issues are frequently different from those of the administration and that a matter of compromise and frequently sensible balance has to be found. . . . I think it simply is as much a matter of respect for other people's points of view as it is your own obligation to do a particular job as best you can. (11 MAN/M)

Attributes of Success
(Promoting Officer Material)

As part of our discussion about patterns of institutional success, we asked the senior managers whether they attempted to promote talented individuals or train them for particular positions. While some managers identified mentoring and general support, others nominated measures resembling nothing so much as an old-fashioned system of patronage. Here they "kept an eye out" for individuals possessing the requisite skills and groomed them for key committees. "We are keeping an eye on her and career-tracking her. . . . she could become chair of the next foundations committee" (1 MAN/M), said one. Similarly:

> I certainly try and encourage people, train wouldn't be the right word, "groom" might be a better word, groom by selecting people who, one feels, might have the potential and the talent by nominating them to key positions. Nominating people to key roles and committees is the most powerful strategy. (5 MAN/M)

What of the senior managers' prior views of success and failure? Here their responses diverged sharply from those prevailing in the universities at large. In contrast to the disaffection among the rank and file, members of the senior executive overwhelmingly believed that people succeeded on the basis of their personal qualities and got left behind because of their failings (see tables 7.2 to 7.4 in chapter 7 for the data). They also differed from academic staff in that they saw success in executive, rather than scholarly, terms. Academic qualities were mentioned relatively rarely as indicators of success, and when they were it was in relation to "active and productive research" (13 MAN/M), rather than teaching. One senior manager even suggested that teaching contributed to failure.

> Well the people who don't get ahead are those who . . . have not continued to develop themselves professionally, and they have used, or fully believe in, the rhetoric that they are teachers. And I think they have . . . this kind of catch-cry of "Oh my teaching is all important" and . . . some of them spend twenty hours a week marking, and I do believe, in some of those cases, it is something they hide behind a little bit. They're all committed to their big marking, they're all committed to the status quo, and that's the female staff as well. They actually believe all the rhetoric. (4 MAN/M)

The attributes endorsed by the senior executive were good common sense, flexibility, motivation, tact, and firmness. They favored staff who could "take courageous decisions and stick to them" (5 MAN/M) and described potential leaders as "fairly tough, able to . . . look someone in the eye and tell them exactly what they think and to lead by example" (2 MAN/M). The notion *of delivery* was also a popular theme: "It's important that we have people who will deliver . . . the characteristics I would look for are: enthusiastic, motivated, delivery" (1 MAN/M). In contrast, the senior managers said the unsuccessful lacked common sense, were narrow, didn't have clear goals, prevaricated, and couldn't adapt to change. They have "an apathy for administration" (4 MAN/M) and "just pick up their pay check basically" (9 MAN/M).

One of the intriguing elements of the senior managers' reflections was the emphasis on *comportment*. They showed a keen interest in the rules of deference

and debate, observing who said what, in what manner, and for how long. They
noted approvingly that the successful "think before they speak" and know "how
to play the committee game" (9 MAN/M). Conversely, they felt that the unsuccessful should "learn to be less time consuming in how long it takes them to say
their ideas" (1 MAN/M) and depicted them as people who

> just harp on about one or two issues, constantly on about this thing, so they
> tend to get ignored after a while; they don't have very original views, they trot
> out clichéd lines perhaps; or they could be people who are constantly criticizing
> and opposing the management. (5 MAN/M)

The suggestion that people who criticize management don't get ahead—*and
deservedly don't get ahead*—came up a number of times. The underlying assumption was that management, by virtue of its position and mandate, could
understand the interests of the university as a whole, while people in separate
divisions and disciplines could not. So it was only by sharing management's
vision that staff could demonstrate they had a grasp of the university "as a total
organism" (10 MAN/M). By the same token, opposition to management signi-
fied a sectional and partisan stance. As one senior manager put it: "It's a bit like
the TV advertisement 'work hard and love your mum!'" and "mum in this case
is the university" (5 MAN/M).

Two senior managers challenged such assumptions about genuine commitment to the university. One suggested that identifying with management was
simply a necessary strategy for those who wanted to get ahead:

> I don't see too many people succeeding who, although they understand the val-
> ues of the university, try to take another line. That doesn't seem conducive to
> being selected for senior positions. So I think what is actually quite critical in
> one's ability to score well in the selection process is to show that one under-
> stands the corporate values of the organization, one has actually internalized
> them and behaves consistently with them. (8 MAN/M)

The other proposed that the executive did not like opposition and that sycophants got ahead. At one point in his interview, he said, "Well, those who don't
get ahead, don't follow the lead of their leaders but speak their own mind. I
think you risk being damned if you do that" (7 MAN/M). Later he returned more
emphatically to the same theme:

> Who gets ahead in this university? Well I was going to say those who piddle in
> the VC's pocket. Certainly, in my view of late, people get ahead because their
> peers or seniors or supervisors or whoever decides that they will get ahead. . . .
> I have this sense that suddenly certain people seem to be great and others not so
> great. Why the hell is this? And then we find out that those who are great have
> been, you know, somehow got the ear of management. But there are other bet

ter people, I believe, who are not tapped on the shoulder. That really has worried me over the last few years. You know it is very difficult for me to say this. (7 MAN/M)

Reflections on Gender and Senior Management (Sailing into Troubled Waters)

We asked the senior managers a number of questions about gender. We inquired whether they thought men and women had different management styles, whether the new corporate measures would affect men and women differently, and why there were so few women in senior positions. Many of their responses have been described in chapters 4 and 5. What we do here is bring these views together, separate from the rest of the academic and general staff. This sheds a slightly different light on what we have previously said.

One of the characteristics of the senior managers' reflections on gender is their *choppy* nature. Up to this point, we have been able to describe distinct patterns in their responses, involving discrete ways of thinking about the new forms of management, particular appraisals of success and failure, established strategies for promoting promising individuals, and so forth. But when it comes to questions that directly bear on gender, it becomes much more difficult to map such patterns. The senior managers' responses swirl around in a turbulent fashion, with contradictory positions and arguments emerging in the same interviews. Why should this be so?

We suggest that the turbulence arises from the structural contradictions of the senior mangers' own positions. They are, on the one hand, *managers* with a mandate to support affirmative action and promote the institution's human resources as a whole. At the same time, they are *males*, empowered to defend a long tradition of organizational practices that benefit men rather than women. Personal factors also come into play, with male networks counterbalanced by strong wives and daughters in some instances. Most of the senior managers, furthermore, would have been aware that feminist researchers were interviewing them.

In any event, and for whatever combination of reasons, the senior managers' responses to the gender question are, as we have said, distinctly *choppy*.

Why So Few?

The question of why there were so few women in senior positions revealed the turbulence of the senior managers' position *par excellence*. Three responded that they didn't see a problem and stuck to that position. Two took the opposing view and solely concentrated on the barriers that prevented women from rising to senior positions. All the rest cross-dressed, shifting between minimizing and affirming the problem.

As reported in chapter 4, those denying the problem maintained that women were either well represented at senior levels or soon would be. This line of argument was advanced by five senior managers, most succinctly by the one who replied, "Well, I think for a start, is it true that there are so few women? I think it's changing rapidly" (4 MAN/M). Another four senior managers effectively talked the problem away by suggesting that the underrepresentation of women was the *natural* outcome of *choices* that females *had* to make. The following comment provides a good example of this line of thought:

> Women by and large, I think, have made alternative choices or maybe society has made the choices for them, so they feel more comfortable with the more conventional role. (3 MAN/M)

The senior manger who talked about the coincidence of basic biological difference and the fact that men had "set the scene" provided the most intriguing of these justifications. His views were discussed at length in chapter 4, so we simply cite them here for the sake of the record:

> For me the evidence is overwhelming that there are fundamental and basic biological and behavioral differences between the genders and that affects how they are going to behave in every situation. . . . . So underlying what happens in organizations is this gender difference. We are not really comfortable unless we behave and operate in tune with our genetic make-up. . . . . Males are more aggressive . . . so in the organization there are going to be elements of that; in the management style, in the conduct of work . . . how they behave on committees, and I think that in that sort of background, where you start with a predominance of males, it can be difficult for women to get ahead. [Later] What I am saying is that where men have set the scene and have set up the process of how to get ahead then there can be the tendency for that style of management to be the style which is accepted. (5 MAN/M)

When the senior managers acknowledged the barriers facing women, they concentrated on interrupted careers and the unequal division of domestic responsibility. Compared with the responses favoring a *woman's choice* interpretation, these reflections carried a greater appreciation of structural forces. One senior manager reflected that home and family responsibilities "still isn't evenly shared" and that women, unlike men, have to "deal with the conflict between, say, a home or family responsibility and the academic pursuit" (8 MAN/M). Another reflected on a woman's world, and in a slightly bewildered way, found it messy and unfair.

I think that male staff tend to be able to carry the work home and just keep on going whereas female staff [have to contend with] a different environment . . . in which they are . . . going home and having to cook a meal and they have child rearing, housekeeping stuff to do as well. (9 MAN/M)

Some of these senior managers also talked about prejudice and homosocial reproduction. One observed that "people are more inclined to select in their own likeness and males dominate the senior positions" (12 MAN/M); another that "while you try to be as objective as possible, you can't do anything about an inherent feeling, say, toward women or different ethnic people. . . . you can never prove it [prejudice] anyway, but I know it exists" (7 MAN/M). This view was more emphatically put by the two senior managers who solely concentrated on the barriers facing women.

I think there is a considerable amount of prejudice against women and in favor of men, which is both explicit and often probably covert, and I think it is generally very hard for women to get to senior positions unless they are so outstanding they just cannot be overlooked. (14 MAN/M)

The competition that women are up against, the opponents, are just too powerful for them at the moment. (8 MAN/M)

We asked senior managers if they attempted to redress the gender imbalance by making particular efforts to promote women. With the exception of the senior manager who said, "I tend to give support to individuals regardless of their sex; I look for individuals who have got the drive, the ability" (9 MAN/M), the rest answered that they did. One followed what was almost a party line when he said:

Generally, I think as a manager, one of the most rewarding things that I can do is help people with ambition and potential and ability to progress and develop . . . and given the gender imbalance that we have, I think it would be true to say that I put an extra effort into that part of the role. (12 MAN/M)

However, this senior manager, like the great majority of his peers, did not pause to consider that the criteria of success might themselves be gendered. Women, if they were to succeed, must succeed on the same basis as men. The culture of management itself was not in question, even when affirmative action principles were well articulated. So the senior manager who said, "we don't have to wait until women have the same experience as men because we would be talking about a hundred years if you go that route. You have to . . . give them the experience . . . and put them into positions and provide the support that is necessary to allow them to manage that position" (8 MAN/M) was still talking about inserting women into the status quo. Only one senior manager saw things differently.

I think there is actually a huge challenge ahead of this university to get a better balance, and to modify the culture. And when one thinks about it, slightly more than half I think, of our customers are female. I see that as a pretty good reason to do something about it. Quite apart from what you might say about the staff and their aspirations. (12 MAN/M)

Whether Men and Women Have Different Management Styles

The senior managers' responses to the question about management styles were all over the shop.[4] Five thought there wasn't a difference between male and female styles; eight, that there was. There were institutional differences operating here. As we noted in the previous chapter, managers at the larger university were more likely to take the latter position, and, indeed, that institution had more women in middle management (a few of whom we interviewed), and women were more likely than men to argue that there were differences in working style. Even so, of the eight arguing that there were gender differences, three argued that women were not as capable as men and five argued that women had something to offer. In their turn, these appositions hinged on the qualities under consideration.

For those downplaying the difference between male and female management styles, *aggression* was paramount. Here senior managers proposed that women could be just like men:

I have several daughters. They don't go to the particular seminars on assertive behavior, but they're all professionals and fairly aggressive with it. My daughters are as aggressive in a professional sense as any males I know, a new breed. (4 MAN/M)

I'm told that women don't like confrontation as much as men seem to relish it, and that could be the testosterone, who knows, but women who get to senior positions, they have demonstrated that they are able to deal with that. I don't see that as a problem for any of the senior women we have. (8 MAN/M)

I remember . . . very vividly what would have been the toughest committee that I have ever chaired since I came to the university, and the questions that . . . were particularly asked of the women candidates by the women were very severe. They were so severe they could have been regarded as inappropriate at times. (3 MAN/M)

In contrast, the senior managers who suggested women didn't cope as well as men emphasized *emotion*, proposing that women were very different from men:

But I have had about three women shed a tear; I have never had a man, now that didn't bother me, I am accustomed to that, so I can cope with that. But I am pointing that out. . . . Maybe it is a good thing to show your emotion that way. I don't know. I have not held that against anybody to say, "You're a poor manager, you can't cope because you shed a tear." But I would say that is about the only difference among male and female academics I deal with. (7 MAN/M)

For the senior managers arguing that women had positive management styles, the common theme was *cooperation*. Females, it was said, had "a greater nurturing role" (13 MAN/M) and had "always accepted a more humanistic role for themselves" (7 MAN/M). One also suggested that women were *better prepared*:

I think there are differences, it is not something I have really given a lot of thought to . . . but women are not as likely to take short cuts to achieve things. I would say that the senior people on the staff that I have dealings with, and they are mostly outside this division, you get the impression that they [women] probably do their homework better or more thoroughly. (2 MAN/M)

When asked whether they thought the new forms of management might affect men and women differently, the senior managers expressed surprise or doubt. Almost half worked their way around the question, rather than answering it directly. Another four appeared nonplussed by any suggestion that the new measures might have a differential impact. One said he couldn't see "any reason why gender should be affected by particular decision making processes" (10 MAN/M); another that he "didn't think that the shift to corporate style and all that sort of thing would make any difference, they would just equally affect men and women" (8 MAN/M). And while two senior managers thought that the new measures *would* have uneven implications, this was *not* because they considered the measures were themselves gender specific. Rather, it was because, relative to men, women didn't have the skills and/or opportunities to take advantage of the new developments:

One of the by-products of the Dawkins' reforms is a more managerial approach which puts more stress on numerical skills, budgeting and planning skills which I would suspect that males have more than females. (1 MAN/M)

I don't think the new measures themselves are gender specific but they could have a differential impact on males or females; let's take the greater emphasis on research output, for example, now to the extent that men have greater continuity and put up a greater score on research performance, they will benefit from that. (5 MAN/M)

Who Am I, the Manager?
(The Captain Reflects)

As well as asking the senior managers about political change, success, management, and gender, we inquired about some personal issues. We asked them whether or not they had planned for their careers, the kinds of sacrifices they had had to make to reach their position and their level of satisfaction with their job.

The Planning Question

Two senior managers said no, they didn't plan: "Things just happened. I'm not that much of a planner," said one (11 MAN/M). At the other end of the spectrum, four senior managers said they planned just about every move. One of them talked about the satisfaction of "setting goals of where I wanted to be at various ages and within a year or two being able to achieve them" (2 MAN/M). Others took up the same theme:

> And you know I always had the view that once I went into academia I wanted to be a professor and I wanted to be a professor by the time I was 40. Well I did become a professor at 42. I knew what I had to do, I had to get research going, I had to get strong administrative ability as well as a wide range of teaching from sub-degree to post-graduate. So I did that. (9 MAN/M)

> I've always very carefully planned the next move and the one after that, in terms of establishing priorities. I came here as a lecturer and God knows that was hard enough. I'd always wanted to be a professor and have a personal chair. When the university brought out its criteria for personal chairs I got hold of them without telling anyone straight away. I deliberately didn't put my name in for the first round but I made sure I was in fairly good shape for the second round. Oh yes, I have been a bit of a zealot in terms of planning. (4 MAN/M)

In between those who trusted in fortune and the planning zealots was a larger group of senior managers who were keen to emphasize that they didn't plan, but were always prepared to take advantage of opportunity. When asked whether he had ever planned his career, one responded, "Absolutely not. I never made any career plans of any significance. The only plan I ever make is to do something that is a challenge and I enjoy doing" (10 MAN/M). Another remarked, "I don't have highly developed career plans, but I do make sure that I am positioning myself for opportunities that will come along" (8 MAN/M). Yet another told us how he thrived on variety:

You see, you learn about yourself as you go along, so when I look back at my career to this point what I have come to realize is that I am a person who likes variety . . . and once I get to know what a particular job or thing is I find a need to go out and find something different, something extra . . . [so] I'd always keep my eye out for other opportunities and be curious about other positions and I'd ask people what they find interesting about what they do; so I'm always looking around for something as I'm always looking around for variety . . . I just look one step ahead. (5 MAN/M)

These attitudes to planning were tied to particular views of the self. The nonplanners said they were not, at heart, ambitious: "Contrary to popular perception, I'm not a very ambitious person" (1 MAN/M). The committed planners owed it to their determination to succeed. "Oh yes, I have been a bit of a zealot in terms of planning" (4 MAN/M). Different to both, the *rise to the challenge* group emphasized their energy and talent: "I would always find something to do if I were not an academic. That gives me a sense of independence and freedom. If you don't have a kind of sense of zest or beauty of life, it's unfortunate" (13 MAN/M).

Sacrifices

I suppose . . . if you want a personal view on that then yeah, you sacrifice to move ahead . . . you do sacrifice quite a lot. A lot of that is personally oriented, family oriented. I don't think there is any doubt about that. (9 MAN/M)

Only one senior manager denied that his work involved any personal losses. "I have never given away any of my hobbies or interests," he insisted, going on to say that he was "dying to get to retirement because there are so many things I want to do" (10 MAN/M). All others acknowledged trade-offs and losses, even if they said these were outweighed by the satisfactions of the job. Some mentioned relinquishing their research, other job opportunities, and money. These losses, though, were overshadowed by the *big three* as far as sacrifices were concerned: collegiality, leisure, and family.

The senior managers mourned the passing of collegiality, even as they argued their separation from the rank and file was necessary. "They no longer invite me to the Christmas dinner," one said sadly (1 MAN/M). Another told us that "one of the things I miss is going to a common room and talking about the world at large, general things" (5 MAN/M). His sense of loss was voiced by many others: "It's part of the job, I can see it is unfortunate, but I do miss the extended group of colleagues around me" (8 MAN/M). This senior manager reflected that

One of the most rewarding things about being an academic . . . is that you are part of a group of colleagues and that tremendous community of inquiry and so

on. . . . once you step out of that, you are into a much more competitive environment where everyone's future depends on how well they perform and how
well they contribute. . . . We have to get runs on the board, and that inevitably
means that you can't be as collaborative and collegial as you would have been.
(8 MAN/M)

Many senior managers talked about the erosion of leisure pursuits, attributing it to the "unconscionable hours" (1 MAN/M) they worked. They expressed a
sense of inevitability on this score, with the loss of leisure described as "one of
the tragedies of the workload" (8 MAN/M). Seen this way, "righting the balance" became a matter of personal responsibility.

My leisure time has been very much taken up by my university work and commitment. I find that during the week I go home and I'm too tired to even con-
template having to do something else. Now I'm not unhappy about it. I'd just
like to get a better balance, to do a bit more. I'm working on it. (5 MAN/M)

The same aura of finality appears in relation to family life. We were told
that wives took the brunt of the family responsibility, that the senior managers
were often away and didn't see much of their children. This, it seemed, was a
fact of the job. In the words of one participant: "One just has to work very hard
so family and all that stuff suffers as a consequence" (12 MAN/M). But what of
the human cost?

Our family life is certainly compromised quite dramatically by the role I am in
at the moment, because the workload is just continuous. I get home at a reasonable hour but I take work home. Almost every day I am working on something
that has to be done tomorrow, and that means when you have children and they
are saying "Give me a bit of help with my calculus," the help they get is there;
but it's not the same as, "Let's sit down for a couple of hours." And I find my
kids are a little bit distant on occasions because they just view me as a person
who comes and goes. (8 MAN/M)

Satisfaction

With very few exceptions, the senior managers did not regret the sacrifices they
had made (or their families had made on their behalf). The losses, they said,
were more than outweighed by the satisfactions of the job. The following senior
manager put this position strongly:

I've never worked so hard in my life. There are so many additional demands on
you. I haven't been home many nights this week. I just love the challenge. I
have said publicly I have the best job in the university. We want to build another campus or two. It's all yours—go and fix it. (10 MAN/M)

The senior managers nominated many sources of satisfaction. At the modest end of the spectrum, one or two simply talked about the pleasure of a job well done: "I'm doing a job that I like now. It's a job I'm suited for and I do it well. I get the impression that most people feel I'm doing very well" (1 MAN/M). Similarly: "I am happy and continue to learn in my role, and I am really very, very satisfied with the position I am in right now, and the work we are doing" (12 MAN/M). Those who made more extensive claims emphasized the satisfactions they gained from a high-profile reputation: "You know I was interacting with some pretty prominent people around the place. You know I felt good" (7 MAN/M). Here is the buzz of "presenting a lot of my research to different boards around the world" (14 MAN/M) and "establishing an international reputation in my own field of research and . . . being invited to give plenary lectures and keynote lectures" (2 MAN/M). As one said:

> I love it. I think it is absolutely fascinating. . . . I mean it is just that constant mix of things that you do and what you do in a day . . . within a day you might be dealing with everything from Mozambique to Sri Lanka to the Scottish Highlands. And you are moving around all the time, bit like a butterfly really. (9 MAN/M)

The senior managers also reflected on their capacity to leave a legacy. They spoke about "creating environments . . . so that other people can realize their potential" (3 MAN/M). In such ways they felt they shaped the new generation:

> I suppose what is the most satisfying thing for me is having been able to make a scientific contribution, and in particular in being able to groom other people, the next generation. I've got three people who will be going to the concert hall tonight, getting doctorates. (4 MAN/M)

Regrets? Just one senior manager spoke about his:

> Yes, it has been sort of lonely. . . . If I had stayed a lecturer or whatever, I think I would have had friends and a social life far different to what I have now. It is a consequence of the job. It is lonely at the top in that respect. It is, and suddenly your life is over and you wonder where it went. (7 MAN/M)

Conclusion
(Putting Down a Feminist Anchor)

At the start of this chapter we asked whether the *we* of senior management represented a single view or masked multiple, and even inconsistent, opinions. Although different views have been revealed in the course of the chapter, we suggest there is, nevertheless, some kind of centripetal force at work, drawing the responses together around a common core.

Let us suppose that we have the senior managers assembled together, not on a desert island, but in a spacious office overlooking the university. Let us also suppose we have asked them to summarize their corporate view. Their answer might go something like this:

What, you want us to summarize all that we have been talking about? All those interviews in one go? Fair enough, we guess that's possible as we do have a collective view on these matters, you know. But we don't have a great deal of time, so listen carefully and keep the squeak on that recorder down.

As we said, the fact of the matter is that political forces have pushed universities into competitive relations and brought about new systems of accountability. We've had to respond to these demands to achieve the best deal for our institutions. It's a fact of life. So we act like a peak executive group, making quick and efficient decisions. The realities of this aren't well appreciated by the rank and file; they just don't grasp the big picture. You asked about who gets ahead and why. Well, we certainly favor people who are motivated and deliver. Like us, they need to have a sense of the "big picture." And overall, we think the university system is pretty fair, and hope that women with drive and talent will succeed, even though we admit there are some fairly hefty barriers in their way at present.

As for those other gender issues you raised, well, sorry, we find it impossible to respond to those. Too metaphysical really, particularly when there are political imperatives to be faced and runs to get on the board. Lastly, on those personal questions, yes, it's true, we've had to make sacrifices along the way. We still do, given the workload; but the satisfactions of the job more than compensate. We really do love the challenge. And now we must rush. The Minister's waiting. Or is it the CEO of Toyota? (Prototype Senior Manager)

The components of this fictional view are too poorly articulated and too open to challenge to suggest an overriding ideology or even hegemonic forces. However, following Foucault (1972), it is possible to see a definite *discursive formation* at work, making sense of the world in particular ways and rendering some things possible and actionable and others not. The discourse of the senior managers affirms pragmatism, corporate strategies, and commitment to the task in hand, and rules out idealism, deliberative democracy, and radical alternatives. Most crucially, its attention to political *realities* obscures the long-term threats now facing the creative and intellectual traditions of Australian universities and the possibility that common action might be taken against them.

How far is the senior managers' discourse separate from the considerations of the rank and file? The answer is equivocal. On some issues, senior managers hold quite different views from the rest of the staff or accentuate what is otherwise a minority response. On others, they more broadly reproduce the spectrum of opinion within the university, at least as far as males are concerned. The first lot of issues includes questions of political change, university management, attributes of success, and levels of personal satisfaction. The second, gender and management, the barriers facing women, planning, and sacrifice. Why the difference in the managers' responses? We suggest the answer lies in their relationship to the two groups of questions.

The first set pertains, directly or indirectly, to the work of the executive itself. In answering questions on this score, the senior managers make sense of their own labor, rendering management practices logical and defensible. In this respect, they articulate ways of "thinking about the nature and practice of government . . . making some form of that activity thinkable and practicable both to its practitioners and to those upon whom it was practised" (Gordon, C. 1991: 3). That academic staff did not accept this rationality was, as we have seen, a source of frustration to the senior managers. It also set their accounts off from the rank and file, who, operating under different conditions, constructed good governance in different ways.

In contrast to the first category, the second set of issues pertains to the *world at large*, incorporating questions about male/female relationships as well as planning and sacrifice. We noted earlier that when asked directly about gender, the senior managers spoke as *men*, as much as—or more than—they spoke as *managers*. So here their responses reproduce the spectrum of ambivalence and contradiction characterizing male responses across the universities, qualified only by their mandate to uphold affirmative action policy. A slightly different pattern emerges on questions of career and sacrifice. Here the responses of the senior managers track those of successful and upwardly mobile males, but depart from the (larger) disenfranchised or oppositional group of men questioning the goals and directions of the university.

Overall, though, a certain stability prevails over the senior managers' responses, and not just for the reasons outlined so far. Their world is indisputably male, and a sense of the social order *as it just is* results from that. The normalness and hence, in a sense, the very inconsequentiality of male patterns underlies the observation that "sometimes at the senior executive group there are some bar jokes told . . . occasionally there are some off jokes. But that's neither here nor there" (1 MAN/M). And a wonderfully unselfconscious sense of a male-centered world is expressed in this senior manager's memories:

> Some of the friends I have got in the university would go out and eat once a month with our wives. . . . Just a group of guys who have got on well together. (2 MAN/M)

Masculine referents lie behind the senior managers' allusions and metaphors, even when they are being denied. "Hell," says one, "I'll slam a woman as much as a man, that's the way it is" (7 MAN/M). During this chapter, we have heard about "being at the helm," "in the engine room," "at AFL matches," "playing the committee game," "making tough decisions," and many more. In chapter 4 we were told about women's absence from the rugby network: "There aren't many women who go to watch the rugby. There is R. and the VC and they catch up with some of the academic staff who are watching. . . . I wouldn't expect to see K. and you there" (1 MAN/M). And against the competitions of the senior managers' world stands the shadow of the supportive wife. We caught sight of her at various points in the interviews, and then she would vanish:

> My wife is my biggest support I suppose. She gives me a fair bit of support and allows me the freedom for work . . . and has some understanding about the fact that I am away a lot and travel a lot and I mean that impacts on the family. (9 MAN/M)

> I draw 99 percent of my support from my wife and my family. That's not very fair on her is it? (4 MAN/M)

What are the chances of women in senior management? We are not optimistic. Since the time the interviews were undertaken, the corporatization of Australian universities has proceeded apace. In the smaller university there was a radical reorganization in which the positions of old style administrators committed to collegiality were lost. Two women were appointed to the newly created executive dean positions, but one soon left for personal and family reasons. Women who speak out against current directions do not get appointed to senior positions, while those who are appointed experience formal and informal sanctions bringing them in line with the senior executive. It is tough at the top and particularly tough, it seems, for the few women who make it there.

On a more optimistic note, we return to the many points of tension, inconsistency, and divided loyalty in the senior managers' responses. Theirs is not a uniform voice, and some of their members are not without sympathy for older academic traditions. Indeed, at times they break rank and display a distinct longing for collegiality, imagination, and the time to reflect. At the same time, the changes and pressures that senior management have had to respond to and are in charge of implementing within their institutions have severely eroded precisely those qualities of academic life that they recall. Few, if any, academics and general staff would recognize in their present working lives the old traditions and values of a university community, and they would not think their managers particularly sympathetic to their plight. It is to their experience of the university as a workplace that we now turn.

Notes

1. Excluded are the managers of faculties, schools and administrative units, and deputy executive deans. Faculty deans often regarded themselves as a halfway house, more closely allied with the academic staff from whence they came, and caught between the demands of their faculty and those of the central university executive. In contrast,

executive deans, with oversight of larger academic divisions often containing several faculties, tended to identify more, and be culturally identified, with central management. At the time of interviewing, the larger university had a divisional structure with executive deans. The smaller university has since moved to a similar structure.

2. Dawkins' reforms are discussed in chapter 1. Basically, these reforms deregulated aspects of funding and governance, shifting universities toward business practices and making them more entrepreneurial, especially in recruiting foreign students and in partnering with industries to develop commercial products.

3. It is interesting that these managers justify their isolated decision making by framing the alternative as requiring input or agreement from *everyone*. The area between *everyone* and *no one*, other than senior managers, is left unexplored!

4. "All over the shop" is an Australian expression meaning all over the factory shop floor or referring, in this instance, to diverse responses.

Chapter 7

The View from Below: Sacrifices and Success in Greedy Universities

"You talk about sacrifices. Show us the wooden cross."
(Junior academic, female: 12 JAC/F)

Introduction

The view from the top looks very different from below. In the previous chapter the account of managers recorded their distinctive view of the organization and themselves—as separate from and above the rest of the institution. Despite the hard work and sacrifices required to succeed as a manager, they were, with very few exceptions, deeply satisfied with their lot. This is the opposite of the story told by the rest of the university staff.

In this chapter we turn to the costs of the normalization of male culture as experienced by those below senior management in terms of sacrifice and success. There is value in juxtaposing the two terms because our respondents had a clear sense that sacrifice is demanded of them not only to get ahead, but just to do their jobs. Equally, as we have seen in the managers' experience, getting ahead and being successful are understood rhetorically and practically to involve *self-sacrifice*. The sacrifices one has to make to stay in an academic career are issues that reoccur in studies on academics. In a study of early career academics,

Bazeley, et al. (1996: 27) emphasize the importance of complete dedication to the research task: "Successful researchers demonstrated a single-mindedness and an unswerving commitment to their research. They were marked by an inner drive and intense focus, often working 70+ hour weeks." McKenna (1997) also makes this connection in her study of women who dropped out of senior positions in the United States. She described the world of work as "a Darwinian system that weeds out those with no stomach for politics, competition, or mono-focused ambition" (McKenna 1997: 51) and went on to say that it is a success value system, which has a subtle and extremely corrosive part to it, where "it's all or nothing and it equates self-sacrifice with success . . . where the system makes no allowance for anything to be more important than work" (McKenna 1997: 54). This chapter looks broadly at the nature of these sacrifices and in-quires into their gendered character before examining what *the troops* think about how fair or unfair the system is in rewarding those sacrifices with success.

For better or worse, contemporary universities are not sheltered from eco-nomic and political change, and we have traced the broader context in which university life has been transformed by an increasingly economistic and mana-gerial ethos. In the previous chapter we also outlined the specific rationales senior managers in the two universities offered for their compliance with these changes. More significantly, these changes have contributed to an intensification of the pressure experienced by staff in universities. Academics, for example, can no longer claim to follow an older monastic model whereby scholarship and research could be pursued without the intrusion of commercial bidding for the latest discoveries or the pressure to make their work directly relevant to the de-mands of industry. At the same time, more and more of an academic's time is now devoted to tasks not associated with research or teaching. This means, in effect, that greater inroads are made into time that would otherwise be spent with families and friends. Social life and health may suffer. General staff, like academics, are being asked to give more time to the university, work overtime and weekends, while not being paid any more money for doing so.

In brief, as pressures on academic and general staff increase due to budget constraints and restructuring of universities, more and more time has to be de-voted to work. This takes its toll on families, friends, and the general health of university workers. In this context and for those who feel the university is de-vouring them, Coser's (1974) term *greedy institution* may be an apt description of the contemporary university.

Universities as Greedy Institutions

Coser depicts a greedy institution as one that makes total claims on its members and seeks exclusive and undivided loyalty from them. "Their demands on the person are omnivorous" (Coser 1974: 4). At the time of writing, the early 1970s,

Coser did not include universities, turning instead to monks, Bolsheviks, Jesuits, and wives/mothers. He explains that such institutions do not themselves coerce participants into total commitment. Rather, there is something about their nature that attracts voluntary compliance. Individuals assent to the lifestyle because it is highly attractive to them. In their turn, greedy institutions encourage their members to devote their total energies to collective tasks. In his chapter on women who devote their lives to the family, Coser (1974: 91) points out that "the more wives sacrifice for the family, the more they are bound to it." Put in another way, "the more one invests in an object, the greater the hold that object has on the person" (Coser 1974: 91).

Franzway (1996) uses Coser's analogy of the greedy institution to describe women and their commitment to their jobs in trade unions. Drawing on Coser's work, she describes these women's almost total commitment in much the same way that Lenin wanted people "who shall devote to the party not only their spare evenings, but the whole of their lives" (Franzway, citing Coser 1974: 129). Coser quotes Victor Serge, another revolutionary author, as saying that "the highest praise that can be bestowed on [a participant in the revolution] is to say that he has 'no private life,' that his life has fused totally with history" (Coser 1974: 131).

Many academics, it can be suggested, have the passion of revolutionaries. They often commit themselves totally to their work, allowing little private life for themselves or their families.[1] Like revolutionaries, they can become dedicated to a cause, whether that cause lies in teaching about new ideas or tracking down a gene in a laboratory. And the more academics invest in their work (not necessarily in the institution), the greater that work has a hold over them. In much the same way as mothers who cannot love enough or cannot give enough to their families, academics cannot give enough to their teaching and research. There are always students who need more help. There are always more books and articles to read. There are always ideas that need to be researched. There is always more research that needs to be published. Acker (1994: 126) used the same analogy of greedy institutions in describing academics saying that "like housework, academic work is never really done."

Academics, like other high-status professionals, have apparent control over their work, but choose to work long hours. It is, though, the nature of this *choice* that needs to be questioned. In part, and as indicated above, it is enthusiasm for their work that attracts academics to the university in the first place and continues to drive them on. But more is involved than this. What frustrates academics today is not so much that intellectual work encroaches on their private lives. This, they would say, has always been so. The problem, rather, is that increasing workloads and demands for greater productivity erode their capacity to do their traditional activities with the quality they value, at the same time as the university increasingly demands that they be involved in detailed administrative and quality-assurance-type work. This kind of managerial accountancy, with the endless form-filling, data collection, and benchmarking it involves, seriously disrupts and overregulates teaching and research. Academics have to put in extra hours, wrestle with how to use their time, and decide what will be sacrificed for what. Increasingly, that part of their work that is meaningful to them is displaced and time is borrowed from leisure, family, and sleep as days are occupied responding to administrative demands. Autonomy is undermined and academics experience loss of an older internal rhythm which allowed them to be creative and reflective about ideas.

Many academics would prefer to be like monks, accountable only to their own curiosity, not to the government. Today, though, it is the pressure to be publicly accountable, to answer to government and/or to management, that is transforming older academic traditions. Academics no longer have the *luxury* to emulate monks who could devote their lives to scholarship. Their jobs are becoming increasingly *proletarianized*, and their professional labor is increasingly managed by administrators. Under the influence of wider economic and political trends, university bosses are calculating productivity and demanding more of it. As universities come to depend more upon private funding, academics are asked to go out into the marketplace and show profits on the cash register. It is the market, and not the quality of creative ideas and scholarship, that is increasingly determining the lives of academics and the work they do.

Overworked

In numerous articles, for example, "The Age of Overwork" (Powell 1995a) and books, for example, *The Overworked American—The Unexpected Decline of Leisure* (Schor 1992), the demands on people's lives and what they have to sacrifice for their jobs (often their health) have been recounted in detail. Australians, in general, increased their working hours from 35.6 hours per week in 1985 to 42.6 hours per week in 1995 (*The Age* 1995). Professionals appear to be working even longer hours: half of the Senior Executive Service, for example, are said to work between 51 and 60 hours a week, and a fifth work more than 60 hours per week (Renfrow 1995).

In the United States, workers today put in 163 more hours per year than they did twenty-five years ago (Moody and Sagovac 1995). In an increasingly competitive environment, occupational stress, both mental and physical, is growing and now affects a third of the workforce. In the first half of the 1980s, stress-related workers' compensation claims tripled and continued to climb (Moody and Sagovac 1995). An American study of more than 250,000 women, accompanied by a scientific, randomly selected survey of 1200 women, found too much stress to be the biggest problem. Over half (59 percent) of these women experienced stress at work and/or in balancing home and work demands

(Jones 1994). In Britain, longer hours and little job security have resulted in stress as a major issue facing professionals (Hugill 1994).

Powell (1995a) reported that the overwork story was substantially the same across the professions and extended to universities in Australia:

> The shakeout of higher education, which began in the late 80s, has seen commercial pressures descend on universities. Increased class sizes, shrinking budgets and the introduction of summer schools have pumped up workloads to the point where many academics prefer to leave the system for the private sector. One Australian National University professor asserted on ABC [Australian Broadcasting Corporation] radio recently that you could not stay on top of science research without working at least 100 hours a week. (Powell 1995a: 1-2)

By 1993 Australian academics were working an average of almost 48 hours per week, an increase of around 3 hours per week since the 1970s (McInnis 1996). Coaldrake and Stedman (1999) reported that the situation since 1993 had placed further strain on the system and that by 1998 student load had risen by a further 17 percent while academic staff numbers remained static or decreased. McInnis (2000) surveyed academics again in 1999 and found that overall work hours had increased by 1.5 hours in the last five years, from an already high base. He noted a dramatic decline in the level of overall satisfaction from 76 to 51 percent and the level of work-induced stress rose significantly from 52 to 56 percent. The National Tertiary Education Union (2000) study found that the majority of staff worked on average a 52.8-hour week. The majority of staff also reported increased workloads since 1996, with most working in departments that had lost staff.

Studies in other countries show similar results. New Zealand found that 80 percent of academics said their workloads had increased in recent years and full-time academics worked an average of 53 hours a week (Boyd and Wylie 1994). Studies in the United States from the late 1980s to the early 1990s (Mingle 1992; Jordon and Layzell 1992; Allen 1994) reported faculty workloads increasing during the last decade and the average hours per week ranged between 53 and 56 hours. In Britain, a workload survey (Court 1994) found British academics working an average of 54 hours per week. Fisher (1994) reported that 75 percent of a sample of British academics felt frequently or always overloaded.

As already suggested, the hours alone are not necessarily the main problem for academics. Rather, it is the longer hours *coupled with* the new administrative tasks and the associated fragmentation of work time (McInnis 1996). The tasks that cause the greatest cynicism are those brought about by institutional competition and accountability (McInnis 1996). In this context, McInnis identified two long-term trends: a decline in the control academics have over the management of their work and increasing fragmentation of tasks:

> The intrusion of excessive accountability processes, the regulation and codifi-
> cation of work practices associated with teaching and research, and the pressure
> for compliance to routine management requirements undermine the primary
> work motives of academics, and paradoxically, put both quality and productiv-
> ity at risk. (McInnis 1996: 10)

When the managerial paradigm for universities that economic rationalism
has produced around the globe is overlaid upon the highly gendered (masculine)
nature of universities as workplaces and organizations, then the costs for women
are high. Previous chapters have confirmed the observation made of university
cultures around the world, that they tend to value and reproduce concepts of
career, academic achievement, and institutional and intellectual work based
upon male life trajectories (Itzen and Newman 1995) and that the pathways to
success tend to be built upon dominant male traits and characteristics (Izraeli
and Adler 1994). The consequences for women academics pervade their work
experience. Morley and Walsh (1995), in a study of British academics, reported
that women at every level actually worked longer hours than men. They quoted
a survey carried out by the Association of University Teachers (1994) which
found that the average working week of a woman professor was 64.5 hours
compared with an average for male professors of 58.6 hours.

Park (1996), in a U.S. study, and Acker and Feuerverger (1996), in a Canadian study, found that women were more likely to spend more time teaching
than their male colleagues and had less time to devote to research and publications. Acker and Feuerverger (1996: 404) report that by *doing good*, "women try
to reach exceptionally high standards by working hard, even at personal expense, and that they make efforts to support and care for colleagues and students
and to be 'good citizens' in their departments." These women, they suggest, *feel
bad* because the academic reward system is out of sync with their efforts. The
overall effect of this context is that the sacrifices which women academics make
to *just do the job*, caught as they are between two greedy institutions, family and
the corporatized university, are already high; and the sacrifices they make to do
the job well, as prescribed by gender, are not equitably rewarded.

Our Findings: An Overall Picture

In the first part of this chapter, we describe the responses to the following composite question: Do staff have to sacrifice certain things to get ahead? Or compromise certain values and interests? If so, what are the things that get sacrificed? Table 7.1 identifies whether or not staff felt that they had to make
sacrifices and the kinds of sacrifices that were made. Staff could respond in
more than one way, so the numbers show the total responses for each category
and thus are greater than the actual number of staff interviewed. The data is
given by gender, and work status (academic or general staff).

Table 7.1 Sacrifice to Get Ahead (by work type and gender) Percentages and (numbers)

	Academics		General		
Sacrifices	Male	Female	Male	Female	Total Nos.
Type of Sacrifice	(N=47)	(N=52)	(N=22)	(N=47)	(N=168)
Personal	51.3 (39)	43.6 (34)	30.6 (11)	42.6 (23)	43.9 (107)
Family	26.3 (20)	20.5 (16)	11.1 (4)	20.4 (11)	20.9 (51)
Social/Leisure/Health	25.0 (19)	23.1 (18)	19.5 (7)	22.2 (12)	23.0 (56)
Work	30.3 (23)	33.4 (26)	25.0 (9)	22.2 (12)	28.7 (70)
Money	5.3 (4)	2.6 (2)	2.8 (1)	0.0 (0)	2.9 (7)
Academic & Prof. Values	25.0 (19)	30.8 (24)	22.2 (8)	22.2 (12)	25.8 (63)
One Chooses	10.5 (8)	15.3 (12)	30.6 (11)	18.5 (10)	16.8 (41)
Strategic Choices	7.9 (6)	8.9 (7)	11.1 (4)	3.7 (2)	7.8 (19)
Resistance	2.6 (2)	6.4 (5)	19.5 (7)	14.8 (8)	9.0 (22)
No Sacrifices	7.9 (6)	7.7 (6)	13.8 (5)	16.7 (9)	10.6 (26)
No Need to Sacrifice Values	7.9 (6)	7.7 (6)	13.8 (5)	16.7 (9)	10.6 (26)
Total Percentages	100	100	100	100	100
Total Responses	(76)	(78)	(36)	(54)	(244)

Of the total number of responses (244), the large majority (177 or 72.6 percent) described some kind of significant sacrifice. A smaller number (19 or 7.8 percent) of responses indicated that staff felt they could choose to make strategic *choices* and thus the sacrifices were to some extent self-inflicted, while 22 (or 9.0 percent) of responses spoke of resistance to the demands placed on them. Finally, 26 (or 10.6 percent) of total responses asserted that staff did not have to sacrifice or compromise values to get ahead.

Somewhat surprisingly at first sight, our data did not indicate any consistent pattern of difference between the responses of male and female staff, either within or between the institutions.[2] (Some interesting points of comparison did emerge, though, around perceptions of success, and these will be commented on later in the chapter.) What was apparent was that many staff, both male and female, believed that the combination of work demands and an increasingly competitive ethos produced an antifamily, antisocial environment that was injurious to their personal commitments and values. Table 7.1 also shows that general staff were somewhat less likely to refer to sacrifices than were academic staff. The data, though, is variable and inconclusive as far as this is concerned.

We start our discussion with the minority of responses that argued that there was no need to make any kind of sacrifice.

No Need to Compromise Values

> I have no idea why we need to sacrifice anything at all. (8 GEN/F)

A total of 26 responses (10.6 percent of total responses) suggested that there was no need to sacrifice values or interests. The numbers of responses from academic and general staff were similar (12 academic responses and 14 general staff responses), as was the breakdown in relation to gender (15 responses from females and 11 from males). If anything, general staff were proportionally more likely to assert that no sacrifices were needed to do their jobs (15.6 percent compared with 7.8 percent for academic staff), but this may well reflect the greater range of general staff jobs. Certainly, the more senior general staff, in administrative rather than clerical grades, were less likely to assert that they made no sacrifices.

In this category there were staff who did not mind working long hours because their work was so central to their lives. The following are an academic and two librarians:

> I see this place as the centerpiece of my life and a benefit of this is a close social life at the workplace. My whole life is here so I'm not sacrificing anything to be here. (8 JAC/F)

> Extra time is not a sacrifice for me. I enjoy doing it, e.g. Open Days, Career Days. It's often expected in my position, although I could say no. I'm in the happy situation that I don't have to worry about children. (9 GEN/F)

> I don't mind spending more hours. It shows dedication and enjoyment. I have to follow through on my supervisor's and manager's ideas. It's never been a problem yet. (10 GEN/F)

There were others who saw the organizational values in their institution as being congruent with their own. This view was more often, but not invariably, expressed by more senior males:

> I don't really think that word, sacrifice, is applicable. For people who work at it for 12 out of 24 hours a day, they get the rewards at the end of it, and I don't

believe I have ever met anybody who has looked back and said "I have had to
sacrifice this to get that" who is successful. It is a question of if you really want
to do this, you really want to get somewhere, and it doesn't matter. (5
S.GEN/M)

I don't think one has to compromise values or interests in this organization. One
may have to be subtle and one may have to be political, but that is a personal
point of view. (21 SAC/M)

I am not sure about compromising values. One can only speak from a personal
point of view and I don't think I have compromised any values or principles in
becoming a head of school. (14 SAC/M)

I think to work effectively in an organization, you don't necessarily have to
compromise your values; I think it's professional to get on with people and try
to get something done, so I don't see it in terms of sacrifice. (11 S.GEN/F)

At the junior end of the hierarchy there were staff (both academic and general) that felt they did not have to compromise their values because they felt that
the university remained true to its democratic traditions:

I certainly don't ever feel that I have had to compromise my values here. (2
JAC/F)

I feel that the values of [my university], which include diversity, mean that I am
valued. I don't have to compromise my values here any more than I would at
another institution. (9 JAC/F)

I don't think you have to compromise your values to get ahead and that's one
of the good things about it—you can get ahead and keep to moral values if you
have them. (12 S.GEN/F)

A General Climate of Sacrifice?

As indicated earlier, the great majority of responses (177 or 72.6 percent) were
from staff who said that they made some kind of substantial sacrifice. In regard
to these responses, one thing was consistently evident. We had asked staff about
what they had to sacrifice in order to "get ahead." Our respondents reminded us
that sacrifices had to be made just to stay afloat:

Curiously, the things we're saying are not the kind of things that you sacrifice
to get ahead, they're things you sacrifice to do this kind of job. (5 SAC/F)

Before describing the different categories of response, we provide a series
of quotes which illustrate the pressures staff are working under and the hours

they expend. We found this to be more characteristic of academic than general staff, but that a number of general staff were also forced into giving long hours and, sometimes, most of their weekends and evenings, to the job.

> This is not a nine to five job. It really is more like a small business where the deli is open 24 hours a day. (12 SAC/M)

> I mean if you are in an academic career, it's a 24 hour a day, seven day a week, 365 day thing, it's not a nine to five period, it's a profession and as a profession it's also a life. (5 SAC/M)

> In terms of the hours that we spend working, you count them up and it is just horrendous. And you think if I were a plumber, I'd earn more money and have less stress. (8 JAC/M)

> There is no way I have ever been able to do my job to my satisfaction in less than 50 to 55 hours a week. (1 SAC/M)

> My job has taken over my whole life; on the weekend and at night the phone is constantly ringing. (11 GEN/F)

> It seems to me that what is required of people today to get ahead, you have to show commitment. You have to be seen to be in the office, you must be seen to be flexible; you mustn't come in at nine o'clock and leave at five, because that is not good. You have to be in early and you have to leave late. You have to be seen occasionally in at the weekend, no matter how far away you live. (6 S.GEN/M)

Two staff members (one academic and one general) described how working extremely long hours becomes a norm and creates pressures to perform at a certain level.

> We tend to be under this pressure—well enculturated, if that's the word, to try to perform to a very high level, an international level, and not wanting to perform anything much less. You're trying to perform in this small university at a strong international level and that's just really hard to do. (11 SAC/M)

> One area is a very go go area and the people at the top are sleeping four hours a night and live for their work. They are extremely high achievers and the young people doing work for them, they just pick up on this culture and try and do the same thing. I see these young people come into this area and getting totally burnt out. . . . it's the culture and it's coming from the top. (13 S.GEN/F)

Staff who talked about sacrifice raised a number of concerns relating to their domestic and private relationships, their personal commitments, their social life and their health, their professional and intellectual interests, and their academic values. We divided these responses into *personal* and *work* sacrifices. Overall, there were more responses in the category of personal sacrifices (107) than in work sacrifices (70).

Personal Sacrifices

Within the category of personal sacrifices, the largest single factor concerned family (51 responses). In addition, we distinguished a broad cluster of personal issues relating to social activities, leisure, and health (56 responses). The common factor behind both these sets of responses was the inroads which work demands made into other commitments.

Personal Sacrifices: Family Life

> I work extra time, work nights, weekends and when I'm asked to do extra work, I can't tell the Dean that I won't do it. I have to give up family time just to have the extra time to do my work. (12 GEN/F)

Contrary to what we expected, almost as many male (24) as female (27) responses were concerned with family sacrifices (see table 7.1). At the smaller university, the proportion of male academic responses mentioning family sacrifice (23 percent of male responses) was higher than the comparable proportion of female academic responses (15 percent of female responses), while for general staff, the pattern was more traditional with 22 percent of female responses concerned with family compared with 5 percent of male responses. At the other university, the proportions of responses were more evenly divided between males and females across both academic and general staff.

Behind these figures lie regret, sadness, guilt, and frustration:

> Well, I carried a very heavy administrative load through the eighties as well as having an active research program and there's no doubt my family just didn't see a great deal of me and that was the time my son was growing up and I think that was to his disadvantage. He might, of course, say it was to his advantage (laughter) but I think it was to his disadvantage. It was to the disadvantage of the family, I think. (9 SAC/M)

> All my leisure time . . . certainly my family. When I started here, I guess the children were a bit younger, five years younger than they are now. When I think about it, it was a phenomenal task in terms of the hours it took. (11 SAC/F)

> Absolutely. I think I have a certain amount of responsibility for the collapse of my first marriage and I am pretty sure quite consciously at that time, now I am speaking bluntly, I was aware that if I was going to continue on the road to

working here that that would have to go. There were extreme time pressures. That might seem like an extreme statement but there is no question that staff here make an enormous commitment to working at this place. (10 JAC/M)

My children are used to phoning me at work; if they don't see me at home, they just ring work. And that is very sad. (6 JAC/F)

The biggest cost comes in probably family relations because I think it would be quite easy to sacrifice a marriage in terms of work. (6 S.GEN/M)

I think the higher you move up the more sacrifices you're expected to make. In my case I've got two small kids and I tried not to work full time and I know that they lose out. I don't have time to spend with them. . . . It's school holidays now and I'm taking a day off tomorrow because I really want to be with them, but I know my workload is still going to be there on Monday. It's always that juggling act, of knowing the work never goes away and one day having pleasure with the family, it just gets to be more at work. So that is a sacrifice. And when you're at work, the kids are wanting to spend time with you. You can never be in both places at once and you feel guilty a lot of the time. (14 S.GEN/F)

As the voices of these staff show, the constant factor, the constant loss, is *time*. It is the pressure to work and the sheer lack of time which eat into family life. The following exchange between three male academics epitomizes this:

Do you have to make sacrifices to do this work? (Interviewer)

Yes, a life. (10 SAC/M)

Your personal life. (9 JAC/M)

Weekends. (8 JAC/M)

I find that my personal life has gone down a lot. The time that I used to spend with my family. I am finding that I was spending less time with my family and more time here. And you know you run around here, you come in on weekends. (9 JAC/M)

The time you do spend with your family, you feel guilty. So it is not quality time. (8 JAC/M)

Personal Sacrifices: Leisure, Social Activities, and Health
As well as sacrificing time with family, staff talked about sacrificing leisure, social activities, and health (56 responses).

Time . . . friendships . . . relationships . . . leisure . . . sleep are the things that
you sacrifice to get ahead, they're things you sacrifice to do this kind of job. (5
SAC/F)

Across both institutions, more academic than general staff made this kind of
response (37 responses compared with 19 responses). It is possible that the experience of stress is more generalized across the academic than the general staff
spectrum—certainly the pressure to work all hours appeared to affect junior as
much as senior academics.

As far as gender was concerned, there were differences between the two institutions. At the smaller university, the responses of females *describing so-
cial/leisure/health* issues outnumbered those of males across both academic and
general staff. Out of a total of 28 responses, 18 came from females and 10 from
males. At the other university, a different picture emerged. Again, 28 responses
fell into this category, but here responses from males (16) outnumbered responses from females (12). This higher representation of male responses at the
latter university owed itself entirely to gender differences among academic staff,
where the number of male responses (11) nominating social/leisure/health issues
outstripped those made by females (4 responses).

In this broad category of personal issues, staff continued to talk about the
work pressures that made inroads into their lives outside the university. This was
particularly the case for academics who spoke of the need to simultaneously
undertake research, teaching, and administrative tasks:

At times it feels that all I've ever done is put my life off until I've got this done
or that done or whatever. Time, I mean, I would rarely work less than a 9 to 10
hour day. Very rarely. During the week I never go to the theatre, a film or dinner. Ever. It's just we've now realized it causes us so much stress, so it's not
worth the angst. (10 JAC/F)

You have to cut back time, you know, time that you would have perhaps gone
out to see a movie or had a dinner out or even just picking up children, you
have to arrange someone else to do it. (11 JAC/F)

Because of the pressure on time, other things suffered, particularly health
and outside interests:

I guess health is the other thing that gets sacrificed. The first two years I was
here I started work at 5:30 every working day and I would not leave before 6 or
7 at night. I worked like that for two years and ended up in hospital. I knew it
was ridiculous at the time, but I couldn't actually see how I could do the job
without putting in those hours. Now I won't put in those hours, although I still
work phenomenal hours but I won't put those hours in with the result that I
now have an ulcer. If I don't put the hours in then I am more stressed, I am so

anxious about everything, I get home every night and there are five hours to get the work done. So that's another thing. (11 SAC/F)

I have got high cholesterol and I'm not greatly overweight, but given that I have high cholesterol, my doctor said I must lose weight, I must modify my diet, I must exercise. Well, I don't have time to exercise and I don't actually have time to plan and make sure I eat the healthy diet I used to eat. Now I am beginning to say to myself "Surely it's actually better not to get the work done and stay alive" but what's been happening is more students, fewer staff, and more administration. (12 JAC/F)

I have given up a whole lot of worthwhile voluntary commitments because I can't carry them any longer, can't do them justice. At our level, I work very, very long hours and have to be available for erratic hours. It's not just the length of time but its unpredictability. (10 S.GEN/F)

So what you are compromising are outside interests, the quality of life outside university and the contacts with people outside the university because of the long hours of working. (2 S.GEN/F)

Work Sacrifices

Although sacrifices regarding the working environment were substantial in terms of numbers (70), there were not as many responses as in the previous category of personal sacrifices (107). Only a small number of these work-related responses were concerned with money (7 responses). Most people talked about work sacrifices in terms of compromising academic values (63 responses).

Work Sacrifices: Money
Seven staff members mentioned the loss of income in taking a job or moving sideways in a university. Four of these responses came from male academics, one from a female academic, and one from a male general staff member.

Well, money too. Outside I could earn twice what I make here. (4 JAC/M)

Oh a lot of people sacrifice salary to get ahead. They go backwards to go forwards, by moving sideways and slightly downwards into another chain, another line of work. You are prepared to go sideways and backwards, sacrificing position and money, to get in the new stream which you perceive will take you further in time. (2 S.GEN/M)

Work Sacrifices: Academic/Professional Values

You have to sacrifice your own personal views as well, I think, often. (6 S.GEN/F)

This category of academic/professional work sacrifices ranged over a number of issues including teaching values, research and the chance to pursue one's own interests, free thinking, critical thought, the opportunity to voice one's opinion, and the threat to an older system of collegiate values. More females (36 responses) than males (27 responses) spoke of these kinds of compromises, and more academics (43 responses) than general staff (20 responses).

A larger number of responses of this kind came from the smaller of the two universities (39 compared with 24). Some of these responses expressed a sense of loss, suggesting that its institutional ethos had deteriorated. The following quote from a senior female academic at this university exemplifies this:

> I was going to say I do have a sense of compromising integrity—of being pushed to the point where there is no other way forward except to compromise on integrity things like . . . I now have meetings with students where half of my brain is saying "I wish they would go away." I don't have time for the social chitchat, whereas 5 years ago I would give anyone who walked in my door the amount of time they needed. Now I'm finding ways of avoiding them, pushing them out, being sharp—all very politely and I'm sure they never realize it. But I'm quite conscious half of my brain is not focusing on what they're saying. A real sense of short-cutting—not to get ahead, but because of the pressures of the job. (5 SAC/F)

This academic's concern with sacrificing *teaching values* was voiced by others. Not having enough time for adequate preparation was a concern:

> I do compromise some values—in terms of not having enough time to prepare well enough for teaching. I am conscious that sometimes lectures are a con job—that they give the impression I know more than I know—I'll refer to an article I've only read briefly etc. And I don't like that. (12 SAC/F)

Our respondents also spoke with some disquiet about staff buying out their teaching, either with consultancy money or research grants, enabling them to prioritize research for promotion purposes:

> An academic's time is being privatized. If you can find money to do certain things you can buy your way out of certain responsibilities. The effect is that teaching often becomes relegated to people who have inappropriate or weak teaching experience. But this also allows people to do the important research that they want to get on with. However, you also begin to research what you think will attract more research money in the future, rather than doing the most interesting compelling research. (20 SAC/M)

> It is a very dangerous occurrence and trend. "Either you sacrifice your career or you sacrifice your teaching." Buying out teaching is the only incentive structure that has been offered. (14 JAC/F)

Sacrificing teaching for research was thus seen to be necessary if one wanted to get ahead:

> I think you do end up sacrificing the teaching for the research, that's if you want to get ahead as an academic in this place. (13 SAC/M)

> If you want to get ahead, you don't put much effort into your teaching, you do an adequate job, but no better. And you put your effort into something that you can quantify, because the other way to look at it is the credit you get for the things that you do really needs to be tradable, so you really need to get credit in something that other people can see. So if you want to get a job somewhere else, if you write on your application that you're a very good teacher, it carries almost no weight at all. (12 SAC/M)

> Teaching gets sacrificed if you want to get ahead. I think people put very little time into teaching. Those people who put a lot of time into their teaching don't get ahead. (5 JAC/F)

The result was a loss of quality, which directly affects students:

> I've seen students really struggling because their supervisor gives them so little time and then they go and get it from somewhere else. So you can get away with a whole minimal teaching and minimal supervision load. (13 JAC/F)

Although these and other responses talked about the privileging of research over teaching, research was not seen to be an unqualified winner. For many of our respondents, *research interests* were sacrificed too. Here, staff spoke about the lack of time for research, the pressure to do certain sorts of high-profile research, and the accent on quantity rather than quality:

> I know that what I also sacrifice in that time is my research time. I get things done because they've got to get done. I sacrifice the time to pursue research interests but also interests in other areas. (10 SAC/F)

> Sometimes you have to sacrifice the sort of particular type of research you'd like to do, because some kinds of research are valued more than others, like a teaching area versus a discipline based type of research or qualitative versus quantitative and those sorts of things. Sometimes you've got to sacrifice your own research program, your own further degrees to cope with the administrative load that tends to get off-loaded onto you. (7 JAC/F)

> You can just write one paper that puts it all in context and is a much more valuable article. But if you want to get ahead, you write the three or four, same ideas. (12 SAC/M)

Very closely related to this was the feeling that *free thinking* and *critical thought* were at risk:

Also there's free thinking time. I'm always project oriented. Occasionally at lunch we pursue certain ideas, but you know that is a luxury. You know that is different from what you are "supposed" to do. (3 JAC/M)

I think my intellectual ability to think for myself is sacrificed. I think when you work for one specific person, you gradually get to think like they do and you are no longer allowed to write in your normal fashion, you have to write the way they do and you are not allowed to use your own common sense. (13 GEN/F)

I think that some people in administration have to compromise their values. What they've compromised is their ability to think independently, or to think critically or to think for themselves. It's like the extent to which people get en-culturated—they come to believe the propaganda. They can't keep themselves separated and say, "yes we're playing this game for DEET [Department of Employment, Education and Training] or the sake of the University's relations with DEET, but we're definitely playing a game." They have to believe and they have to try and convince you to believe . . . that quality assurance is OK. (5 SAC/F)

As the last quote suggests, this undermining of critical thought was closely related to a situation in which staff compromised or kept silent about their *political values*. This, in its turn, was seen to produce a compliant culture. There were numerous responses on this score. Staff referred to "sacrificing integrity to get ahead" (8 S.GEN/F); "making sure you get on with the superiors at the senior level. And say the right things as well" (2 GEN/M); "being prepared to keep silent and not be at loggerheads" (5 GEN/F); and "sacrificing your own personal views" (6 S.GEN/F). It was this issue of sacrificing political dialogue that involved some of the most extended discussion among respondents, and especially among the general staff:

You constantly have to bite your tongue. Maybe it is freedom of speech. Maybe sometimes you see structures in place that are so obviously counter productive but they serve the particular people. It becomes very difficult to challenge or even suggest alternatives, so maybe that is what gets sacrificed. (3 GEN/M)

One thing I have noticed here is that you have to be very careful politically with what you say. You can't go to a meeting and just tell them what you think. We would go to meetings with the VC and I would say: "we've got to tell them this." "No, you can't tell them that, they won't want to know that." "But that is the truth." "No, no mate, you can't tell them that. You've got to be very careful with what you say." And that was impressed upon me all through the years to the stage that we would discuss things before we would go into a meeting because you had to be very careful about what you said. (7 S.GEN/M)

You are asked to make compromises, and often, and they are what I would call, just below a noticeable difference. They are little. And you think, "oh well, all right, ok, I don't really like it, but hey it's not a really big one," but you ignore the fact that these are cumulative really. And you suddenly wake up and after fifteen thousand compromises you are in a position that you would never have dreamt about. If somebody had said, "I want you to be in that position," you would have said, "Get lost. Never going there. That's completely against my whole value system." But by this creeping set of below-noticeable difference compromises, you have suddenly found that you are there. (15 S.GEN/F)

If you are prepared to compromise your values and your interests, then yes, you will get ahead. Obviously universities are under pressure to pass students or whatever and if you speak up against that, then obviously it doesn't go down very well. Everybody knows these things go on, but never want to admit them, yeah. (8 GEN/F)

There are values that are compromised as well, I am sure. You become part of the sycophantic culture in the school and make sure that you don't make too many waves, except little prima donna wavelets when somebody is looking at you, you know. (8 S.GEN/M)

Closely related to this, and underlying the angst which characterizes many of these responses, was the feeling that *collegiate values* were under threat:

It's the people that start getting very ruthless, get very selfish, that actually get ahead. They sacrifice that sense of camaraderie, the fulfillment of being a valued member of a team. This type of behavior affects the whole working environment because people begin to be suspicious of each other and become very cynical about sharing. So it sets off a whole chain reaction. (15 JAC/F)

You have to sacrifice those values that lie outside a narrow construction of self-interest and those which are not individualistic. All those areas of social and even those collegiate values are compromised by a structure which only rewards individual achievement. (8 SAC/M)

A Half Sacrifice? The Case of the Strategic Choice

Some academics and general staff at the smaller university (a total of 19 responses) felt that they could make strategic choices about whether to compromise or make sacrifices. (No one at the other university mentioned making strategic choices.) More academics (13) than general staff (6) said they were strategic about their choices, and these responses were fairly evenly divided between the sexes.

Most staff here talked about the way they rationalized their time and set priorities:

> You begin to research what you think will attract more research money in the future, rather than doing the most interesting and compelling research, which is a strategic compromise. (20 SAC/M)

> Well obviously you have got to make certain choices as to where you put your energies. You don't have to think of those as sacrifices, they are choices. If you want to spend a lot of time doing other things, like getting involved with your family, then you're not going to have that same time and energy to put into your work. If you want to be rewarded in your job you have to be prepared and able to commit a lot of time. (19 SAC/M)

> The sacrifices I have made have been ones I've been willing to compromise, like research, because I wanted to give more to other priorities. (11 JAC/M)

There were also two specific examples of staff choosing to move away from feminist research to *safer* disciplines or research topics which would allow their work to be more readily acknowledged within the university. These responses point to the struggle certain disciplines have to enter in order to gain status within the academy. The staff concerned talked about making "a sort of compromise to gain some strategic advantage" (2 SAC/F) and the realization that it was better to "play down the feminist work" within Australia (4 SAC/F).

Refusing to Sacrifice

> I refuse. I would have to sacrifice my family and I refuse to do that, and sacrifice my beliefs, my values and I refuse. I've said that there's no way I'm going to sacrifice myself to get any higher. I know I can, I've been told, but I'm not going to, I refuse to. That's my principles and I'm happy where I am. (16 S.GEN/F)

> In the business school they have all just hopped into uniforms and I refuse to have a uniform. How stupid. I'd join the army if I wanted a uniform. But I am frowned upon as a rugged individualist! (8 S.GEN/M)

We turn finally to the distinct group of staff (a total of 22 responses) who said they refused to make sacrifices. These staff members acknowledged that this could mean that they would not get ahead as a consequence. The *resisters* were fairly evenly divided between the two universities, between general and academic staff, and males and females.

There were two consistent themes among these resistant responses. First, there was a refusal from the staff to devote the time demanded of them:

> I won't put in 60-70 hours a week into [my university]. I did that for a time and all I got was a kick in the teeth. I don't take work home. I mean, it would be absolutely rare. And that is largely due to bad experience. (4 S.GEN/M)

> Yes, I just made it clear that I wasn't willing to make that sort of sacrifice. If they want that kind of sacrifice made, they should describe the job in that way. If you, you know, want to know what your family looks like . . . (9 S.GEN/M)

> I have for various reasons decided not to compromise my time for work activities. I feel that I needed a balance in my life. I have decided to work between 8 in the morning and 6 at night and still retain another life outside of those hours. (13 SAC/F)

Second, there was a determination to maintain their own values:

> I loathe hypocrisy. Integrity is very important to me. I haven't got ahead, but I have a better reputation and more credibility because of my integrity. (1 S.GEN/M)

> A lot of people hang in there but I just made the decision then, I am not going to give my values away. That's the thing. I am not going to compromise my values. I probably won't get very far as an academic. (16 JAC/F)

> I have seen people being pushed to the point where something makes them draw a line. But you are conscious if you draw a line, and I have. There are some things that maybe you are going to lose out on because you refuse to go to a meeting after a certain time, or you just can't deliver on a particular project. It is a calculated decision but you are conscious that if you did just roll over and go along with it, then things would probably work out better for you, be more comfortable for you. It may flow over from the academic culture where there is this blurring between what's work time and what's home time and it flows into the general staff culture as well. (3 S.GEN/F)

We conclude with one academic who suggested that resistance to some of the trends discussed here could be increasing:

> I think one of the good things about Humanities is there is a kind of well articulated resistance in the school to some of the worst business-friendly and entrepreneurial tendencies in administration. There has been some pretty well organized resistance and that's really coming from the top, from the senior blokes who don't like it very much. (17 JAC/F)

From Sacrifice to Success?

The overall picture of these two universities is disquieting. They resemble the greedy institutions Coser says are omnivorous of their loyal workers. The over-whelming picture is of staff working long hours, being away from their family and abandoning community interests. The extent of the staff's sense of sacrifice was very clear, and it was predominantly about sacrifices for the job itself, rather than for career advancement.

There was, though, in the responses to our question on "what sacrifices staff made to get ahead," a twist to our research expectations. We had set out to in-quire into the *differences* between institutions, between men and women, and between academic and general staff. What emerged was more to do with *equivalence*. The differences between the two institutions were not great, either quantitatively or qualitatively.[3] The same voices, the same concerns, echoed across campuses. And although slightly more females than males and slightly more academic than general staff talked of the sacrifices they made, the differ-ences were not great between the sexes and some were surprisingly reversed (for example, when more academic men than women complained about sacrificing family to the job).

We could explain this by reference to the power and invisibility of the nor-malization process: that academics, both men and women, expect to be com-mitted to their profession and thus to sacrifice personal life and family to some extent; that what is being complained about is the intensification of the degree and extent of sacrifice which has impacted on men as well as women; or that women, taking up a profession that is in both a generalized and specific way shaped by a normalized masculine culture, expect the sacrifice to be heavy and to be worth it. We cannot say for certain, but the shared and generally equivalent account of sacrifices provided by our respondents begs further analysis.

At the most concrete level, we can ask whether women and men are simi-larly placed in relation to these intensified organizational demands. Are women and men equally able to devote extremely long hours to their paid work? Given the cultural and social expectations about women's domestic responsibilities, does the *work all hours* ethos have the same meaning for women and men?

A recent study of 3872 academic and general staff in Australia found that 50 percent of women academics were the main carers for their children com-pared with 4.3 percent of men. Despite this difference in domestic responsibili-ties, the research found that women valued their careers no less than men do and were equally committed to research. In essence, the findings of the study suggest that universities provide a good academic job for women if they want to behave like men, but that most women do not want to behave like men (Probert, Ewer, and Whiting 1998).

As well as these material factors, we can question the actual terms of neo-liberal economic reforms. As we have shown in previous chapters, embedded within these reforms is a masculinist discourse and, further, a peak masculinist discourse (one that operates from the top of the organization). It operates to normalize high workloads and a prime commitment to the institution. Such things are what a *good* university staff member, desirous of promotion, does. It's simply part of the game, part of reality; it's the way the world is. Dame Leonie Kramer drew on this kind of reasoning when she attempted to explain why so few women reach senior management positions in Australian universities. She claimed that "women go limp" when "the going gets tough" (Powell 1995b: 1). Eveline analyses this assertion with its evident sexual metaphor, suggesting that

> The cultural lack of desire story situates women as lacking in mental and cultural affinity for the work. Striking in their very ordinariness, the codes of normality forming this story are nonetheless difficult to break: senior personnel must be "highly committed," "single-minded," and prepared to contribute "more than a forty hour week"; general agreement that "it's a *hard* job," often used in selection panels, was tantamount to saying that "we want a man for this job," . . . while to be a successful academic "you have to be selfish and arrogant" to complete research. (Eveline 1996: 72)

Neoliberal economic reforms produce particular patterns of inclusion and exclusion. As part of this process, these reforms hide the political and social choices that shape organizational culture, render the process invisible, and make it almost impossible to consider other alternatives. These reforms accentuate the private/public divide and undermine any movement toward the greater participation of males in families even when, as we have seen, they complain about the extent to which the intensification of work has further encroached upon their limited family life. A neoliberal economic agenda rules against collegiality and mutuality and against the hope that care for workers can be coupled with productivity and creativity. In all these ways, it runs directly counter to socialist and feminist agendas. It also disenfranchises all those, men and women, who subscribe to even a modicum of these aspirations. In this context, it may not be surprising that the gendered responses to our question of how fair the systems of rewards were reaped greater gender differences than did the question of sacrifices—it may not be that women see themselves to be sacrificing more, but that they see the system as rewarding them less for the sacrifices they make. Indeed, the merit system, as we saw in chapter 4, may have already discounted the sacrifices women make, and in a double move, it made women less meritorious because of the expectation that they *must* manage the competing demands of the two greedy institutions—home and the university.

The Attributes of Success: The General Picture

In two successive questions, we tested our respondents' views of how fair or unfair they thought the system of rewards and opportunities to be. In phrasing the questions, we were, first, mindful that different sections of the university community have very different opportunities for, and systems of, advancement. The general staff working within Australian universities have nothing to match the stepped career trajectory (from a base-level tutor through to a professor) of academics. For general staff there may be a much shorter, or no, career ladder. In addition, advancement may be through appointment, rather than promotion or reclassification, as happens when academic staff shift across into senior university management roles. Second, however, we wanted to capture a broader notion of success and career advancement than that defined by promotion or reclassification systems. There are informal, less material ways in which an individual might be successful (for example, having influence) and rewarded (through recognition, respect, or expanded opportunities). Thus we asked: "Who gets rewarded in this university? What characteristics do such people have?" "What are the characteristics of those who don't get ahead?"

Having done so, however, it is problematic to conflate or compare the responses of academic and general staff because the organizational structures and expectations governing the two groups can be so different. For that reason, the discussion of gender differences in perceived attributes of success which follows takes the academic staff as a case study. The attitudes of academic staff to attributes of success are in marked contrast to those of management. The views of managers (a good proportion of whom had had academic careers before shifting to university administration) have already been discussed in chapter 6, but we include the managers' data in the tables below to make the comparison explicit.

In responding to our questions, academic staff revealed how fair they felt the system to be. The characteristics they ascribed to those who got ahead and those who failed to make it were almost invariably *evaluative* in nature. That is, they incorporated an assessment of whether the attributes of success and failure deserved the institutional response they received. To say, for example, that the successful are "dedicated researchers" while the unsuccessful are "cruisers" suggests that the system is reasonable, handing out its rewards justly. Conversely, to describe the successful as "single-minded writing machines," while those left behind are "all-rounders who care for their students," implies that the system is flawed and unfair. As these examples suggest, evaluative statements were systematically linked across both sets of our questions. Positive comments about those who succeeded were paired with negative descriptions of the unsuccessful. Equally, negative descriptions of the successful had their correlates in positive assessments of the unsuccessful.

The overall picture is shown in table 7.2 where we divided the responses we received to the two questions into two groups: those indicating satisfaction (the system is reasonable) and those expressing disquiet (the system is flawed).

The data in table 7.2 provide an approximate index of disaffection. (Levels of disaffection are positively associated with a higher ratio of responses in the *system is flawed* to the *system is reasonable* section of the table.) In this context, we draw attention to the following points:

- For our respondents as a whole, the responses indicating disaffection (209) were 1.5 times greater than those expressing satisfaction (131). It should be noted, however, that the composite figure obscures the fact that levels of disaffection were much greater at the smaller university. In the smaller institution, the dissatisfied responses were double the satisfied ones, whereas in the larger institution, satisfaction and dissatisfaction were expressed in roughly equal measure.
- Disaffection was highest among female academics. In their case, disaffected responses (110) outweighed satisfied responses (31) by a ratio of 3.5:1.
- For male academics, disaffected responses (77) outweighed satisfied responses (46) by a ratio of approximately 1.7:1.
- Managers' responses to these questions reversed the picture. In their case, satisfied responses (54) outweighed disaffected responses (22) by a ratio of almost 2.5:1.
- These results were fairly consistent between the two questions, although male academics and senior managers tended to harden their respective views as they shifted from discussing those who got ahead to those who did not. That is, as the percentage figures for each cohort within each question in table 7.2 show, academic men were more likely (and senior management less likely) to present the system as flawed as they considered those who did not get ahead.

Before proceeding, two points need to be made. First, *responses* and *respondents* are approximately, but not precisely, equivalent.[4] Second, and perhaps more importantly, within each broad category (*satisfied* and *disaffected*), responses show different views and political rationalities. As we described previously, the recent changes to university education have had variable effects on the staff, impacting differently on contract tutors, tenured academics, and managers. The diametrically opposed perceptions of academics and managers evident in table 7.2 provide a very stark example of this diversity of viewpoint. These differences are played out in the responses we received, within, as well as between, the satisfied/disaffected distinctions.

Table 7.2 Perceptions of Fairness (by gender and position) Percentages and (numbers)*

	For those who get ahead			For those who do not get ahead			Total
	FA (52)	MA (47)	SM (25)	FA (52)	MA (47)	SM (25)	
The system is reasonable	22.6 (17)	40.3 (27)	65.9 (27)	21.2 (14)	33.9 (19)	77.1 (27)	(131)
The system is flawed	77.3 (58)	59.7 (40)	34.1 (14)	78.8 (52)	66.1 (37)	22.9 (8)	(209)
Total Percentages	100	100	100	100	100	100	

Notes: FA = female academic; MA = male academic; SM = senior management (only 5 of the 25 were female).
The numbers in parentheses at the top of the table refer to the total number in each group who were interviewed.
* In addition to the results tabulated here, there were five noncommittal responses from respondents at one of the two universities: three academic men said that getting ahead in their university was simply a matter of luck, and two academic women from the same institution raised the issue of incompetent staff being moved sideways or promoted to "get them out of the way where they could do least damage." This was not presented as evidence of the fairness or unfairness of the system, but rather an acknowledgement of the difficulties of removing staff who were not good at some aspect of their work.

Satisfied Responses: "The System Is Reasonable"

The sense that the system is reasonable incorporated the belief that institutional discrimination was absent. A male dean commented:

> In my view we have a pretty meritocratic system where people are by and large promoted on the basis of ability and I don't see any kind of gender bias here. Maybe I'm blind, but in my view people are promoted on merit. (15 MAN/M)

Some acknowledged that things might be imperfect, but maintained that matters were improving:

> There has been a fair change in recent times in the way in which the promotion system works. In the olden days it was totally geared towards research and, of course, research is a very important component of the university. But I think the university has taken steps in the right direction to try and redress the balance of the system. (6 SAC/M)

With this text as a backdrop to discussions of success as seen through the promotion system, most respondents knew that research was the preeminent way to succeed in terms of academic promotion and, thus, they concentrated on the attributes of individuals in terms of gaining advancement in the organization.

We have already noted the obvious preoccupation of managers with attributes of organizational success (they provided 59 percent of the responses in this category while they represented only 20 percent of our sample). As discussed in chapter 6, among the managers success was interpreted as obtaining positions of power within what was seen to be a neutral and beneficent university system. Above all else, this was seen to hinge on possessing a "university-wide perspective." It was argued that staff promoted to senior administrative positions had to rise above the sectional interests of their own schools or research portfolios. In sharp contrast, academics tended to think about success in terms of "the good academic." Male academics were far more inclined to provide accounts of academic success that suggested that the system was fair and reasonable than were female academics. Nearly two-thirds of all academic respondents in this category came from men.

Table 7.3 Perceived Attributes of Success (by gender and position)

		The System Is Reasonable Numbers					
	FA (52)	MA (47)	SM (25)		FA (52)	MA (47)	SM (25)
Those who get ahead are:				**Those who do not get ahead are:**			
Good academics	11	21	10	**Poor academics**	7	14	9
Good at research; able to obtain grants; hard and productive workers.				Lacking in ability in teaching and research; lazy; the cruisers and trudgers; apathetic about administration; do not project themselves, and/or are content/disinclined to pursue a career.			
Good organizational members	6	6	17	**Poor organizational members**	7	5	18
Well liked, charismatic people; those with a university-wide view and ability; highly committed to their jobs; willing and responsive; good planners; they are fairly rewarded by the system.				Unable to get on with others; uncomfortable with university goals; prone to speaking out of turn; politically naïve; inflexible and narrow; poor strategists; refuse to do administration; do not develop themselves professionally.			
Totals	17	27	27	**Totals**	14	19	27

Notes: FA = female academic; MA = male academic; SM = senior management (only 5 of the 25 were female). The numbers in parentheses at the top of each column refer to the total number in each group who were interviewed.

The keys to academic success were said to be research output, hard work, and productivity, while the main characteristics of managerial prowess were identified as the capacity to get on with others and having a university-wide perspective. Those who failed to advance academically were perceived to be unproductive and lacking in motivation; those unable to rise to positions of managerial influence were perceived to have difficulty in getting on with others, to be poor strategists, and narrow in outlook. Table 7.3 provides the details.

The Attributes of Academic Success
Discussions about the qualities needed to be a successful academic were centered on research. To be a good researcher not only involved "original research," but also "getting big research grants." Productivity and hard work were the keys:

> Productivity is the big word that hits me in the face. (18 JAC/F)

> Well, the people who [get ahead] have actually performed if you like, the people who are active in their various teaching/research and administrative tasks. (5 SAC/M)

Conversely, people who fail to get ahead were said to be those who

> Lack publications. They may accomplish a lot of research, but not write it up. (19 JAC/F)

Respondents made various distinctions between those who failed to get ahead, and these are represented below in the words of two senior academics and two deans. At the very bottom of the heap were those who simply put in no effort at all: the cruisers and the drudgers.

> There are also some people who are prepared just to cruise, just achieve what they have to, and that's it. (14 SAC/F)

> Laziness. By that I mean that they really take advantage of the system for some reason. They are not big on research, but it's a question of what they are big on. And sometimes you have to look pretty hard. (16 MAN/M)

There was also a larger category of staff who failed to progress, not so much because they were lazy, but because they were disinclined to put in the long hours needed to pursue a successful career. They were basically said to be content with their lot. Such people, it was reasoned, might be competent academics, perfectly within their rights. But they couldn't expect to gain the rewards, which would, and should, accrue to staff who did put in the required effort. They were represented by those who

> maintain a certain casualized structure to their lives. They don't ever prepare a paper, or sit on a committee, or do any homework. So they don't do any of the extra work. They do their basic 40 hours a week. There may be some very good

reasons why they don't do that. But they can't expect to compete with those people who are putting in that much more. (19 SAC/M)

There are some, I think, who take a conscious decision that they are not interested in promotion . . . they are decent colleagues, they are decent teachers, they do some research from time to time, and generally speaking they don't strike me, anyway, as wanting to go to a higher level. They don't want to work that hard. I'm not sure that laziness is quite the right word for it, because they do the minimum of what is expected of them and they do it decently. (17 MAN/M)

These responses echo the comments some staff members made in response to the question on why there were so few senior women and, again, emphasize how merit is derived from effort and spoken of in ways which obscure the deeply gendered context of such a connection. It is with no surprise that, as we turn from the satisfied to the dissatisfied, women's voices begin to be heard.

Disaffected Responses: "The System Is Flawed"

Responses in the disaffected group were 50 percent greater than those in the satisfied category. Female academics predominated, accounting for 53 percent of disaffected replies (as against 24 percent of satisfied responses). In contrast, male academics exhibited a more even profile providing 37 percent of disaffected and 35 percent of satisfied responses. (And in an even sharper contrast, management provided just over 10 percent of disaffected responses in comparison with their 41 percent share of all satisfied responses.)

Disaffected responses were of three kinds. The first concentrated on the relationship between academic success and individual attributes. The second focused on organizational issues, particularly patterns of institutional tradition and privilege. The third identified various forms of direct and indirect discrimination.

Table 7.4 shows that the responses of female academics predominated in *(a)* critiques of the successful careerist (57 percent of responses) and *(b)* identifying patterns of discrimination (52 percent of responses). It also indicates that male academics joined their female colleagues in equal, or almost equal, numbers in *(a)* characterizing those who do not get ahead as the "nice people" and *(b)* challenging the characteristics of the peak culture. On both these issues, the proportion of academic males speaking out outweighed the proportion of females.

Table 7.4 Perceived Attributes of Success (by gender and position)

			The System Is Flawed Numbers			
	FA (52)	MA (47)	SM (25)		FA (52)	MA (47)	SM (25)
Those who get ahead are:				**Those who do not get ahead are:**			
Careerist	23	12	5	**Balanced**	21	17	1
Selfish and single-minded; ruthless and aggressive; self-promoters; those who get grants and farm out teaching; high fliers.				Unselfish, all-rounders; those who put more effort into teaching than research; people who have a life outside the university; modest people who do not blow their own trumpet; nice people who are not entrepreneurs.			
Fit the peak culture	23	22	5	**Cross the peak culture**	7	6	1
Members of the in-group; people in the know; those who work the system, who are visible; people who are part of the establishment; corporate economic rationalists; middle-aged men.				Those who do not fit the organization and do not toe the company line; people who have high values not shared by management; people who challenge things; those who have crossed the wrong person.			
Favored by the system	12	6	4	**Subject to discrimination**	22	14	6
Served by the old boys' network; those who have important patrons or who symbolize the favored classes, e.g., Aborigines and women.				People in dead-end jobs; those without Ph.D.'s; women; junior women; feminists; those with the wrong research records; staff in the Arts Schools; good staff in declining disciplines.			
				Not encouraged to do so	2	0	0
				Senior management fails to encourage staff to apply for promotion; lack of support for career development.			
Totals	58	40	14	**Totals**	52	37	8

Notes: FA = female academic; MA = male academic; SM = senior management (only 5 of the 25 were female). The numbers in parentheses at the top of each column refer to the total number in each group who were interviewed.

The Attributes of Academic Success

Disaffected responses portrayed the successful in strongly antagonistic and individualistic terms. The winners were said to be preoccupied with projecting their image in the right places. They are "very aggressive in promoting themselves" and intent on "positioning themselves right," "saying the sorts of things the administration wants to hear." The notion of "strategic sense," so important in the satisfied responses, was recast as simple self-aggrandizement.

In a similar fashion, productive hard workers were transformed into "single-minded writing machines" who cared only about their own careers. The successful are

> often very selfish people who devote themselves to their research at the cost of their colleagues who take on the administrative roles that they courteously, or otherwise invisibly, or otherwise incompetently manage to avoid. (2 MAN/F)

> I feel that the people who make it here are very single-mindedly career-oriented people. . . . The ones I consider career achievers are determined, aggressive and pretty hard working. (4 JAC/M)

Unlike many of the respondents in the satisfied group, these staff believed that the effort put into teaching remained largely unrecognized. Some argued that it had a shockingly low priority at this institution. Others maintained that while lip service was paid to it, being a good teacher was not the way you get ahead. Accordingly, the successful were those who farmed out their teaching:

> People who get rewarded are those who have a good research and publication record and can afford to buy themselves out of teaching and have other people, like me, do those jobs for them. (20 JAC/F)

> My real answer to this question is that it is the ruthless workaholics who are sort of willing to be completely non-collegial and reduce their teaching loads as much as possible and to teach in areas which directly feed into their areas of research. As far as kinds of people, it is people who are willing to walk over people who receive greatest advancement. This type of behavior is related to increased research output which, in the long run, gets people ahead. (8 JAC/F)

In contrast, the unsuccessful were represented as balanced, unselfish people who put more effort into teaching or servicing others than research. In this vein, a female academic commented that

> There is a group of people in this school who don't get ahead. And the reason they don't get ahead is because they are servicing the school and not themselves. They do services of immeasurable benefit for the school. They don't get rewarded because they don't have publications, . . . they don't do things that are highly visible. (1 SAC/F)

In parallel, a dean argued that

> There is also a group of individuals who are extremely idealistic and extremely hard working and are quite scholarly but who don't put their single minded energy into their personal research, which you have to in order to get on. They are

people whose arms you can twist to take on administrative jobs because they accept that it is for the good of the school or the good of the university. (18 MAN/M)

The Organizational Attributes of Success

Respondents thought that particular kinds of people were likely to rise to positions of influence. These people fitted "a certain kind of masculine culture." They belonged to the establishment in both dress and outlook.

> The people I see rewarded are the ones who wear crisp white shirts, classy ties, suits, who often come to this university from fairly senior positions and with well established networks in their profession, knowing how to speak the "managerial language" and all of them move on to a full professorship or vice-chancellorship. (10 JAC/M)

> They are people who don't rock the boat at all. I think they are extremely conservative in their orientation of what a good thing is to do and they exhibit a certain deference pattern where they are always trying to find out what it is that, say, the VC wants. (2 SAC/F)

In line with this, respondents talked about the penalties of speaking out and the ways in which the institution silenced opposition.

> The ones who don't get ahead and don't get the positions of authority are the ones who have spoken out against certain issues. For example, there was a colleague who . . . got into total opposition to the VC and he was snubbed. An absolute different kind of marginalized individual is another colleague who was a bit of a maverick, speaking up, in an alternative style—that kind of image has followed him for years. And there are other colleagues who have been associated with Women's Studies and it was seen to be too radical. If you speak up and you do things directly in opposition, or that are seen to be threatening, you don't get ahead. (2 SAC/F)

> I think there is a really "sinister" feel to much of university work. I begin to think of this notion of a "company person" . . . with the drive towards this "company person," you increasingly narrow the limits of the kinds of criticism which have been the hallmark of university work. (12 JAC/M)

Institutional Discrimination

A large number of responses (42) discussed institutional discrimination. Women made up more than half of the responses (22 or 52 percent). Twenty centered on hierarchy, six on academic and/or research specialization, and sixteen on gender and/or family commitments. We take hierarchy first:

> Getting grants will make you successful, some of my colleagues have told me. The tricky bit when you are way down the system is being given the time to sit and think about doing this. (2 JAC/M)

Discussions around research or academic specialization suggested that certain institutional practices meant that some areas were systematically favored over others:

> There is a "scientific model" in place at the university which is used to monitor who advances and who does not. By the very nature of scientific research (conducive to team work and getting more publications), this helps those in the sciences. (18 SAC/M)

> Research must be published in the four brownie point journals, irrespective of how excellent your research is. (15 SAC/M)

Responses concerning discrimination on the grounds of gender covered mobility and family commitments, the position of junior women, hostility to women undertaking feminist research, and the continuation of entrenched patterns of behavior. We end this part of the chapter with a selection of these comments from several junior academic women and a male dean:

> If you stay in one place, you get ahead. I lose at least a year every time I move. People don't get ahead if they have babies, travel and work in different places. (21 JAC/F)

> We have had a number of women leave this school. They have all been really bright women who have gone elsewhere to get promotion and they've explained [to me] that there's no interest in feminism, no recognition of it as important theoretically, and so if you're in that field you don't get recognition. (17 JAC/F)

> Women are also limited by throwaway comments. People who have a certain view of the world, that make throwaway comments that put females down. . . . I certainly remember such comments on the promotions committee, and I've heard them from time to time on other committees, whether they be selection committees or others. They tend to be, you know, just put down jokes. (6 MAN/M)

Conclusion: The Basic Processes of the Organization

There is no doubt that to be a successful academic you have to be highly committed to your work. However, as this chapter shows, both men and women are working above and beyond the call of duty; they are sacrificing their families, their friends, and their health. Universities in contemporary Australia have fallen under the sway of neoliberal restructuring, which means that they are being reduced to a core of permanent, tenured staff and many part time and short term contract staff. This puts increased pressure on that core of tenured staff and impoverishes the working conditions of part time staff. People working in universities are becoming alienated from their institutions because of unrealistic workloads and an increasingly competitive environment. This is especially so for those who do not want to compromise their values or *play the game*. One has to wonder if these are the kinds of working environments that are conducive to creativity or in which most people would want to participate. And one has to hope that the intensified pressure on all workers might inspire a social movement toward healthier working environments that will achieve something feminists have long argued for and that will allow both men and women the chance to have lives outside their work.

It is clear from this chapter that gender constructs patterns of academic and managerial success. At the same time, the dynamic works the other way around—these patterns of success construct gender. Recent changes to university education—the intensification of labor, the accent on productivity and output, managerialism, and the instrumentalities of economic rationality—have different implications for men and women. But it is also true that these processes cross gender boundaries and cannot be reduced to them.

For almost all women, a choice, or at least some kind of trade-off, needs to be made between female consciousness and success. Conversely, for men, masculinity and patterns of university prowess may be more closely allied. But the fact that disaffected males outweighed the satisfied and that men were more outspoken than women in their condemnation of the establishment shows that exclusionary forces cannot be neatly arranged along gender lines. The economic rationale behind the current changes to university education means that many males—particularly those who, for whatever reason, are unwilling to play the publication or managerial stakes—will get left behind. Only a few men can, by definition, belong to the peak culture. And as Connell (1994: 5) argues, the very term *hegemonic masculinity* means precisely that "there are also subordinated masculinities, marginalized masculinities . . . and complicit masculinities." We argue, then, that the patterns of success described here reflect, above all, the aspirations and consciousness of a managerial elite. The members of this elite form their own culture separate, and sometimes actively distanced from the organizational rank and file male or female.[5]

This chapter illustrates how university life is organized around particular notions of success. Despite their different evaluations of the situation, our respondents commonly argued that success is defined in terms of productivity and that the product is, above all, the *paper*. The processes by which this output is rendered possible—through keeping the institution running and teaching the current and future generation of researchers—are rendered invisible. In a profoundly gendered fashion, production is privileged over reproduction; output over process. Simultaneously, these definitions of excellence promote particular patterns of gendered behavior. Glimpses of these have been provided here. The gendered patterns of disaffection underwrite the apparently gender free account of common sacrifices. So while there are the successful academics devoted to producing more research and undertaking less infrastructure—maintenance and teaching—work, men are the more satisfied of these. And while there are large groups of disaffected staff, both male and female, who question the values of the institution but keep working at it anyway, women are the greater number.

Notes

1. In recent union meetings at one of the universities that participated in this study, there was discussion about limiting the amount of time academics worked to 45 hours. The motion was defeated because most people in the room felt they would not achieve their personal goals or the demands placed on them by the institution if they did this.

2. The differences between the two universities were not consistent or appreciable, but the larger institution had a higher proportion of its total responses indicating that sacrifices were made than did the smaller, more traditionally collegial institution (79 percent of the responses at the larger university in comparison with 67 percent of the responses at the smaller university). This difference was almost entirely accounted for by the higher proportion of responses indicating strategic choices or resistance at the smaller university (22 percent of responses) compared with the larger university (8 percent of responses).

3. In explaining this, we suggest that the impact of neoliberal reforms and the global trends to reduce public funding leading to restructuring of public institutions minimizes the historical differences between universities, wiping out traditional affiliations in the name of the market. Furthermore, the imperatives it utters, its obsession with calculation, and its normative expectations concerning productivity are, in one sense, gender-blind. Everyone's work is to be calculated in market terms. The story, however, cannot rest there. Having acknowledged that neoliberal reforms treat men and women similarly in demanding both particular kinds of work and a particular orientation to work, we still need to inquire into the gendered implications of current practices.

4. On some occasions, respondents returned to the same theme in a different way at a later point in the interview. If he or she was not merely persisting with the original line of thought, two responses (in relation to the same general theme) were registered against the respondent. Nor does the distinction between *satisfied* and *disaffected* responses directly transfer to *satisfied* and *disaffected* respondents because a small number of the staff provided responses that carried across both categories.

5. This separation produces, and is reproduced in, the previously quoted management view that the main body of academic staff are "spectators" and "whistle-blowers" outside main university business (10 MAN/M). (See note 3 above.)

Conclusion

A Critical and Conserving Agenda for Universities

Introduction

We referred to Richard Sennett's book, *The Corrosion of Character*, in our introduction. He describes the new capitalism, flexible capitalism, which changes the nature of work and the idea of a career. In this new capitalism, he suggests, workers have to be willing to take risks and to move from job to job. He argues that the disadvantages are no security, no anchoring into a workplace, and no loyalty to the employer or the company. Sennet (1998: 137) ends his book with grave concerns about the survival of community and asks the question: "What value is the corporation to the community, how does it serve civic interests rather than just its own ledger of profit and loss?" That is the kind of question we want to conclude with in this book: What value is the university to the community and how does it serve public interests rather than just its own survival as a commercial enterprise?

In addition, we ask: "How can the university best serve the workers who inhabit the institutions? How can their quality of working life be more satisfying?" We approached this topic about gendered universities in globalized economies from a feminist perspective, critiquing the masculinist culture that pervades universities across the world. We also began with a critique of corporate globalization and its impact on pubic sector institutions, including universities. In this last chapter, we want to offer what we believe is a way forward, despite our pessimism about the way global practices are changing our workplaces. We want to see how we can grasp the tools of globalization and use them for more constructive ends.

What sorts of values might a university cherish and try to perpetuate in the community? How should it operate as an organization? Sennett writes about the importance of trust and a sense of commitment to one's place of work. He believes that the lack of mutual trust and commitment erodes the social bonds that are necessary for the workings of any collective enterprise such as a university. It is his, and our, insistence that while current circumstances may have left the notion of a community of scholars behind, universities need to bring scholars together in the pursuit and delivery of knowledge.

In this final chapter, we start by linking some of our findings from the Australian case studies to the wider literature. We then discuss the barriers to, and possibilities of, change. We end by outlining our own agenda for change. These ideas are offered in light of our awareness that each university has to develop its own agenda. Each university has its political history, its geographical context, its gender mix, and its cultural background. However, there are times when we can learn from each other, and we hope that this book and its suggestions may benefit others seeking to make universities more equitable, supportive, and thus pleasant places to work.

The Australian Case Studies and the Wider Literature

The Male Norm and Masculinist Culture

In chapter 4, we described how male practices operate as the *norm*, both in the sense that they form the pivot around which expectations and evaluations revolve, and in that they are seen to be ordinary, normal, and taken for granted and, in this sense, invisible. Because the normalization of male culture is embedded in the structures, everyday practices, and consciousness of staff, it is often hard to reveal or bring to consciousness. Quite often the people we interviewed, even when committed to some form of gender equality, spoke of the disadvantages of women, but failed to see men as advantaged by the core processes of the institution. In this way, explanations direct attention away from men and their advantages within a male culture.

It was the responses of senior managers that most clearly revealed the characteristics of the male culture—and, more specifically, the peak male culture. We drew particular attention to this in chapter 6. The qualities that came to the fore revolved around performance, competition, conformity to the corporate mission, and *delivering outputs*. What they did *not* talk about were processes, cooperation, social critique, and care for others. It was also notable that when asked directly about why women were underrepresented in senior positions, most male managers either denied that this was so or fell back on socio-biological or historical explanations.

Perhaps there are no surprises here. After all, and as we acknowledged in chapter 2, have universities not *always* been designed primarily for men by men? Has the scholar not always been coded male? The answer is yes. However, we also noted that there have been important changes in the *type* of male norm that is operating and in the *kind* of masculinity at play. We suggest that there has been a move from a traditional form of patriarchy, redolent of the establishment club, to a new form of entrepreneurial patriarchy with all the trappings of the corporate boardroom. The point is that both settings are uncomfortable places for women, but uncomfortable in different ways. Part of the aim of this book has been to reveal the particular discomforts arising out of the new forms of entrepreneurial patriarchy. On this, the women in our study talked about the loss of collegiality; the erosion of leisure and community contacts; the threat to children, partners, and friendships as time collapsed around them; and the pressure to undertake profitable research far removed from their own interests.

Although much has been written on the changes to university culture (see chapters 1 and 2 for reference to this literature), there is comparatively little that conceptualizes these changes in terms of male culture. Attention, rather, has been directed to the impact of globalization and neoliberal reforms per se. There are, though, some exceptions. Useful insights can also be found in studies of shifts in corporate culture outside universities. We start with these.

In his extensive study of the changes in the British civil service over the last century, Hearn (1999) recognizes the power of men to set the ideological agenda, suggesting that "managers and men managers do not just organize the organizational, technical and personnel matters in their charge; significantly, they set and create the ideological scene, although of course not without resistance" (Hearn 1999: 125). The masculine characteristics of prevailing forms of management are well described by Kerfoot (1999). She describes the new managerialism as intensely goal-driven, subjected to a yardstick, and suggests that males are more drawn to this type of management. To succeed as managers, individuals, whether male or female, have to become more masculine. In sum, Kerfoot (1999: 189) observes that "for many managers, 'being a manager' and 'being masculine' are near synonymous."

In line with this, Ozga and Walker (1999: 107) suggest that the new managerialism reflects a particular formation of masculinity that is "competitive, ritualistic, unreflexive and false." Coming alongside, Surowiecki (2001: 46) describes the new American CEOs as "the Green Berets of corporate management," the "swaggering outsider who rides into town to clean up the mess" that a previous CEO left behind. They exude a "CEO hubris" that allows them to take charge and make decisions that Surowiecki (2001: 46) suggests are not necessarily in the company's best interest.

In our research, the views from the top and from the bottom suggest a deepening gulf between the corporate managers in universities and the workers they manage. We used the term *peak culture* to describe the values and practices of senior managers. From our findings, we conclude that the term is even more appropriate than we originally envisioned. The attention of senior managers is focused on what they see as the bigger picture. They are generally less attentive to the well-being and health of what lies beneath them, often irritated by the rumblings that come from the academic and general staff. Because of the political and financial pressures driving greater corporatization, university managers, willingly or otherwise, have discarded many traditional educational values. Many of those we interviewed thought there was a growing mismatch between a good education and the product of the client-oriented rhetoric of the corporation, much of which is concerned with commercial promotion. Below the peak, the pressures are intensifying as staff do more and more, with less and less.

Another study bearing directly on our arguments has been undertaken by Martin and Meyerson (1998). Drawing on the work of Connell (1995) and Foucault (1979), these authors explored the way in which organizations define men and masculinity as the standard by which normality is defined. Analyzing the experience of high-ranking women in a technology company where technical expertise is rewarded (somewhat similar to universities that reward knowledge and scholarship), they observed that power relations between the sexes in this context were reinforced by a myriad of micro-processes.

> Gender inequality was seen as the product of a series of institutionalized practices, including the placing of allegedly unqualified group members in desirable jobs as a reward for loyalty; the need for forceful, brutally honest, even semiviolent argumentation in meetings; and the allocation of challenging work to those who promoted themselves most actively. These ostensibly gender-neutral practices were gendered. Conformity to these norms was generally more problematic for women, in part because many men and some women, . . . disapproved when women engaged in the stereotypically male behaviors, such as aggression and competition, that were expected in this context. (Martin and Meyerson 1998: 339)

It is these very behaviors, aggression and competitiveness that are the language of success in today's corporate universities. Such factors, as we suggested in chapter 2, help to explain why there are so few women in senior positions in universities. The top is simply not a comfortable place for them to be. In Sondheimer's terms, "Professorial chairs apparently, were designed to accommodate only masculine frames" (cited in Meehan 1999: 36).

A number of recent studies reveal how women experience these cultural patterns and the exclusionary processes that accompany them. In Spurling's (1997) research into women in senior posts in British universities, participants variously described the new managerialism as "academic machismo" (in traditional universities) and "machismo of the business culture" (in new universities) (Spurling 1997: 44). They depicted the cultural barrier as "not so much banging your head against a glass ceiling as grappling with a smoke screen" (Spurling 1997: 45), aptly describing the confusing and subtle messages that are often given to women in universities. Similarly, the women in Morley's (1999) study of British, Swedish, and Greek academic females spoke of the male-dominated nature of their universities, using terms like competitive, aggressive, and individualistic. A Swedish university lecturer said: "It is a male climate . . . totally. Absolutely. Yes. It is. . . . no emotion, you know? You have to be egoistic. . . . You have to sit down, close your ears and just write" (Morley 1999: 82). Another Swedish associate professor said: "The University is one of the worst hierarchical, patriarchal structures that exists. So it's pretty awful for everybody, quite honestly, but given that women are at the bottom, it is even worse for them" (Morley 1999: 86). One British senior lecturer commented on the maleness of the management team in her university in these terms: "It's very macho . . . very macho. . . . We've got a male vice-chancellor and then you've got his little threesome of deputies, you know—all men. And very, very macho. I mean we used to have a guy who was even more macho. . . . it's deeply male" (Morley 1999: 84).

Powney and Weiner (1992) discuss the patterns of inclusion and exclusion generated by the male norm in British universities in their book, *Outside of the Norm*. A good description comes from a black female academic who explains her inability to engage in standard management practices: "University management structures are highly middle class, white and male dominated . . . [I find myself] as a black working class woman outside of the norm of being acceptable on three counts: class, race and gender" (Powney and Weiner 1992: 40). Collier, a pro-feminist law professor, also draws attention to the exclusionary characteristics of the male norm, maintaining that "what needs to be addressed is the 'gender regime' of organizations themselves, the complex system of cultural norms and institutional arrangements 'that keeps men tethered to an increasingly demanding workplace and women professionally marginalized and economically dependent'" (Collier 2001: 12).

These patterns of inclusion/exclusion can affect men as well as women, but are experienced in different ways. This is revealed in Goode's (2000) research. Goode asked both men and women about the culture in British universities. While both genders described the culture as alienating, women more often referred to it as a *male* culture, while men often used a variant on the phrase, if your face fits. Some examples of women's responses include

- macho, aggressive management style, where the only acceptable management is that defined by a male mind-set;
- exclusion exists for those not willing to join in the macho long-hours culture;
- masculine research culture which determines funding priorities;
- a male culture, which can be quite intimidating at first because the scarcity of women can make you feel exposed. (Goode 2000: 269)

Men talked about

- gerontocratic and patriarchal professoriate;

- men in grey suits run the place (badly);
- there is a small mafia of academics who aspire to important administrative positions. They are making life hell for everyone else;
- bullying those whose faces do not fit: move to smaller office, move to office isolated from colleagues, move to unpleasant duties, and keep tabs on their movements. (Goode 2000: 269)

Success, Sacrifice, and Compromise

Many of the participants in our study, male and female, were highly critical of the attributes of success in their universities. The successful academic was typified as a "single minded writing machine," unmindful of student and collegial responsibilities, while those who rose to senior managerial positions were often brusquely typified as sycophants and toadies. Another (and less obviously invidious) characteristic was strategic thinking—that is, planning your career ahead, knowing where you want to go, and getting there. Some of the men in our study gave very clear expositions on this. Recollect the senior manager who related: "And you know I always had the view that once I went into academia, I wanted to be a professor and I wanted to be a professor by the time I was 40. Well, I did become a professor at 42. I knew what I had to do . . . so I did it."

Most women do not think of themselves in that way. Many have to plan around their families and their partners and do not have the luxury of thinking about their career as a linear trajectory. Edwards (2000: 315) observes that female careers are characterized by a distinct lack of autonomy; they follow the tracks of the "accidental academic" and the "unplanned career." In a similar vein, Morley (1999: 170) describes how difficult it is for many women to follow age-related linear career expectations, as their professional lives are characterized not by "a series of carefully planned, rational, measured steps," but by the "contingent, rarely linear, sometimes accidental and often serendipitous."

Numerous participants in our study commented on the long hours and total commitment to the job that made it virtually impossible for most women to succeed in the current climate (the same applies to those men who commit themselves to being equal partners in raising children). Weiner (1996: 64) suggests that those who survive and flourish in British universities are now "the youthful, the energetic, the entrepreneurial and those with few domestic commitments who are able to work long hours." Goode (2000: 273) reports a similar comment by a respondent: "I do feel that the professorial network in the UK is a closed club that tolerates women but does not support them as the senior members would support a 'bright young man' (usually younger and pushier)." Goode (2000: 272) also mentions how males shut out female aspirants to top jobs through "*networks of sporty maleness.*"

Importantly, the participants in our study said that they had to make considerable sacrifices just to stay afloat—let alone getting to the uncomfortable top. As dwindling public funds force universities to become more corporatized, the ever-increasing workloads leave many academics frustrated that they cannot maintain quality standards that they used to have in the past. Their personal integrity and professionalism are challenged when there is simply not enough time to do a good job. There is no longer any leisure to reflect deeply about academic decisions, unless it is extracted from the time that should be spent with students, family, and friends or in contributing to the community. Many talked of working all the time, like the respondent who said: "University life was like working in a deli that is open seven days a week, 24 hours a day." A British female academic made the same point: "I always work actually, evenings, Saturdays, Sundays, holidays, all the time I do something" (Morley 1999: 166). As a consequence, our participants emphasized the leisure loss, sacrificing family and friends, and the damage to their health.

Their talk of exhaustion is echoed over and over again in the related literature. A senior woman in Spurling's (1997: 44) study maintained that "Exhaustion is inevitable for senior women. What you have to avoid is burn-out." Bone (1997: 25) similarly talks about the sacrifices that staff are making in British universities: "The pressures on all staff in higher education now are significant. . . . The solution is too often found in working long hours and foregoing leisure." Morley (1999) adds another dimension to this by considering the additional labor that is involved if women are committed to challenging the sexism in the university. She identifies this additional workload as both material and emotional. One senior lecturer succinctly described her experience: "I think the major disadvantages [of teaching about how the system marginalizes women] affect me rather than the students or the institution. . . . I think I'm tired" (Morley 1999: 163).

The picture looks bleak. What are the prospects of change?

The Prospects of Change

Room to Move?

Many writers in Australia and the United States suggest that the current situation of overwork and academic erosion is likely to continue. In spite of budget surpluses, both conservative and liberal governments have continued to reduce the public funding of universities. In parallel, many feminist writers are pessimistic about changing the masculinist norms in American and Australian universities (Kolodny 1998; Martin and Meyerson 1998; Blackmore 1999). While individual feminist administrators can make small changes within their universities, Kolodny (1998) admits that it is difficult for someone with progressive and feminist ideals to take on a leadership role because most institutions of higher education remain structurally male. She describes a number of case studies of antifeminist intellectual harassment of female academics in American universities. More cases have occurred since Kolodny's writing. Many writers are concerned that this type of harassment has not ceased and see the university as an institution that continues to violate its moral imperative. They regret that universities are sacrificing their potential to serve as models of just institutions.

Delanty (2001), however, is more optimistic about the future of universities in this global era. He describes universities as standing at the crossroads between serving market goals and social goals. He believes that the university has the strength of its experts and the technology today to develop critical citizens. Writing within the context of globalization and academic capitalism, he remarks: "The global age, with its foundations in communication technology, offers great opportunities for the enhancement of citizenship by making possible wider participation of citizens" (Delanty 2001: 127). He argues that academics in universities should use "their relative autonomy to humanize technology and to recreate new expressions of citizenship" (Delanty 2001: 128). He also asserts that globalization can become a force of cosmopolitanism by promoting the self-transformation of cultures through a critical engagement with each other.

A number of writers have also described their visions for universities in the twenty-first century against the background of globalization. However, they have not identified globalization as a force for positive change. Describing the impact of globalization, Gidley (2000) asserts that it has been largely responsible for bringing the traditional humanistic dimensions of the university to an end. She argues the need for universities to reclaim their core purpose, creating higher order knowing and the ability to synthesize and integrate fragmented pieces of knowledge. In a similar vein, Inayatullah (2000) imagines a more communicative postcapitalist vision of what it is to be human. As Inayatullah emphasizes, in creating universities that can develop alternative futures, dissent is pivotal. He notes the need to limit the excesses of any civilization and to create spaces to reflect on society. In this context, Milojevic (2000) presents a feminist alternative by placing education and parenting at the center of society. She suggests that with such a focus on parenting and education and on future generations, this would not only transform education but also society in general. She argues, "The rush to obtain more money and more power and the urge to dominate would be replaced with a more sustainable approach, focused on cooperation" (Milojevic 2000: 180). In addressing the future of the Caribbean university, Hickling-Hudson argues that the *soul* of the university would be the tradition of scholar activism. In focusing on this, she delivers a strong social justice message, arguing for the need to strengthen "the 'soul' or essence of the university through the commitment of its scholar-activists to the development of communities, and the restructuring of politics and the education system" (Hickling-Hudson 2000: 150).

Even though these future scenarios are rather idealistic, there is some support for these alternative visions in the growing concern about the impact of globalization on communities and the inequities created by relying on a free market ideology. These concerns can be found if we consider the political trajectory over the past two decades. In the 1980s and early 1990s, it did not seem to matter too much whether an ostensibly left- or right-oriented government was in power in most Anglo-American countries. These governments ushered in changes that led to accepting the global practices of privatization, marketization, and new managerialism. All made radical changes to the way universities were organized and to the lives of academic workers. Currently, though, there are concerns about whether the move to the New Right has gone too far, with too great a loss to public services. For example, Henderson (2001) reports that privatization in Australia delivered little improvement to the financial performance of most government businesses. Even in the United States, where the efficacy of the market is most trusted, there are beginning to be questions about privatization and deregulation. After the September 11 attacks, US politicians considered replacing private providers of airport security systems with federal security screeners. During the summer of 2001, Californians experienced a crisis in the generation of electricity that was blamed on the deregulation of the system, and there were calls for re-regulation. In Britain, New Labour is considering giving students tuition grants again or providing a system that will reduce the burden of educational debt on the individual student. And in both Britain and Australia, the political parties of the left are considering raising higher education funding, rather than continuing to drain the system of public funding as has occurred in the United States where the result has been the escalation of tuition fees over the last decade.

The possibility that there is *room to move* is reflected in the fact that many feminist writers have put energy into considering how to transform the academy in Australia, Britain, the United States, and in other countries around the world (Deem and Ozga 2000; Morley 1999; Kolodny 1998; Morley and Walsh 1995; Yeatman 1993). Their calls for change are similar to some mentioned above. They center on nonpatriarchal management practices, participatory organizational structures, accessible and supportive management styles, and redistributive agendas aimed at reducing inequality and promoting fairness. What these writers open up is the possibility of a space in which women academics and managers can contribute to universities in a creative and constructive way.

Actions Taken by Senior Women

What, then, have some of the women at the top tried to do? Deem and Ozga's (2000) study sheds some light on this. At a time when tertiary institutions were being transformed by globalization agendas, Deem and Ozga wanted to know whether female senior managers could introduce equity principles. In order to find out, they interviewed forty women academic managers in the United Kingdom who described themselves as feminists or strongly committed to equal opportunities. While Deem and Ozga concluded that it would be difficult to make major transformations inspired by feminist values at the institutional level, they were more sanguine about feminist change at micro levels. They found that the feminist managers they interviewed were more likely to adopt so-called soft management skills, such as consultative and collaborative approaches. Compared with their male colleagues, these women were more likely to treat management as a way of shaping education in a more equitable direction, rather than a vehicle for enhanced personal status.

Walton (1997) similarly found that British women at the top of higher education institutions departed from the new forms of masculine management. They spoke, for example, of their ability to get people to work as a team rather than "throwing one's weight around and laying down the law to get things done" (Walton 1997: 80). Another principal talked about rejecting "the old macho management styles of the past generation" and replacing them with "creativity, communication, vision, symbolism and even love" as characteristics of good, modern management (Walton 1997: 81). According to Prichard, these instances in which small groups of women in senior positions attempt to create different organizational patterns are most often occurring in the new post-1992 universities, where women are "challenging masculine taken-for granted ways of doing and way of being" (Prichard 1996, cited in Goode 2000: 245).

Much has been written about mentoring and encouraging greater participation by women in the internal decision-making process of universities (Eggins 1997; King 1997). We initiated a mentoring program in our university in the mid-1990s. It successfully mentored two women into senior management. More pessimistically, though, we question whether such strategies are likely to result in a feminist transformation of the organization's management practices. Gordon (1991), in the book *Prisoners of Men's Dreams*, concludes that women become entrapped by male norms. She found that increasing the numbers of women in management did not, in itself, change the nature of the organizations. *Individual* successes do not denote significant *cultural* change. In parallel, Deem and Ozga (2000) warn that even women with strong feminist values can "acquire values infused with 'macho' masculinities and the management narratives of business organizations." Further, many "find themselves spending their time trying to stave off undesirable changes rather than introducing new positive change" (Deem and Ozga 2000: 154).

Eggins (1997) is more optimistic about the possibilities of success. In her review of U.S. programs designed to increase the number of women in higher education, she found that the percentage of women in leadership positions rose from a low base of 5 percent in 1975 to 10 percent in 1984 and to 16 percent in 1995. She records how, in 1977, the office of Women in Higher Education created The National Identification Program for the Advancement of Women in Higher Education. She then identifies a number of ways in which this program, along with federal legislation and federal agencies, increased women's leadership in higher education. While she does not discuss whether the institutions themselves were transformed, there are various pieces of research that suggest positive change.

King (1997) describes a network program that was launched in England in 1990, which was similar to The National Identification Program in the United States. The program was called *Through the Glass Ceiling*, with its architects observing that

> Increasingly, although slowly, women are entering the upper echelons of management in higher education. They move into a predominantly male world and many find themselves operating in a radically different culture, with different perceptions and assumptions, excluded from all sorts of male networks. It can be argued that women can, and do, bring clear and different skills to management, as well as the more traditionally professional skills. These "female" characteristics, which may be for example, about delegation, working in teams, sharing credit, high social and interpersonal skills, are shared by some men and are highly regarded in some management systems, but can be undervalued in the traditional British male management and institutional culture. (King 1997: 94)

In this context, it is also useful to recall Astin and Leland's (1991) account of the ways in which seventy-seven American female educational leaders made a difference between the 1960s and the 1980s. While this research describes a previous epoch in the history of universities, it demonstrates that change is possible, and that energetic, determined, and visionary women are vital. Astin and Leland found that many of the female leaders had been forged through commitments to social justice (the Depression, World War II, civil rights movement, antiwar protests, and trade union activities). Besides having a passion for justice and social change, some described their ability to conceptualize, to generate ideas, to see the bigger picture, and to make things happen. "They described themselves as visualizers" (Astin and Leland 1991: 70). Astin and Leland (1991: 108) maintain that these women's leadership was empowering and "mobiliz(ed) a collective action toward the common good."

It appears that, despite the challenges encountered, individual leaders can, and do, make a difference. Eveline (2000) details how Fay Gale, the vice-chancellor of the University of Western Australia and the second female to hold a vice-chancellorship in Australia, enacted a number of equity procedures that made the university a more comfortable place for women. She increased the number of women at professorial level and above from two to sixteen and moved the university from the bottom rung of Western Australia's equity index to the top. Eveline quotes one tribute to Fay Gale when completing her term in 1997:

> I admire Fay so much for the way she has stuck to her commitment to equity in the face of considerable opposition by a very vocal minority. I have been at UWA for nearly 20 years and, as a woman in academia, I at last feel this is a comfortable place for women to be. (Eveline 2000: 10)

Men Working for Change

What of the men who want to challenge current forms of masculinity and work for fairer and more human outcomes? There appear to be some managers who can genuinely work for the benefit of women. This was apparent at MIT, for example, where a male dean took immediate steps to redress the inequities uncovered by the committee. One senior woman faculty member described the outcome of this collaboration (between tenured women scientists and administrators) as "more progress for women faculty at MIT in one year than was accomplished in the previous decade" (MIT 1999: 9). Another woman, describing the change in her professional life, noted:

> I was unhappy at MIT for more than a decade. I thought it was the price you paid if you wanted to be a scientist at an elite academic institution. After the Committee formed and the dean responded, my life began to change. My research blossomed, my funding tripled. Now I love every aspect of my job. It is hard to understand how I survived those years—or why. (MIT 1999: 9)

Important here is work by pro-feminist male academics who are deconstructing masculinities and investigating ways of transforming management (Collinson and Hearn 1994; Clarke 1999; Hearn 1999; Moodley 1999). Clarke (1999) raises the question of how men can challenge masculine ways of doing management. Drawing inspiration from the idea that masculinity is a fluid concept and can be changed, he describes how he attempted to bring about a positive and ethical transformation both in his own work and the organization as a whole. While this attempt was not entirely successful, Clarke began to get a clear handle on some of the reasons he found the changes difficult to make. He realized, for example, that "as a man, the preservation of privacy, the maintenance of firm boundaries between the public and personal, and the primacy of acting and thinking over feeling are significant codes of masculine conduct" (Clarke 1999: 175). Moodley, in trying to unmask the male "man-ager," adds another point: "In talking of 'men,' 'masculinity' and 'masculinities,' it is particularly important to continually contextualize the discussion in power and power relations, especially since men have come to see power as a capacity to impose control on others . . . the domination of men over women" (Moodley 1999: 225).

Our Agenda for Change

In chapter 1 we spoke of four traditional university values currently under threat: democratic collegiality; professional autonomy and integrity; critical dissent and academic freedom; and the public interest value of universities. As part of our *critical and conserving* agenda, we now reassert the importance of these values and push them in a feminist direction.

Democratic Collegiality

A number of social theorists (Carter and Stokes 1998; Giddens 1998; Unger 1998; Weale 1999) have recently written about different forms of democracy and the virtues that the democratic process can instill in citizens. They advocate democracy because it is through the process of democratic deliberation that participants are forced to formulate their arguments in a principled way and respect different positions. Newson (1998) argues strongly about the importance of promoting democratic values and practices within universities, the more so given our current political climate. She maintains it is the university's role to promote democratic life and develop democratic sensibilities to "enable citizens to be thoughtfully influential over the affairs of the world" (Newson 1998: 310). There is less consensus on what form that democracy should take (see Currie 1999 for further discussion). We will not go into this debate here, but affirm that representative democracy, where all sectors of the university community are involved, will create the best forum to understand an issue.[1]

From a feminist perspective, three things stand out about democratic processes. First, the importance of democracy as an active vehicle of social justice, not just a debating club. Second, the relationship between democracy and power inequalities. We recognize that democratic processes have the capacity to silence and marginalize in the very process of promoting participation. So it is *particular* forms of democracy we are interested in: that is, those that represent a broad spectrum of the community; weight the voices of the less powerful; respect difference; and encourage listening as much as the speech act. Third, we insist on the importance of the relationship between democracy and community. Today most universities have grown so large that it is difficult to think of them as one community. But without some sense of belonging, the whole thing is hollow.

Crucially, the community in question must be one in which people of different gender, ethnicity, age, and political convictions are equally at home. A feminist democratic community is an inclusive one, and this means paying attention to difference, rather than assuming similarity. This attention needs to be recognized in material as well as intellectual ways: in the timing of meetings and the hours people are expected to work, for example, as well as the conventions of speech and debate.

Professional Autonomy and Integrity

A well-established principle is that the integrity of a university depends upon the integrity of its scholars. This integrity, in its turn, depends upon honesty in scholarship and developing consistently high standards in assessing one another's work. It is important for academics to exercise independent judgment where there is no self-interest involved. On this, Polster and Newson (1998) write about the notion of disinterest or open-mindedness. They insist that scholarly inquiry should not be influenced by any particular interests that are served by the results. Bone (1997) notes that in surveys of employee expectations of their leaders, integrity features as a key characteristic. "Such integrity is understood as consistency and dependability, moral and intellectual honesty, with beliefs and values in evidence in day-to-day operations" (Bone 1997: 23).

What are the particular implications of this for women? One of the findings of our study was that women were more likely to be in teaching or research areas that did not accord with the establishment view and were less likely to trade or compromise their integrity. "Playing the game"—whether by fixing the form or figuring out the most strategic road to success—was far more readily accepted as "just a matter of being realistic" by our male than female participants.

So a feminist commitment to professional autonomy and integrity insists that such values cannot be pitched purely at the level of the individual scholar (who, note, is historically coded male). They need to enter into all the material practices of university life. For example: promotion procedures should encourage honest and reflective assessment, rather than impressive CV production; quality assurance should promote a genuine and reasonable accountability, rather than monitoring for the sake of the record; funding decisions should reflect intellectual contribution and the mission of the university, rather than the areas of profit—and so forth. The devil is in the detail and the detail, as women know, needs to be right. After that, the rhetoric will take care of itself.

Critical Dissent and Academic Freedom

Academic freedom is a key legitimating function of the university. It underpins the desire to search for alternatives to the current paradigms of knowledge and encourages academics to be the social conscience of a nation. When this principle is in good health, academics are given the freedom to teach with passion and introduce controversial ideas that will challenge students to be more critically thinking citizens. Geeta Singh (2001), writing in defense of academic freedom in *The Age* newspaper, argues that "in accepting an academic position, a person accepts a moral obligation to the purpose of the university as an institution, and the purpose of the university is free intellectual inquiry." In a similar vein, Said (1994, cited in Morley 1999: 4) points out that the "challenge of intellectual life is to be found in dissent against the *status quo*." This idea is also articulated in Britain's Higher Education Quality Council Report (1994: 315): "Universities are organizations like no other; they are institutions where the principal product is *dissent*, or opposition to received wisdom" (Said 1994, cited in Morley 1999: 4).

Perhaps one of the more distressing costs of the corporate university is an apparent lack of respect for staff. While this is not an uncommon feature of capitalist workplaces and arguably has been part of the experience of general staff in universities, the devaluing of intellectual skills is a relatively new phenomenon. Certainly, a climate of open debate and intellectual rigor can be an uncomfortable and demanding environment for a manager who just wants to get things done. However, to neglect the intellectual strengths and expertise of one's employees would seem to be counterproductive, even in the corporate culture's own terms.

Throughout this book we have touched on the ways in which the commercialization of academic life has affected traditional values, most particularly these qualities of critical dissent and academic freedom. On this, Collier (2001) asks: "If the market is the measure of all things, and if only the 'fittest' institutions *and individuals* are likely to survive, where does such an economic rationalist discourse leave the 'inquiring soul' of the academic?" (Collier 2001: 20, emphasis in the original). Marginson's (1997b) answer, which relates to the importance of democratic collegiality and is in line with well-established feminist principles, is to give greater priority to solidarity and cooperation, to nonmarket and noncompetitively inspired communities. As unions around the world protect their members from attacks on academic freedom, it is important to recognize the power of solidarity as a way of protesting current directions in higher education and the consequences they have for academic freedom.

The Public Interest Value of Universities

In chapter 1 we mentioned the role taken by Olivieri in speaking publicly about her fears concerning the safety of a certain drug. If academics like Olivieri are not willing to protect people's rights and interests and pursue their research without fear or favor, how will the public know about the effects of a range of public interventions, whether political, social, environmental, or economic?

Polster and Newson (1998) argue that unconditional funding is necessary to ensure that the public interest is maintained. This means, for the most part, that funding has to come from government. However, other arrangements can be made so that corporations can give money to universities without directly funding specific projects. This kind of untied funding has been used with some success in government-to-government aid where Third World countries have requested that aid be given to their countries without all the strings attached to the donor country.

Academics are more likely to be able to argue from a position of disinterest if they are not being paid by corporations or subject to governing bodies that attempt to debar them from inquiring into issues that concern the public. It is noteworthy that since the September 11 terrorist attack and the engagement of the United States in a *new war,* there have been threats of dismissal and disciplinary action taken against faculty members who have criticized US foreign policy at teach-ins. Efforts to silence criticism and dissent occurred at the City University of New York, University of Texas at Austin, MIT, the University of North Carolina at Chapel Hill, and the University of Massachusetts at Amherst. A proposed advertisement to protect academic freedom (sent via e-mail from the Center for Economic Research and Social Change, Chicago, October 31, 2001) urges all members of the academic community to speak out strongly in defense of academic freedom and civil liberties. It concludes: "At a moment such as this we must make sure that all informed voices—especially those that are critical and dissenting—are heard."

We believe that there is an enduring need to assert the role of universities in developing active and critical-thinking citizens. Smith and Webster (1997) argue that university education is about creating thoughtful citizens. Universities, they say, must be concerned with

> the conduct of critical enquiry and rational debate, nurturing abilities such as a capacity to distinguish opinion from evidence and to evaluate an argument dispassionately, to learn independently and in groups, to develop abilities to present coherent arguments, to improve the sophistication of one's thinking, to open one's imagination and reflexive capabilities, to improve analytical capacities and to think conceptually. (Smith and Webster 1997: 108)

Crucially, and as part of our feminist agenda, we also argue that the educated individual is one who develops tolerance and compassion. We want tomorrow's citizens to work for social justice. Malah Singh (2001) argues how important it is to conceive of universities with broader social purposes to facilitate social justice and work for the social transformation of society. She speaks from a South African perspective where there is a role for universities in the agenda for social reconstruction. The South African Report, *Towards a New Higher Education Landscape*, endorses this view:

> The role of higher education in the defense and advancement of democracy is closely related to promoting good citizenship. . . . Such a role is also intrinsically related to higher education's ability to deliver programmes that are essential to the promotion of a critical citizenry, and to ensure that the higher educa tion system is firmly rooted within South African society and its particular development challenges. (South African Higher Education Task Team 2000: 10)

And One More . . .

While the four values outlined above have been traditional to universities, as feminists we would add one more, one that has traditionally been neglected by public institutions and private corporations alike. It is the need for employing organizations to take a better account of the personal lives and private responsibilities of their employees. Traditionally, paid work, because it has been dominantly cast as men's work, has been organized with scant regard for the rhythms and responsibilities of caring for oneself and one's family. This is the work that has been women's work and largely still is, even though women are participating in paid labor and pursuing careers alongside men. In chapter 4, we showed that even when administrators and academic staff were cognizant of the structural burden facing female colleagues, they were unable to conceive of the *university* as being able to redress the problem. For so long as that view persists, women will be disadvantaged. The increasing pressure of working within universities will make it more difficult for women with families to pursue academic careers. It will also make it more difficult for men with families who embrace the egalitarian ethos of sharing domestic responsibilities with their partners to take on the increased workloads that universities demand today.

A crucial component of our feminist agenda relates to the creation of a more caring, collegial, and family- and community-friendly ethos within the university. Universities need to take a more responsible role in this matter. The hours that staff and students work need to be in tune with their commitments to their kith and kin, friends, and local communities. Only then will academics, whether male or female, be able to integrate their professional and personal lives and make the university/community connection actually *work*.

These issues affect all of us, female and male academics, as we strive to conserve the essential values of universities and push them in new and fairer directions, more respectful of difference. We want universities to pursue social goals that work toward greater justice and more caring communities, both within the academy and outside of it. Our goal is a more just and equitable society and a more caring university community.

Notes

1. One contentious issue concerns the kind of decisions taken to democratic councils for debate. Every academic decision does not need to go there. An obviously vital matter is the annual budget, which should be available for thorough discussion.

Appendix

Interview Protocols

Staff Interviewee Protocol

General Career Question

1. We would like you to think about your career. How satisfied do you feel with your working life?

2. Over the course of your career, have you ever sat down and planned your career?

Attributes for Success

3. Who gets ahead in this university? What attributes do they have?

4. What are the characteristics of those who don't get ahead?

5. Do staff have to sacrifice certain things to get ahead? Or compromise certain values and interests? If so, what are the things that get sacrificed?

6. Do you see any barriers that are placed in the way of individuals?

Perceptions of Gender in Organizational Culture

7. Do you think men and women have different styles of working and create a different atmosphere in the workplace?

8. Why do you think there are so few women in senior positions?

Perceptions of Fairness

9. Do you think the system of promotion and/or reclassification at your university is fair?

10. Do you think benefits and duties are fairly distributed?

Power

11. How would you describe those who have power? What attributes do they have?

12. What sort of power and influence do you have?

Collegiate Support Groups

13. From where in the university do you draw most of your support? (secondary probes—mainly women or men? If answer is no: where do you get your support from?)

14. How do you maintain contact with them?

Management Interviewee Protocol

Managing Change

1. There have been a lot of changes in higher education over the past few years. How do you think they have affected managerial styles at your university?

2. Do you think that these current changes are likely to affect male and female staff (academic and general) differently?

Attributes for Success

3. Who gets ahead in this university? What attributes do they have?

4. What are the characteristics of those who don't get ahead?

5. Do staff have to sacrifice certain things to get ahead? Or compromise certain values and interests? If so, what are the things that get sacrificed?

6. Do you see any barriers that are placed in the way of individuals?

Perceptions of Gender in Organizational Culture

7. Why do you think there are so few women in senior positions?

8. Do you think there is a problem with the number and position of female staff? If so, which strategies do you think could benefit women?

9. In your experience, do men and women have different styles of working? If so, what's the nature of these differences?

Personal Strategies in Relation to Staff Career Development

10. Do you see it as your particular responsibility to give opportunities to women and/or to encourage particular women to apply for higher positions? Have you done either of these things?

11. More generally, and in an informal way, do you "train" people for particular positions? Encourage those you feel have potential? If so, in what sort of way?

Career Planning

12. We would like you to think about your own career. Overall, how satisfied do you feel with your career path to date? What is the most satisfying thing for you?

13. Over the course of your career, have you ever sat down and planned your career? Hoped to get to the kind of position that you hold now?

Life at the Top

14. Staff in senior management positions have to interact with a number of different groups and wear many hats. Are you conscious of having to cross boundaries? How do you manage that?

15. People at the top of organizations are often described as isolated or, as the phrase goes, "Lonely at the top." Does this describe you?

16. From where in the university do you draw most of your support? (secondary probe—mainly women or men?)

17. How do you maintain contact with them?

References

Acker, J. 1990. "Hierarchies, jobs, bodies: A theory of gendered organizations." *Gender and Society* 4 (2): 139-158.

Acker, J., and D. R. van Houten. 1974. "Differential recruitment and control: The sex structuring of organizations." *Administrative Science Quarterly* 19 (2): 152-163.

Acker, S. 1994. *Gendered Education: Sociological Reflections on Women, Teaching and Feminism.* Buckingham and Philadelphia: Open University Press.

Acker, S., and G. Feuerverger. 1996. "Doing good and feeling bad: The work of women university teachers." *Cambridge Journal of Education* 26 (3): 401-422.

Affirmative Action Agency. 1993. *Annual Report 1991-1992.* Canberra: Australian Government Publishing Service.

Age, The. 1995. Editorial. "Too much work?" November 2: 17.

Allen, H. L. 1994. "Workload and productivity in an accountability era." In *The NEA 1994 Almanac of Higher Education.* Washington, DC: National Education Association Publishing: 25-38.

Allport, C. 1996. "Improving gender equity: Using industrial bargaining." *NTEU Frontline* (Autumn): 5-8.

Anderson, H. 2001. "France finds more time for the good life." *The Weekend Australian,* January 27-28: 20.

Annandale, E., J. Clark, and L. Allen. 1998. "Interprofessional working: An ethnographic study of an English hospital trust." Paper presented at the International Sociological Association 14th World Congress of Sociology, Montreal, Canada, July-August.

Association of University Teachers (AUT). 2001. *Analysis of Staff Record Data for 1998-9 by HESA.* London: AUT.

Astin, H. S., and C. Leland. 1991. *Women of Influence, Women of Vision: A Cross-Generational Study of Leaders and Social Change.* San Francisco: Jossey-Bass Publishers.

Australia Institute. 1999. "Quality of life in Australia: An analysis of public perceptions." Discussion Paper. September, Canberra: Australian National University.

———. 2001a. "Reith proposals erode public service professionalism." Media Release. February 28, Canberra: Australian National University.

———. 2001b. "Commercialism and academic freedom." Discussion Paper. March, Canberra: Australian National University.

Australian Bureau of Statistics. 1994. *The Labour Force. Cat. No. 6203.0.* Canberra: Australian Government Publishing Service.

Bacchi, C. 1990. *Same Difference: Feminism and Sexual Difference*. Sydney: Allen and Unwin.

———. 1999. *Women, Policy and Politics: The Construction of Policy Problems*. London: Sage Publications.

Baragwanath, C., and J. Howe. 2000. "Corporate welfare: Public accountability for industry assistance." Discussion Paper. Canberra: The Australia Institute, Australian National University.

Barlow, M. 2000. "The corporate colonization of higher education. Notes from Queen's Day on globalization and higher education." Ottawa, January 21, The Council of Canadians, at www.canadians.org (accessed February 20, 2000).

Barraclough and Company. 1995. "Experienced insights: Opinions of Australian managers, ideals, strengths and weaknesses." In *Enterprising Nation: Renewing Australian Managers to Meet the Challenges of the Asian-Pacific Century*. Vol. 1. Research Report of the Industry Task Force on Leadership and Management Skills, Canberra: Australian Government Publishing Service: 521-584.

Barsoux, J.-L. 1987. "From dinner jacket to straight jacket–what kind of manager does industry need?" *The Times Higher Educational Supplement* 767 July: 13.

Bazeley, P., L. Kemp, K. Stevens, C. Asmar, C. Grbich, H. March, and B. Ragbir. 1996. *Waiting in the Wings: A Study of Early Career Academic Researchers in Australia*. Canberra: Australian Government Publishing Service.

Beaman-Smith, K., and M. Placier. 1996. "The interplay of gender in the careers of white female and male senior professors." Paper presented at the annual meeting of ASHE (American Society for Higher Education), Memphis, Tennessee, October 30-November 2.

Bellas, M. 1994. "Comparable worth in academia: The effects on faculty salaries of the sex composition and labor-market conditions of academic disciplines." *American Sociological Review* 59 (December): 807-821.

Bittman, M., and J. Pixley. 1997. *The Double Life of the Family*. St. Leonards, NSW: Allen and Unwin.

Blackmore, J. 1989. "Educational leadership: A feminist critique and reconstruction." In J. Smyth, ed. *Critical Perspectives on Educational Leadership*. London: Falmer: 93-129.

———. 1992. "More power to the powerful: Corporate management, mergers and the implications for women of the reshaping of the 'culture' of Australian tertiary education." *Australian Feminist Studies* 15: 65-89.

———. 1993. "'In the shadow of men': The historical construction of administration as a 'masculinist enterprise.'" In J. Blackmore and J. Kenway, eds. *Gender Matters in Educational Administration and Policy*. London: Falmer: 27-48.

———. 1999. *Troubling Women: Feminism, Leadership and Educational Change*. Buckingham, England: Open University Press.

Blackmore, J., and J. Kenway, eds. 1993. *Gender Matters in Educational Administration and Policy*. London: Falmer Press.

Bone, J. 1997. "Women and the ethics of leadership in higher education." In H. Eggins, ed. *Women as Leaders and Managers in Higher Education*. Buckingham, England: The Society for Research into Higher Education and Open University Press: 17-27.

Bottery, M. 1992. *The Ethics of Educational Management*. London: Cassell.

Boyd, S., and C. Wylie. 1994. *Workload and Stress in New Zealand Universities*. Wellington, New Zealand: Council for Educational Research and The Association of University Staff of New Zealand.

Brooks, A. 1997. *Academic Women*. Buckingham, England: Open University Press.

Brooks, A., and A. Mackinnon. 2001. "Introduction: Globalization, academia and change." In A. Brooks and A. Mackinnon, eds. *Gender and the Restructured University*. Buckingham, England: Open University Press: 1-11.

Burton, C. 1987. "Merit and gender: Organisations and the mobilisation of masculine bias." *Australian Journal of Social Issues* 22 (2): 424-435.

———. 1991. *The Promise and the Price: The Struggle for Equal Opportunity in Women's Employment*. Sydney: Allen and Unwin.

———. 1997. *Gender Equity in Australian University Staffing*. DEET/Evaluations and Investigations Program/Higher Education Division. Canberra: Australian Government Publishing Service.

Cameron, K. S., and D. R. Ettington. 1988. "The conceptual foundations of organizational culture." In J. C. Smart, ed. *Higher Education Handbook of Theory and Research*. Vol. 4. New York: Agathon Press: 356-396.

Carter, A., and G. Stokes. 1998. *Liberal Democracy and Its Critics*. Cambridge, England: Polity Press.

Castleman, T., M. Allen, W. Bastalich, and P. Wright. 1994. *Limited Access: Women's Disadvantage in Higher Education Employment*. South Melbourne: National Tertiary Education Union.

Center for Economic Research and Social Change. 2001. "Academic freedom ad." Received by e-mail, October 31, 2001.

Chliwniak, L. 1997. *Higher Education Leadership: Analyzing the Gender Gap*. Washington, DC: George Washington University in cooperation with the Association for the Study of Higher Education, ASHE-ERIC Higher Education Report 25 (4).

Clark, S. M., and M. Corcoran. 1986. "Perspectives on the professional socialization of women faculty: A case of accumulative disadvantage?" *Journal of Higher Education* 57 (1): 20-43.

Clarke, J. 1998. "Thriving on chaos? Managerialism and social welfare." In J. Carter, ed. *Postmodernity and the Fragmentation of Welfare*. London and New York: Routledge: 171-187.

———. 1999. "A personal encounter: Exploring the masculinity of management through action research." In S. Whitehead and R. Moodley, eds. *Transforming Managers: Gendering Change in the Public Sector*. London: University College London Press: 166-183.

Clinton, W. 2000. ABC News Interview. Australian Broadcasting Corporation. December 22.

Coady, T. 1996. "The very idea of a university." *Australian Quarterly* 68 (4): 49-62.

———, ed. 2000. *Why Universities Matter: A Conversation about Values, Means and Directions*. St. Leonards, NSW: Allen and Unwin.

Coaldrake, P., and L. Stedman. 1999. "Academic Work in the Twenty-first Century." Occasional Paper Series. Higher Education Division, Department of Education, Training and Youth Affairs. Canberra: Commonwealth of Australia.

Cockburn, C. 1990. *In the Way of Women: Men's Resistance to Sex Equality in Organisations*. London: Macmillan.

Collier, R. 2001. "Gender, the academic career and work-life balance: Women, men and the 'private life' of the law school." Paper presented at the LSA Conference, Budapest, July 4-7.

Collinson, D. L., and J. Hearn. 1994. "Naming men as men: Implications for work, organization and management" *Journal of Gender, Work and Organization* 1 (1): 2-22.

Connell, R. W. 1987. *Gender and Power: Society, the Person, and Sexual Politics*. Stanford, CA: Stanford University Press.

———. 1994. "States, powers and genders." Paper presented at the XIII World Congress of Sociology, Symposium on Feminist Challenges to Social Theory, Bielefeld, Germany, July 19.

———. 1995. *Masculinities*. Cambridge, MA: Polity Press.

———. 2000. *The Men and the Boys*. Cambridge, England: Polity Press.

Coser, L. 1974. *Greedy Institutions: Patterns of Undivided Commitment*. New York: Collier Macmillan.

Court, S. 1994. *Long Hours, Little Thanks. A Survey of the Use of Time by Full-Time Academic and Related Staff in the Traditional UK Universities*. London: Association of University Teachers.

Croham Report 1987. *Review of the University Grants Committee*. Cmnd. 81. London: HMSO.

Currie, J. 1996. "The effects of globalisation on 1990s academics in greedy institutions: Overworked, stressed out and demoralised." *Melbourne Studies in Education* 37 (2) (November): 101-128.

———. 1998. "Impact of globalization on Australian universities: Competition, fragmentation and demoralization." Paper presented at the International Sociology Association 14th World Congress of Sociology, Montreal, July 26-August 2.

———. 1999. "Alternative responses to globalization practices in universities: The value of democracy." Paper presented at the Conference on Re-Organizing Knowledge: Trans-forming Institutions, Knowing, Knowledge and the University in the 21st Century. Amherst, Massachusetts, September 17-19.

Currie, J., and J. Newson, eds. 1998. *Universities and Globalization: Critical Perspectives*. Thousand Oaks and London: Sage Publications.

Currie, J., H. Pears, and B. Thiele. 1998. "Tertiary and TAFE Organisational Cultures in Western Australia: How Is Murdoch University Perceived?" Unpublished report, Murdoch University, Perth, Western Australia.

Currie, J., and L. Vidovich. 1998. "Microeconomic reform through managerialism in American and Australian universities." In J. Currie and J. Newson, eds. *Universities and Globalization: Critical Perspectives*. Thousand Oaks: Sage Publications: 153-172.

Dawkins, J. 1988. *Higher Education, A Policy Statement. The White Paper*. Canberra: Australian Government Publishing Service.

Davis, J. 1996. "Paying several pipers: The funding of universities." *Australian Quarterly* 68 (4): 9-23.

Deem, R., and J. T. Ozga. 2000. "Transforming post-compulsory education? Femocrats at work in the academy." *Women's Studies International Forum* 23 (2): 153-166.

Delanty, G. 2001. *Challenging Knowledge: The University in the Knowledge Society*. Buckingham, England: Society for Research into Higher Education and Open University Press.

Denniss, R. 2001. "Measuring employment in the 21st Century: New measures of under-employment and overwork." Discussion Paper. Canberra: The Australia Institute.

Diamond, M. 1991. "Dimensions of organizational culture and beyond." *Political Psychology* 12 (3): 509-522.

Dines, E. 1993. "Overview: Women in higher education management." In E. Dines, ed. *Women in Higher Education Management*. Paris: UNESCO.

DuBrin, A. J. 1994. *Essentials of Management*. Cincinnati, OH: South-Western Publishing.

Edgar, D. 2001. "Bottom line motherhood." *The Australian*, Wednesday, May 2: 11.

Edwards, R. 2000. "Numbers are not enough: On women in higher education and being a feminist academic." In M. Tight, ed. *Academic Work and Life: What It Is to Be an Academic and How This Is Changing.* Amsterdam: Elsevier Science: 307-333.

Eggins, H. 1997. "Reaching for equal opportunities: Models from Australia and the USA." In H. Eggins, ed. *Women as Leaders and Managers in Higher Education.* Buckingham, England: The Society for Research into Higher Education and Open University Press: 121-127.

Eveline, J. 1994. "The politics of advantage." *Australian Feminist Studies* 19: 129-154.

———. 1996. "The worry of going limp: Are you keeping up in senior management." *Australian Feminist Studies* 23 (2): 65-79.

———. 2000. "Sex matters: A case of gender and authority in Australian university leadership." Paper presented at the European Conference on Gender and Higher Education, ETH, Zurich, September 12-15.

Farish, M., J. McPake, J. Powney, and G. Weiner. 1995. *Equal Opportunities in Colleges and Universities: Towards Better Practices.* Buckingham, England: Open University Press.

Finch, J. 1983. *Married to the Job: Wives' Incorporation in Men's Work.* Sydney: Allen and Unwin.

Fine, M. 1994. "Dis-stance and other stances: Negotiations of power inside feminist research." In A. Gitlin, ed. *Power and Method: Political Activism and Educational Research.* London: Routledge: 13-35.

Fisher, S. 1994. *Stress in Academic Life: The Mental Assembly Line.* Buckingham, England: Society for Research into Higher Education and Open University Press.

Flynn, N. 1990. *Public Sector Management.* London: Harvester Wheatsheaf.

Foucault, M. 1972. *The Order of Things: An Archaeology of the Human Sciences*, New York: Vintage.

———. 1979. *Discipline and Punish: The Birth of the Prison.* A. Sheridan, trans. New York: Vintage/Random House.

Franzway, S. 1996. "Union women: Living in greedy institutions." Paper presented at the 6th International Interdisciplinary Congress on Women, Adelaide, Australia, April 21-26.

Gale, F. 1997. "Introduction." In F. Gale and B. Goldflam, eds. *Strategies to Redress Gender Imbalance in Numbers of Senior Academic Women.* Nedlands: University of Western Australia: 1-4.

Gherardi, S. 1994. "The gender we think, the gender we do in our everyday lives." *Human Relations* 47 (6): 591-610.

Giddens, A. 1998. *The Third Way: The Renewal of Social Democracy.* Cambridge, England: Polity Press.

Gidley, J. 2000. "Unveiling the human face of university futures." In S. Inayatullah and J. Gidley, eds. *The University in Transformation: Global Perspectives on the Future of the University.* Westport, CT: Bergin and Garvey: 235-245.

Glazer, J. S. 1997. "Affirmative action and the status of women in the academy." In C. Marshall, ed. *Feminist Critical Policy Analysis II: A Perspective from Post-Secondary Education.* London: Falmer Press: 60-73.

Goode, J. 2000. "Is the position of women in higher education changing?" In M. Tight, ed. *Academic Work and Life: What It Is to Be an Academic and How This Is Changing.* Amsterdam: Elsevier Science: 243-284.

Gordon, C. 1991. "Governmental rationality: An introduction." In G. Burchell, C. Gordon and P. Miller, eds. *The Foucault Effect: Studies in Governmentality*, Chicago, IL: University of Chicago Press: 1-51.

Gordon, S. 1991. *Prisoners of Men's Dreams: Striking Out for a New Feminine Future.* Boston: Little, Brown and Company.

Graham, W. 2000. "Academic freedom or commercial license?" In J. L. Turk, ed. *The Corporate Campus: Commercialization and the Dangers to Canada's Colleges and Universities.* Toronto: James Lorimer and Company: 23-30.

Grant, J., and P. Porter. 1994. "Women managers: The construction of gender in the workplace." *The Australian and New Zealand Journal of Sociology* 30 (2): 149-164.

Halford, S., and P. Leonard. 1998. "New hospitals, new work, new people?: Identity, gender and profession in a changing health service." Paper presented at the International Sociological Association 14th World Congress of Sociology, Montreal, Canada, July-August.

Hall, S., L. Parker, J. Currie, and H. Pears. 1998. "Tertiary and TAFE organisational cultures in Western Australia: How is Curtin University perceived?" Unpublished report, Murdoch University, Perth, Western Australia.

Harris, P. 1999. "Changing patterns of governance: Developments in Australian public hospitals and universities." *Policy Studies* 20 (6): 255-272.

Hatch, M. J. 1993. "The dynamics of organisational culture." *Academy Management Review* 18 (4): 657-693.

Hearn, J. 1992. "Changing men and changing managements: A review of issues and actions." *Women in Management Review* 7 (1): 3-8.

———. 1999. "Men, managers and management: The case of higher education." In S. Whitehead and R. Moodley, eds. *Transforming Managers: Gendering Change in the Public Sector.* London: University College London Press: 123-144.

Hecht, J. 1994. "Today's college teachers: Cheap and temporary." *Labor Notes* 188 (November): 6.

Henderson, I. 2001. "Little to show for reforms." *The Australian*, June 12: 10.

Heward, C. 1994. "Women and careers in higher education: What is the problem?" In L. Morley and V. Walsh, eds. *Breaking Boundaries: Women in Higher Education.* London: Taylor and Francis: 11-23.

Hickling-Hudson, A. 2000. "Scholar-activism for a new world: The future of the Caribbean university." In S. Inayatullah and J. Gidley, eds. *The University in Transformation: Global Perspectives on the Future of the University.* Westport, CT: Bergin and Garvey: 150-159.

Hilmer, E. 1993. *National Competition Policy: Report by the Independent Commission of Inquiry.* Canberra: Australian Government Publishing Service.

Hirsch, W. A., and L. E. Weber, eds. 1999. *Challenges Facing Higher Education at the Millennium.* Phoenix: The American Council on Education and Oryx Press.

Hirst, P., and G. Thompson. 1995. "Globalisation and the future of the nation state." *Economy and Society* 24 (3): 409-442.

———. 1996. *Globalisation in Question: The International Economy and the Possibilities of Governance.* London: Pluto Press.

Hoare, D. 1995. *Higher Education Management Review. Report of the Committee of Inquiry.* Canberra: Australian Government Publishing Service.

Howard, J. 2001. "Backing Australia's ability. An innovation action plan for the future." Government Statement. Canberra: Department of Industry, Science and Resources, January 29.

Husu, L. 1999. "Gender discrimination in the promised land of gender equality: Academic women in Finland." Paper presented to the 7th International Interdisciplinary Congress on Women, Tromso, Norway, June 20-26.

Hugill, B. 1994. "A civil service on its last legs." *Observer, Focus*, May 29: 22.

Illing, D. 1998. "Women lag in salary stakes." *The Australian, Higher Education Supplement*, Wednesday, May 6: 37.

———. 1999. "Long haul to top for women in academe." *The Australian, Higher Education Supplement*, Wednesday, April 14: 42.

Inayatullah, S. 2000. "Corporate networks or bliss for all: The politics of the futures of the university." In S. Inayatullah and J. Gidley, eds. *The University in Transformation: Global Perspectives on the Future of the University*. Westport, CT: Bergin and Garvey: 221-233.

Itzen, C., and J. Newman. 1995. *Gender, Culture and Organizational Change*. New York: Rougtledge.

Izraeli, D., and N. Adler, eds. 1994. *Competitive Frontiers: Women Managers in a Global Economy*. New York: Routledge.

James, P. 2000. *Burning Down the House: The Bonfire of the Universities*. North Carlton, VIC: Association for the Public University with Arena Publications.

Jarratt Report. 1985. *Report of the Steering Committee for Efficiency Studies in Universities*. London: CVCP.

Jobs Letter Editors. 1997. "The word is workfare," Letter No. 58, April 18. *Trends*. Auckland, New Zealand: The Jobs Research Trust: 1-2.

Johnsrud, L. K. 1993. "Women and minority faculty experiences: Defining and responding to diverse realities." *New Directions for Teaching and Learning* 53: 3-15.

Jones, R. 1994. "Women at work: High stress, low pay." *Tallahassee Democrat*, Saturday, October 15: 1 and 9A.

Jordon, S. M., and D. T. Layzell. 1992. *A Case Study of Faculty Workload Issues in Arizona: Implications for State Higher Educational Policy*. Denver: Education Commission of the States, State Higher Education Executive Officers Association.

Kelly, P. 2001. "Truth cure for Hansonitis." *The Weekend Australian*, February 24-25: 23.

Kelly, L., L. Regan, and S. Burton. 1992. "Defending the indefensible? Quantitative methods and feminist research." In H. Hinds, A. Phoenix and J. Stacey, eds. *Working Out: New Directions for Women's Studies*. London: Taylor and Francis: 149-160.

Kemp, D. 1999. *New Knowledge, New Opportunities: A Discussion Paper on Higher Education Research and Research Training*. Canberra: Commonwealth Government, Department of Employment, Education, Training and Youth Affairs, June.

Kerfoot, D. 1999. "The organization of intimacy: Managerialism, masculinity and the masculine subject." In S. Whitehead and R. Moodley, eds. *Transforming Managers: Gendering Change in the Public Sector*. London: University of College London Press: 184-199.

King, C. 1997. "Through the glass ceiling: Networking by women managers in higher education." In H. Eggins, ed. *Women as Leaders and Managers in Higher Education*. Buckingham, England: The Society for Research into Higher Education and Open University Press: 91-100.

Kohler, A. 2000. "Globalization: The great leveller." *The Australian Financial Review*, Weekend, November 25-26: 3.

Kolodny, A. 1998. *Failing the Future: A Dean Looks at Higher Education in the Twenty-first Century*. Durham: Duke University Press.

Krakower, J. Y., and S. Niwa. 1985. *An Assessment of the Validity and Reliability of the Institutional Performance Survey*. Boulder, CO: NCHEMS.

Kuh, G. D., and E. J. Whitt. 1988. *The Invisible Tapestry: Culture in American Colleges and Universities*. Washington, DC: ASHE.

Lafferty, G., and J. Fleming. 2000. "The restructuring of academic work in Australia: Power, management and gender." *British Journal of Sociology of Education* 21 (2): 257-267.

Lakoff, G., and M. Johnson. 1980. *Metaphors We Live By*. Chicago, IL: University of Chicago Press.

Lie, S. S., L. Malik, and D. Harris, eds. 1994. *The Gender Gap in Higher Education*. World Yearbook of Education 1994. London: Kogan Page.

Limerick, D., and B. Cunnington. 1993. *Managing the New Organisation: A Blueprint for Networks and Strategic Alliances*. Chatswood: Business and Professional Publishing.

Lingard, B., and B. Limerick. 1995. "Thinking gender, changing educational management." In B. Limerick and B. Lingard, eds. *Gender and Changing Educational Management*. Rydalmere, NSW: Hodder Education: 1-10.

Lingard, R., and F. Rizvi. 1998. "Globalization, the OECD, and Australian higher education." In J. Currie and J. Newson, eds. *Universities and Globalization: Critical Perspectives*. Thousand Oaks and London: Sage Publications: 257-274.

Luke, C. 1994. "Women in the academy: The politics of speech and silence." *British Journal of Sociology of Education* 15 (2): 211-230.

Lund, H. 1998. "A single sex profession? Female staff numbers in Commonwealth universities." *Commonwealth Higher Education Management Report*. London, September 1.

McClure, P. 2000. "Participation Support for More Equitable Society." Final Report of the Reference Group on Welfare Reform. Canberra: Australian Government Publishing Service.

McInnis, C. 1996. "Change and diversity in the work patterns of Australian academics." *Higher Education Management* 8 (2): 105-117.

———. 1997. "Academics and professional administrators in Australian universities: Dissolving boundaries and new tensions." Paper presented at the Annual Conference of the Association for the Study of Higher Education, Albuquerque, New Mexico, November 7.

———. 1999. *The Work Roles of Academics in Australian Universities*. Canberra: Department of Education, Training and Youth Affairs, Evaluations and Investigations Programme, Higher Education Division.

———. 2000. "Towards new balance or new divides? The changing work roles of academics in Australia." In M. Tight, ed. *Academic Work and Life: What It Is to Be an Academic, and How This Is Changing*. Amsterdam: Elsevier Science: 117-145.

McKenna, E. P. 1997. *When Work Doesn't Work Anymore*. New York: Delta.

Madden, M. 1999. "Academic administration in small colleges: Lessons from feminist psychology." Paper presented at the 7th International Interdisciplinary Congress on Women, Tromso, Norway, June.

Mant, A. 1994. "Scrum mentality sidelines women." *The Australian*, June 3: 3.

Marginson, S. 1996. "Competition in higher education in the post-Hilmer era." *Australian Quarterly* 68 (4): 23-35.

———. 1997a. *Markets in Education.* St. Leonards, NSW: Allen and Unwin.

———. 1997b. "How free is academic freedom?" *Higher Education Research & Development* 16 (3): 359-369.

Marginson, S., and M. Considine. 2000. *The Enterprise University: Power, Governance and Reinvention in Australia.* Cambridge, England: Cambridge University Press.

Martin, R., ed. 1998. *Chalk Lines: The Politics of Work in the Managed University.* Durham and London: Duke University Press.

Martin, J., and D. Meyerson. 1998. "Women and power: Conformity, resistance, and disorganized coaction." In R. M. Kramer and M. A. Neale, eds. *Power and Influence in Organizations.* Thousand Oaks and London: Sage Publications.

Massachusetts Institute of Technology (MIT). 1999. *A Study on the Women Faculty in Science at MIT.* Cambridge: MIT.

Maynard, M. 1994. "Methods, practice and epistemology: The debate about feminism and research." In M. Maynard and J. Purvis, eds. *Researching Women's Lives from a Feminist Perspective.* London: Taylor and Francis: 10-26.

Meehan, D. 1999. "The under-representation of women managers in higher education: Are there issues other than style?" In S. Whitehead and R. Moodley, eds. *Transforming Managers: Gendering Change in the Public Sector.* London: University of College London Press: 33-49.

Menard, L., ed. 1996. *The Future of Academic Freedom.* Chicago, IL: University of Chicago Press.

Milojevic, I. 2000. "The crisis of the university: Feminist alternatives for the 21st century and beyond." In S. Inayatullah and J. Gidley, eds. *The University in Transformation: Global Perspectives on the Future of the University.* Westport, CT: Bergin and Garvey: 176-186.

Mingle, J. R. 1992. *Faculty Work and the Cost/Quality/Access Collision.* Denver, CO: Education Commission of the States, State Higher Education Executive Officers Association.

Mitchell, S. 1996. *The Scent of Power: On the Trail of Women and Power in Australian Politics.* Sydney: Harper Collins Publishers.

Miyoshi, M. 1998. "Globalization, culture, and the university." In F. Jameson and M. Miyoshi, eds. *The Cultures of Globalization.* Durham, NC: Duke University Press: 247-270.

Moodie, G. 1994. "Leaping tall organisational boundaries in a single bound." Paper presented to the 18th AITEA Conference, Adelaide.

Moodley, R. 1999. "Masculine/managerial masks and the 'other' subject." In S. Whitehead and R. Moodley, eds. *Transforming Managers: Gendering Change in the Public Sector.* London: University College London Press: 214-232.

Moody, K., and S. Sagovac. 1995. *Time Out: The Case for a Shorter Working Week.* Detroit: A Labor Notes Book.

Moore, K. M., and M. D. Sagaria. 1993. "The situation of women in research universities in the United States." In J. S. Glazer, E. M. Bensimon and B. K. Townsend, eds. *Women in Higher Education: A Feminist Perspective.* Needham Heights, Mass: Ginn Press: 227-240.

Morley, L. 1995. "Measuring the muse: Creativity, writing and career development." In L. Morley and V. Walsh, eds. *Feminist Academics: Creative Agents for Change.* London: Taylor and Francis: 116-130.

———. 1999. *Organising Feminisms: The Micro-Politics of the Academy.* London: Macmillan.

Morley, L., and V. Walsh. 1995. "Introduction." In L. Morely and V. Walsh, eds. *Feminist Academics: Creative Agents for Change*. London: Taylor and Francis: 1-21.

Moses, Y. 1997. "Salaries in academe: The gender gap persists." *The Chronicle of Higher Education*, 44 (16) (December 12): 60.

National Tertiary Education Union (NTEU). 2000. *Unhealthy Places of Learning: Working in Australian Universities*. South Melbourne: The National Tertiary Education Union.

Newman, J. 1995. "Gender and cultural change." In C. Itzin and J. Newman, eds. *Gender, Culture and Organizational Change*. London: Routledge: 11-29.

Newson, J. 1998. "Conclusion: Repositioning the local through alternative responses to globalization." In J. Currie and J. Newson, eds. *Universities and Globalization: Critical Perspectives*. Thousand Oaks: Sage Publications: 295-313.

Nicholls, J. 1996. "Tuition fees and the future of higher education." *Australian Quarterly* 68 (4): 30-48.

O'Connor, O. 2000. "Resistance in academia." Paper presented to NAWE International Conference on Women in Higher Education, New Orleans, Louisiana.

Olivieri, N. 2000. "When money and truth collide." In J. L. Turk, ed. *The Corporate Campus: Commercialization and the Dangers to Canada's Colleges and Universities*. Toronto: James Lorimer Publishers: 53-62.

Olsson, S., ed. 1992. *The Gender Factor: Women in New Zealand Organisations*. Palmerston North: Dunmore Press.

Osborne, M. 1998. "Facts and figures still show little room at the top for women in science in most EU countries." Paper presented to the European Union Women and Science Conference, Brussels, April.

Ozga, J., and L. Walker. 1999. "In the company of men." In S. Whitehead and R. Moodley, eds. *Transforming Managers: Gendering Change in the Public Sector*. London: University of College London Press: 107-119.

Park, S. M. 1996. "Research, teaching and service: Why shouldn't women's work count?" *Journal of Higher Education* 67 (1): 46-84.

Poiner, G. 1991. "Women and the academic profession: Questions of equality and opportunity." Working Paper. In *Women's Studies Number 1*. Kingswood, New South Wales: Women's Research Centre, University of Western Sydney: np.

Polster, C. 2000. "The advantages and disadvantages of corporate/university links: What's wrong with this question?" *Missing Pieces II: An Alternative Guide to Canadian Post-Secondary Education*. Ottawa: Canadian Centre for Policy Alternatives: 180-185.

Polster, C., and J. Newson. 1998. "Re-claiming our centre: Towards a robust defense of academic autonomy." Paper presented to the Higher Education Commission of the World Congress of Comparative Education Societies, University of Cape Town, Cape Town, South Africa, July 12-17.

Powell, S. 1995a. "The age of overwork." *The Weekend Review*, April 8-9: 1-2.

————. 1995b. "Dame Leonie gets 'limp' comment rebuff." *The Australian*, August 8: 1.

Powney, J., and G. Weiner. 1992. *Outside of the Norm*. Rev. ed. London: University of the South Bank.

Press, E., and J. Washburn. 2000. "The kept university." *The Atlantic Monthly* 285 (3) (March): 39-54.

Probert, B., P. Ewer, and K. Whiting. 1998. *Gender Pay Equity in Australian Higher Education*. South Melbourne: National Tertiary Education Union.

Probyn, E. 2002. "Pleasure and power should come together." *The Australian*, February 13: 35.

Quiggin, J. 1998. "Social democracy and market reform in Australia and New Zealand." *Oxford Review of Economic Policy* 14 (1): 76-95.

Rai, K. B., and J. W. Critzer. 2000. *Affirmative Action and the University: Race, Ethnicity and Gender in Higher Education Employment.* Lincoln: University of Nebraska Press.

Ramsay, E. 2000. "Gender employment equity for women in Australian universities–recent research and current strategies." Paper presented to the European Conference on Gender and Higher Education, ETH, Zurich, September 12-15.

Readings, B. 1996. *The University in Ruins.* Cambridge, MA: Harvard University Press.

Rees, S. 1995. *The Human Costs of Managerialism.* Leichardt, NSW: Pluto Press.

Renfrow, P. 1995. *An Assessment of the Senior Executive Service in the Australian Public Service.* Canberra: Australian Government Publishing Service.

Samover, L. A., and R. E. Porter. 1995. *Communication Between Cultures.* New York: Wadsworth Publishing.

Sassen, S. 2000. "Spatialities and temporalities of the global: Elements for a theorization." In A. Appadurai, ed. *Globalization.* Special Edition of *Public Culture* 12 (1) (Winter): 215-232.

Saunders, P. 2001. "Household income and its distribution," Centenary Article. In *Year Book Australia 2001.* Canberra: Australian Government Publishing Service.

Schaef, A. W. 1985. *Women's Reality: An Emerging Female System in a White Male Society.* San Francisco: Harper and Row Publishers.

Schneider, A. 2000. "Affirmative action's impact on academe has been minimal, a new book argues." *The Chronicle of Higher Education,* March 24: A20.

Schneider, R. 1993. "Search for a glass ceiling." *Public Manager* 22 (1): 38-40.

Schor, J. B. 1992. *The Overworked American: The Unexpected Decline of Leisure.* New York: Basic Books.

Sennett, R. 1998. *The Corrosion of Character: The Personal Consequences of Work in the New Capitalism.* New York: W. W. Norton and Company.

Shore, C., and S. Roberts. 1993. "Higher education and the panopticon paradigm: Quality assessment as 'disciplinary technology.'" Paper presented at the Society for Research into Higher Education Conference, Brighton, England, December 14-16.

Sinclair, A. 1994. *Trials at the Top: Chief Executives Talk about Men, Women and the Australian Executive Culture.* Melbourne: Melbourne University, Melbourne Business School.

Singh, G. 2001. "Talking points." *The Age,* Wednesday, July 18, at www.theage.com.au/cgiin/print_article.pl?path=/education/home/education_news/2001 (accessed September 3, 2001).

Singh, M. 2001. "Re-inserting the 'public good' into higher education transformation." Paper presented to the Globalisation and Higher Education: Views from the South Conference, Cape Town, South Africa, March 27-29.

Sklair, L. 2001. *The Transnational Capitalist Class.* Oxford: Blackwell Publishers.

Smith, J. 2000. *Tax Expenditures and Public Health Financing in Australia.* Canberra: The Australia Institute.

Smith, A., and F. Webster. 1997. "Conclusion: An affirming flame." In A. Smith and F. Webster, eds. *The Postmodern University? Contested Visions of Higher Education in Society.* Buckingham, England: Society for Research into Higher Education and Open University Press: 99-113.

Smith, C., and J. Hutchinson. 1995. *Gender: A Strategic Management Issue.* Sydney: Business and Professional Publishing.

South African Higher Education Task Team. 2000. *Towards a New Higher Education Landscape.* Report on Higher Education. Pretoria, South Africa.

Spender, D. 1980. *Man Made Language.* London: Routledge and Kegan Paul.

Spurling, A. 1997. "Women and change in higher education." In H. Eggins, ed. *Women as Leaders and Managers in Higher Education.* Buckingham, England: The Society for Research into Higher Education and Open University Press: 38-48.

Still, L. V., C. Guerin, and W. Chia. 1992. "Women in management revisited: Progress, regression or status quo?" *Women in Management Series,* paper no. 16. New South Wales: Faculty of Commerce, University of Western Sydney.

Surowiecki, J. 2001. "The financial page: Bad company." *The New Yorker,* March 12: 46

Tancred, P. 1998. "Recreating the professions: Women transform traditional structures." Paper presented at the International Sociological Association's 14th World Congress of Sociology, Montreal, Canada, July-August.

Tancred-Sheriff, P. 1985. "Women's experience, women's knowledge and the power of knowledge: An illustration and an elaboration." *Atlantis* 10 (2): 109-117.

———. 1988. "'Semi-nationalism' in higher education: Women in Canadian and Australian universities." *Australian Universities Review* 2: 14-19.

Tudiver, N. 1999. *Universities for Sale: Resisting Corporate Control over Canadian Higher Education.* Toronto: The Canadian Association of University Teachers and James Lorimer and Company.

Turnbull, S. 1999. "France bucks the toiling trend." *The Weekend Australian,* October 30-31: 32.

Unger, R. M. 1998. *Democracy Realized: The Progressive Alternative.* London: Verso.

Vidovich, L., and J. Currie. 1998. "Changing accountability and autonomy at the 'coalface' of academic work in Australia." In J. Currie and J. Newson, eds. *Universities and Globalization: Critical Perspectives.* Thousand Oaks: Sage Publications: 193-211.

Walton, K. D. 1997. "UK women at the very top: An American assessment." In H. Eggins, ed. *Women as Leaders and Managers in Higher Education.* Buckingham, England: The Society for Research into Higher Education and Open University Press: 70-88.

Ward, B. 2000. "The female professor: A rare Australian species–the who and how." Paper presented at the European Conference on Gender and Higher Education, ETH, Zurich, September 12-15.

Weale, A. 1999. *Democracy: Issues in Political Theory.* Basingstoke, England: Macmillan Press.

Weiner, G. 1996. "Which of us has a brilliant career? Notes from a higher education survivor." In R. Cuthbert, ed. *Working in Higher Education.* Buckingham, England: Open University Press/SHRE: 58-68.

Wenzel, S. A., R. T. Blackburn, and C. Hollenshead. 1997. "Respect: A critical issue for women faculty." Paper presented at the annual conference of the Association for the Study of Higher Education, Albuquerque, New Mexico, November.

West, R. 1998. *Learning for Life: Final Report, Review of Higher Education Financing and Policy.* Higher Education Financing and Policy Review Committee, Canberra: Australian Government Publishing Service.

West, C., and D. H. Zimmerman. 1987. "Doing gender." *Gender and Society* 1 (2): 125-151.

White, K. 2000. "Being ignored: A case study of women in the professoriate in Australia." Paper presented at the European Conference on Gender and Higher Education, ETH, Zurich, September 12-15.

Wieneke, C. 1988. "Room at the top? An analysis of the position of senior women in college administration in New South Wales." *Journal of Tertiary Educational Administration* 10 (1): 5-17.

———. 1995. "Managing women: Positioning general staff women in Australian universities." *Journal of Tertiary Education Administration* 17 (1): 5-19.

Wilson, B., and E. Byrne, eds. 1987. *Women in the University: A Policy Report.* St Lucia, Queensland: University of Queensland Press.

Yeatman, A. 1990. *Bureaucrats, Technocrats, Femocrats: Essays on the Contemporary Australian State.* Sydney: Allen and Unwin.

———. 1993. "The gendered management of equity-oriented change in higher education." In D. Baker and M. Fogarty, eds. *A Gendered Culture: Educational Management in the Nineties.* Melbourne: Victoria University Press: 14-26.

Index

academic capitalism, 182
academic freedom, 8, 29-30, 49, 186, 188-90
accountability, 30, 143, 188. *See also* Australia; performance indicators; performativity; quality assurance; universities
Acker, 44, 46, 62, 63, 64, 69, 71, 83, 141, 144
affirmative action, 37, 43, 72, 74, 80, 84n7, 125, 127, 135. *See also* gender equity
Anglo-American countries, 14, 27, 36, 183
Asia-Pacific Economic Cooperation (APEC), 16
Australia, accountability in, 38, 116-17, 134, 144; as a clever country, 20; economic rationalism in, 26-27; and higher education, 19, 20-25, 143;responses to globalization, 7, 14, 31-32; restructuring in, 171. *See also* government response to globalization
autonomy, 14, 180, 182; institutional, 16, 17, 29; professional, 28-29, 142, 186, 187-88

Bacchi, 7, 63
benchmarking, 142
Blackmore, 3, 38, 40, 44, 46, 58, 64, 181
Brooks, 3, 48
Burton, 40, 44, 46, 58, 64

Canada, 27, 36
careers (careerism), 6, 9, 89, 100, 130, 144, 159, 165-68; and gender, 2, 3, 15, 39, 47, 105, 159, 180, 191. *See also* planning; women and career paths
centralization. *See* decision-making. *See also* decentralization; managerialism
City University of New York, 189
Cockburn, 46, 62, 186
collegiality, 2, 5, 29, 92, 103, 111, 118-19, 189; decline of, diminishing, 34, 36, 54, 111, 131, 136, 160, 177, 186; need to strengthen, 119
Collier, 3-4, 189
commercialization of universities, 24, 111, 119, 189
competition, 17, 32, 36, 54, 117, 176; competition policies, 14-15, 17, 140; competition and

211

About the Authors

Jan Currie, Ph.D., is an associate professor in education at Murdoch University, specializing in comparative education and sociology of education. Her research interests include gender and work and higher education policy. She has recently coedited (with Janice Newson) *Universities and Globalization: Critical Perspectives* (Sage, 1998) and co-authored *Global Practices and University Responses* (Greenwood, 2002). In the last ten years, she has had journal articles in *Melbourne Studies in Education, Australian Educational Researcher, Gender and Education, Discourse, Australian Universities' Review, Women's Studies International Forum, International Review of Women and Leadership,* and *Comparative Education Review.*

Bev Thiele, Ph.D., is an associate professor in women's studies at Murdoch University. Her research interests include women and their paid and unpaid work, working fathers of young children, the politics of midwifery and birth, and feminist theories of the body. She is the Asian and Australasian Regional Editor for *Women's Studies International Forum.* Her publications include entries on work and family lifecycle for the forthcoming *International Encyclopedia for Women's Studies,* several major consultancy reports on Alternative Birthing Services in Western Australia, an article on feminist theory and bodies for a special commemorative issue of *Canadian Journal of Women's Studies* on the life and work of Mary O'Brien, and the series of publications with Jan Currie and Patricia Harris from the Gender and Organizational Culture project.

Patricia Harris, Ph.D., is an associate professor in sociology at Murdoch University. Her research interests include social policy, social justice, and gendered work. She is a member of the Editorial Board of the *Australian Journal of Social Issues.* Her recent publications include a co-authored book, *Poststructuralism, Citizenship and Social Policy* (Routledge, 1999) and the journal articles: "Changing patterns of governance: Developments in Australian public hospitals and universities" in *Policy Studies,* and "Displacing market rationalities" in *Just Policy.* She has also published in the following journals: *International Journal of Contemporary Sociology, Gender and Education,* and *Australian and New Zealand Journal of Sociology.*